Jesus
and the
New Testament

Dr. Charles Vogan

Copyright © 1998 Charles R. Vogan Jr.
All rights reserved

Scripture taken from the HOLY BIBLE, NEW INTERNATIONAL VERSION, Copyright © 1973, 1978, 1984 International Bible Society. Used by permission of Zondervan Bible Publishers.

ISBN 978-0-6151-3930-2

Ravenbrook Publishers

A subsidiary of
Shenandoah Bible Ministries

www.shenbible.org

Contents

Introduction	3
Background Information	
Literature	7
History	38
Geography and culture	53
The Ministry of Christ	73
The Apostles – the interpreters of Christ	121
The Old Testament and the New Testament	151
Step Three	185
What the New Testament Teaches	215
How to study the New Testament	245
Appendices	
Led by the Spirit	261
Names of Christ	324
Prophecies of Christ	328
The Miracles of Christ	339
The Parables of Christ	341
Old Testament references in the New Testament	343

Introduction

The New Testament is the Christian's book. The Lord gave the first Scriptures (the Old Testament) to the Jews, and that has also become a book for the Church. But what happened when Jesus came, and the revelation that the apostles got of him, is a new source of truth for the Christian Church. Without the New Testament we would be as ignorant of Christ as the Jews were (if not more so, since the Gentiles didn't even possess the Old Testament that witnesses to Christ).

The New Testament is the finished revelation of Christ. We learn most of the doctrine about Christ in the Old Testament, but that's not enough to give us the full picture of Christ that we need for salvation. In the New Testament, however, not only do we get a complete explanation of the foundation that the Old Testament was laying down, but we also learn the final mystery of Christ that God had in reserve for the Church age.

If we could sum up the message of the New Testament, it would be this:

**The New Testament reveals the New Man
and how we become one with him.**

Jesus is literally our salvation from sin and death. In him we see the perfect man, prepared for eternal life. And we find out how we can be united to him and ourselves take part in every aspect of Jesus' present existence.

Introduction

But in order to see all of this in the New Testament, we have to be ready for the way it chooses to teach us. First, in the Gospels we are introduced to the Savior and what his works and teachings are. Then the apostles give us deeper insights into the Christ for our life of faith in him; because without their interpretations of the life of Christ, we would probably miss the point about Jesus if we read only the Gospel accounts. And finally we will learn about the new Heavens and the new earth that Jesus is going to set up – we see this in the prophecies of the New Testament.

If we study the New Testament aright, we will not only understand how the two Testaments fit together, but we will see the grand scheme that sweeps from the beginning of God's first creation to the new Creation. All along the way, Jesus is the key to our being part of this. He really did mean what he said when he told us, "Apart from me you can do nothing." (John 15:5)

Background Information

The Literature of the New Testament

The New Testament was written in what's called Koine (pronounced, COIN-ay) Greek. Greek was the language of a far-ranging empire (due to Alexander the Great and his conquest of the then-known world) and of course took on various forms according to the need. In scholarly circles the intellectuals used what's called Attic Greek, and there were other dialects of Greek language. But on the streets the common people spoke street Greek, or "vulgar" (Koine) Greek, for everyday business.

What's interesting about this is that the Lord chose this kind of Greek to communicate the Gospel to the world. Instead of choosing the language of the intellectuals, he chose the language of the lowest of society. He obviously wanted everyone to understand the message of Jesus; it's not for scholars and universities, but for housewives, businessmen, slaves, schoolchildren, politicians, and fishermen – everyone in society. Like the message, which found no difference between "barbarian or Greek, slave or free," the type of Greek used would have been easily understood by everyone who heard the Gospel.

The language used wasn't the only thing about the New Testament that put it within the intellectual reach of everyone in society. The authors themselves came from all walks of life. Matthew was a tax collector, a man who probably had some education (otherwise the Romans wouldn't have put him in a position of trust). Luke was a medical doctor, and thought to be

The Literature of the New Testament

Greek himself – he would represent the intellectuals. Paul was the Jewish intellectual who was trained at Gamaliel's feet; his writing wouldn't have had the polish that native Greek writers had (Paul wasn't interested in that anyway! – 1 Corinthians 2:4; 2 Corinthians 10:10), but they are full of logical and doctrinal arguments that Jewish scholars were good at. John, James, and Peter were unlettered fishermen. The education they received was from Jesus; if they could write letters to the churches which ranked with Paul's more professional level, it was because they were touched by the Spirit and given the Word of God which elevated their otherwise common way of speaking.

That raises another point. Even though the writers of the New Testament books contributed their unique backgrounds and points of view, the books themselves were the product of the Holy Spirit who steered the writing a certain way. Some people don't like this idea, as if the writers need to be free to get things wrong about Jesus – or at least give us their own opinions! But God didn't want them to write their own account of what happened; the Church needs the *truth* about Jesus, so the Spirit stepped in and made sure that the witnesses saw that truth and recorded it faithfully. No mistakes here! Therefore we believe that the New Testament books were projects that both God and man worked on, with the Lord being the main editor. Nothing that was unique about any particular writer was allowed to change the message of the Gospel in any way; nothing of man took away from the power of the incarnation and ministry of the Living Word. In other words, a miracle happened: though the writers wrote down their accounts thinking that they were simply telling the story from their point of view, God actually directed their writing to serve his own purposes.

> Above all, you must understand that no prophecy of Scripture came about by the prophet's own interpretation. For prophecy never had its origin in the will of man, but men spoke from God

as they were carried along by the Holy Spirit. (2 Peter 1:20-21)

The result was a book that Christians believe perfectly shows us the Lord Jesus in his true glory. The New Testament needs nothing in addition to convince us of the truth, nor is there anything in it that doesn't serve that end.

Types of literature:

Just like the Old Testament, the New Testament has various *types* of literature. Although the Bible is sacred literature to God's people, and its purpose is to enlighten and save the soul, it's still a fact that it uses different ways of going about that job.

- **History:** The Gospels and Acts are the main history books of the New Testament. They tell the story of Jesus' life and ministry as well as some of the details about the disciples, the Jews in that day, and a little of the Roman world.

    History is never just a bare account of events. Whoever writes history is selective about what details to tell, if nothing else. But usually history goes even further than telling about events. The historian will usually *interpret* the events – he helps the reader see the events from his own perspective. In some circles this is called propaganda, but not every form of propaganda is negative. For instance, the United States thinks that the Revolutionary War was not only right and necessary, but a noble thing to do – it was a time when people formulated the concept of living under laws of "liberty and justice for all." Great Britain would disagree, however! Their account of the same events would be entirely different from the American account (though hopefully they've gotten over it by now!)

In the New Testament we are dealing with the most important thing that has ever happened in the history of the world. But if we would ask the Jews what *they* think of Jesus' life and ministry, they would write a history of Jesus that would dishonor him: they don't believe in him, nor do they want to be saved by him. So of course their history would use the same historical events to show us Jesus in an entirely different light than a Christian would. The Romans, though they had no personal ax to grind like the Jews did, would have even less to say about the importance of Jesus in world history; in fact, he probably would never have gotten in their history books.

Even the apostles would have disagreed with each other about Jesus if the Spirit didn't make sure they all wrote the same things about him. Paul would have gone back to his old rabbinical days and judged Christ in light of a scholar's standards, while Peter and John would naturally have chosen to preach a Jesus who appealed to the common man. Without Divine guidance, the histories of the New Testament would have confused the Church and given us an unreliable picture of who Jesus really was.

But the Spirit made sure that wouldn't happen. When the apostles wrote their histories of Christ, God put *his own* interpretation into their works. The writers weren't telling us what *they* thought of Jesus, or what they saw as important in Christ, but what *God* sees as important. This is history from God's perspective, not man's. The reason this is important is that, when it comes to spiritual issues, man will pick out only what suits him. Anything that threatens his sinful life will get cut out of the story. And anything that gives him the freedom to turn his back on God at convenient times will be primary material for his history.

So we don't know what Jesus looked like physically. We don't know his personal habits. We don't know much at all about his family, or even how much education he received while growing up. These details are purposely left out because they would add nothing to our faith in him; they would only interest the curious and get in the way of the story. The Lord wants us to see the *glory* of Christ, the side of Christ that we need to be saved from sin and death. Anything that happened in his life that paints that side of him – building a spiritual kingdom, his rebukes to sinners, his miracles for the sick and poor, his spiritual training for the disciples, his single-minded determination to destroy our spiritual enemy – that's what God included in the Gospels. These are the things that God wants us to think about. We need *this* Jesus in our lives, not the Jesus that modern newspaper reporters would have written about.

- **Prophecy:** Prophecy is a hot topic in today's circles, and not just in the Church. Most people think that prophecy is simply telling the future; some think that it's facing people with the Word of God. But actually, if we define prophecy in those ways, we would have to include many people who obviously aren't God's prophets!

A prophet is a person whom God sends to us to tell us of the *coming Kingdom*. In the old days when two armies were about to engage in battle, they would send out representatives to parlay and trade insults. That's the same situation that we have in the war between two spiritual kingdoms. God is coming to this earth to destroy the kingdoms of the world – and he has sent out his representatives – the Prophets – ahead of the army. They have told our world that the King is coming, that they saw his hosts gathered behind him ready to do battle. They warned the nations that this King is going to destroy all the wicked and put an end to the dark kingdoms of sin and death all over the world. Then when the old is swept away, the King will set up a new Kingdom of righteousness, peace and justice – which this world hasn't seen since the beginning of Creation.

We find the messages of God's prophets not only in the Old Testament but in the New Testament as well. Perhaps the best-known example was John the Baptist. We have to realize that he was a prophet of God: his message was an ultimatum, a threat from the approaching King, to lay down our arms now and repent before it's too late. John was the advance man for Jesus who came so soon afterwards that the people had little time to think about his warning.

There are other prophetic passages in the New Testament. Paul spoke of the Kingdom of

The Literature of the New Testament

Christ: hints about when it would come, what it would be like when it came, what would happen to the believers at that time, what would happen to the wicked, and many other details of the Kingdom. His warnings to heed the message and repent had all the power and urgency of the Old Testament prophets.

Jesus, of course, was a Prophet as well as the King of the coming Kingdom. He came to set up the foundations of that Kingdom, but the work wasn't all finished in his life here. He left earth to assume the throne of the universe, and behind him the Spirit carries on the work of building the Church. But the day is still coming when the Lord will return to finish the work he started; on that day he will do away with the wicked, reward the righteous, destroy the old creation, unveil the new creation, and turn the entire finished Kingdom over to God the Father. During his entire ministry he warned people of these coming events.

John the apostle wrote a powerful prophecy that actually shows us the King setting out from Heaven to do battle against the kingdoms of the earth. If we had any doubts about earlier prophetic warnings, the verbal "video" that John shows us in the book of Revelation should (and often does) terrify the reader about the coming judgment.

- **Apocalyptic:** We can define this word as a vision of things to come, using symbolic language and prophecy. It's a type of literature like the others, and therefore we have to know how to read it if we want to really understand what it's talking about.

There are several places in the Gospels that use apocalyptic literature (see Matthew 24 for an example) but the primary example is in the book of Revelation. Here we find symbolism that has confused the Church ever since the time it was written.

Symbols are powerful ways of conveying truth. But if we don't want to be confused by them, we have to understand how to handle them. If we are determined to ignore symbols in the text of the Bible, then we will have to interpret everything literally – which means that we'll end up saying ridiculous things about God and ourselves! For example, I've heard literalists say that Jesus really is a physical, animal lamb who his standing on the throne in Heaven, because that's what Revelation says about him:

> Then I saw a Lamb, looking as if it
> had been slain, standing in the center
> of the throne. (Revelation 5:6)

Now if Jesus really was an animal lamb, that would contradict not only the witness of the apostles who saw him *as a man* ascend to the throne in Heaven (Acts 1:9), but the testimony of John the Baptist who called Jesus a lamb *symbolically,* not literally.

> The next day John saw Jesus coming
> toward him and said, "Look, the Lamb of

The Literature of the New Testament

God, who takes away the sin of the world!" (John 1:29)

Students who understand the point about Jesus being called the Lamb of God know that the message of the entire Bible points to his sacrifice, not his physical nature, whenever it talks about him being a lamb.

Another example: In Revelation it talks about the mark of the beast that his subjects will be forced to accept, on their foreheads and their hands.

> He also forced everyone, small and great, rich and poor, free and slave, to receive a mark on his right hand or on his forehead, so that no one could buy or sell unless he had the mark, which is the name of the beast or the number of his name. (Revelation 13:16-17)

There are many Christians who feel sure that this means a physical mark – or even a computerized device – to control people in our society, so that nobody can "buy or sell" food or other necessities of life. So they feel that their physical well-being, and even their spiritual standing before God, is threatened by modern powers who reportedly are experimenting with either mind control or computerized tracking systems.

But in the very next chapter we read this:

The Literature of the New Testament

> Then I looked, and there before me was the Lamb, standing on Mount Zion, and with him 144,000 who had his name and his Father's name written on their foreheads. (Revelation 14:1)

Now this, most Christians would agree, is a *spiritual* mark on God's people. We even have a passage that tells us that the Spirit is the mark that God gives Christians when they believe.

> And you also were included in Christ when you heard the word of truth, the gospel of your salvation. Having believed, you were marked in him with a seal, the promised Holy Spirit, who is a deposit guaranteeing our inheritance until the redemption of those who are God's possession—to the praise of his glory. (Ephesians 1:13-14)

My point is this: if the mark in Revelation 14:2 is spiritual, why is the mark on the devil's people physical? If the mark on Christians is a sign of their salvation, why is the marking on the wicked something that has nothing to do with their souls? The more obvious interpretation of Revelation 13 is that the mark on the wicked is a spiritual mark just like the mark on God's people. Being on the forehead is symbolic of the lies of their father (who is called the "father of lies", see John 8:44), just as the mark on God's people is that they believe the truth of Christ. (1 Thessalonians 2:13)

The Literature of the New Testament

If we hope to understand this symbolic literature, we have to come up with a more consistent way of interpreting it. We can't willy-nilly pick and choose what we want to be spiritual and what we want to be physical. There are rules of interpretation that will keep us from making serious mistakes. One rule is to look back through the rest of the Bible and see if it can shed any light on what the symbol might mean – and usually when we take the time to do this, we will find something. *The Bible is its own best interpreter.*

Apocalyptic literature has to be approached with care, but when we find solid footing in how we study it, it can give us powerful aspects on the truth that ordinary historical or doctrinal accounts would be hard put to match. As they say, a picture is worth a thousand words.

- **Theology:** Paul is a master of doctrine and theology. He was trained in rabbinical circles, he knew the Scriptures backward and forward, and was trained in debate. It's in his letters that we find our Christian faith laid out in principles and doctrines. There are also other places in the New Testament where the writer gets into doctrine.

There have been many well-meaning Christians who shy away from doctrine, especially in our century. Their reason is that simple Christianity isn't a matter of scholarly debate or intellectual exercises. It's just a matter of believing in the Lord and obeying him in everyday life. But their fears are actually unfounded. Though it's true that some people would love to reduce Christianity to an intellectual exercise, our faith is made up of certain truths about God, ourselves, the world we live in, and the future of the wicked and the righteous. It all has a great deal to do with how we *live*.

There are times when we have to set down on paper the truths that we believe in, so that we know we are believing in the right things. If we never checked to see what God is really like, how do we know we're not worshipping a false god? If we don't check to see if we all agree on the basic truths of our faith, how can we be sure that we're not joining hands with people who have turned their backs on a holy God and are making a mockery of Christ's sacrifice? The truth keeps us walking in the straight and narrow road of truth. Those who want to join us there have to accept certain truths that the Bible says are absolutely true and necessary for our faith. Those who don't want to accept those truths have no right to claim the name Christian. We can tell, by the use of doctrine, who belongs in our group and who doesn't.

> They went out from us, but they did not really belong to us. For if they had belonged to us, they would have remained with us; but their going showed that none of them belonged to us. (1 John 2:19)

Another reason we have to be careful about doctrine is that our enemy would love for us to believe lies, not the truth. Our faith isn't a game. The truth of God protects us from the severe

The Literature of the New Testament

spiritual damage that the devil can inflict on us if we make the mistake of turning to false doctrines.

Probably the reason that some believers distrust the word "doctrine" is that they're worried that it will stay in the head and not affect the heart. They're right – for doctrine to be useful to us, it has to affect our emotions, it has to direct us in the way of life and make us holy. Dry doctrine that doesn't change one's soul from sin and death to light and life is useless doctrine. But doctrine – the truths of God's Word – is what changes the heart! A believer can't just love God by his own efforts, or change his life of sin to a life of righteousness by trying on his own. What makes the heart love God is the truth about God that shows us *what* we love and *why* love for him is appropriate. A life of holiness is only possible when we find out how we can achieve that life – truth informs the heart and directs it in the right way. Doctrine informs the heart, guides it, rebukes it, and makes sure it glorifies God appropriately. Without doctrine our hearts would fall into free emotion, ignorant and dangerous, which would (and too often does) follow any god who promises the "believer" a good emotional time.

- **Biography:** Obviously the Bible includes biography – it gives details of the lives of many of the important people at the beginning of the Church. But as we have already seen above, the New Testament wisely focuses on just those details that will build our faith in Christ – not satisfy our idle curiosity. The biographies of the New Testament are disappointing in their lack of details on personal traits of the disciples and Jesus. But the story that it tells about their spiritual walk is exactly what we need to know in order to please God in our own lives.

Bible biography is useful in this way: it shows us ordinary mortals struggling with spiritual issues and either winning through or losing. Also, the Bible is careful to show us *why* they win or lose. We can't get this kind of detailed information even about our closest friends! The Spirit shows us the ugly side of human nature without any apologies or embarrassment, because we need to see the worst of sinners coming face to face with Jesus and being healed of their sin. We see the inner struggle of their souls, and the spiritual healing that Jesus does in their hearts. This information will save us – that's why we're interested in the story. That's why it was written in the first place. God had no interest in recording for all time the events of people's private lives just to entertain historians. He picked these stories, and these people, because what God did in their lives is exactly the same thing he intends to do in our lives.

Peter and Paul are perhaps, besides Jesus himself, the central characters in the story of the Bible. We learn more of their lives than any of the other followers of Jesus. But we do learn some things about such people as Nicodemus, Matthew, Pilate, John Mark, Mary Magdalene, and many others. The point to keep in mind is that God is being selective in the Bible about who he shows us and why. Each person's story reflects a new aspect of God's work of salvation among men, and how each person responded to God either positively or negatively. We're being given an opportunity to learn how to deal with this same God.

Manuscripts:

Jesus came as the living Word of God (John 1:1), and he revealed the truth of God to us so that we might be saved. The words of Jesus themselves became the written Word for us.

He spoke in Aramaic, because that's what all the Jews of his time used as their common tongue. We're not sure if he knew Hebrew (probably he did), but he wouldn't have had to know it in order to read the Scriptures — remember that they had already been translated into Aramaic by his time.

An interesting detail that reveals the mix of languages in their culture is the account of the sign posted on top of Jesus' cross:

> Pilate had a notice prepared and fastened to the cross. It read: JESUS OF NAZARETH, THE KING OF THE JEWS. Many of the Jews read this sign, for the place where Jesus was crucified was near the city, and the sign was written in Aramaic, Latin and Greek. (John 19:19-20)

It was an era of empires, and business flourished between widespread cultures. It was natural for everyone to know at least two languages (as is true in Europe today, for example).

God times his works so that they will have the greatest possible effect. In this case, the Gospel came at one of the critical times of human history: never before could the message

The Literature of the New Testament

of the Gospel spread so rapidly and easily from one end of the civilized world to the other, and the common languages had a lot to do with that.

The disciples, charged with the task of carrying the news of Jesus to the world, naturally wrote their books in the language that the most people would understand: Greek. And they didn't use classical Greek, the language of the poets and theater and upper society. They used the Greek that the common man on the street would understand — "vulgar" or common Greek, what we know today as Koine (*pronounce*: COIN-ay) Greek. They took these Scriptures and taught them to farmers, milkmaids, blacksmiths, housewives, slaves, and other "lower class" people who would understand the message and, by faith, receive it.

At times we find a fascinating interplay of languages in the text that, if we only work with English, we would miss. For example, the story of Jesus questioning Peter about his love for him (John 21:15-18) was written in Greek, by the apostle John. But Jesus and Peter originally had this discussion in *Aramaic*. In Aramaic there is only one commonly-used word for "love"; but in Greek there are two — "phileo" (brotherly, friendly love) and "agape" (self-denying love). In John's account, he shows that Jesus asked if Peter had "agape" love for him, and Peter said that he did have "phileo" love for him. Since there was only one Aramaic word that they both used, John is using the different Greek words to show us what each speaker *meant*. With this linguistic trick, he reveals to us the true state of Peter's heart — something that we wouldn't have known otherwise if we had listened in on the original conversation.

This is a portion of John's Gospel, written in Greek (this is John 1:1-5):

Ἐν ἀρχῇ ἦν ὁ λόγος, καί ὁ λόγος ἦν πρός
τόν θεόν, καί θεός ἦν ὁ λόγος.

οὗτος ἦν ἐν ἀρχῇ πρός τόν θεόν.

πάντα δι᾽ αὐτοῦ ἐγένετο, καί χωρίς αὐτοῦ ἐγένετο οὐδέ ἕν. ὃ γέγονεν

ἐν αὐτῷ ζωή ἦν, καί ἡ ζωή ἦν τό φῶς τῶν ἀνθρώπων·

καί τό φῶς ἐν τῇ σκοτίᾳ φαίνει, καί ἡ σκοτία αὐτό οὐ κατέλαβεν.

Two of the Gospels (Matthew and John) were written by original disciples (that is, men given in the "official" list of disciples who first followed Jesus — Matthew 10:2-4, Mark 3:16-19, and Luke 6:13-16). Mark was a follower of Peter, and therefore he got his stories from an eyewitness. Luke was a follower of Paul, but he also collected information from eyewitnesses:

> Many have undertaken to draw up an account of the things that have been fulfilled among us, just as they were handed down to us by those who from the first were eyewitnesses and servants of the word. Therefore, since I myself have carefully investigated everything from the beginning, it seemed good also to me to write an orderly account for you, most excellent Theophilus, so that you may know the certainty of the things you have been taught. (Luke 1:1-4)

This illustrates a very important point about the books of the New Testament: this information came from men who saw and heard Jesus Christ when he lived on earth. This is special testimony, therefore, something that the Church has never had since then. What they tell us about him is the foundation of our faith, the standard of truth about him. It is for good reason that Paul says we are —

The Literature of the New Testament

> ... fellow citizens with God's people and members of God's household, *built on the foundation of the apostles and prophets*, with Christ Jesus himself as the chief cornerstone. (Ephesians 2:19-20)

We are not allowed to deviate from the apostolic writings in our faith. Therefore their writings are critical to us.

Most of the books of the New Testament were really intended as letters, sent to congregations around the Roman Empire. The Epistles, for example, are obviously personal letters to churches. But you can be sure that these letters became prized property; everyone would want a copy of their own to study and meditate on. In fact, churches would hear about a particular letter that one church had received, and request a copy for themselves. Soon there were copies of the New Testament letters floating around all over the place.

The initial excitement of Christ's life and resurrection produced shock waves in the Roman Empire. People from all walks of life, even some of the imperial family, became believers. Churches sprang up everywhere, converts numbered in the hundreds of thousands, and of course everyone wanted to hear and see the stories about Jesus.

This produced a market for written material. Soon there were other books appearing besides the ones that the apostles themselves wrote. Some of them were simply sermons and lessons on the life of the Lord, but some were, unfortunately, false Gospels written by impostors. Some of them had ridiculous stories in them and they weren't hard to judge as false (one of them told the story of Jesus, as a child, making birds out of clay and then breathing life into them!). Others were quite good and caused a lot of confusion in the Church. Which books were they supposed to believe in?

The Literature of the New Testament

The situation got so bad that the leaders in the Church decided to hold meetings to determine what books (out of the hundreds that existed) God wanted them to call Scripture and what books were only productions of men. After a lot of discussion, in 367 AD they finally came up with an authoritative list — which they called the **canon** of Scripture. This list of books is what makes up our Bibles today. You may be interested in knowing that they argued long over whether several books should be in the canon — for example, James, Jude, 2 Peter, and 2 and 3 John. (If you remember, Martin Luther, as late as 1500 AD, himself wondered whether the book of James should be in the canon!)

Their rule was this: they would include whatever books claimed (and proved) apostolic authorship. Usually a letter had the apostle's name on it, sometimes tradition proved that it came from a certain apostle, and sometimes there was internal evidence in the letters themselves (for example, Peter's testimony of Paul's writings in 2 Peter 3:15-16). But that still leaves a couple of doubtful books, most notably Hebrews (which is still a point of argument in our day!) since it doesn't say who wrote it. So they also used some spiritual sense and included any book that obviously had divine authority in its message. That effectively eliminated most of the books that were circulating then, good and bad, and forever fixed the books that we have now as the New Testament Scriptures.

People wanted to record information permanently long before they had such exotic materials as paper and copier machines and computers and printing presses. So they had to use whatever was available in their non-technological world.

The first types of writing was done on stone, both by painting and carving. Since carving lasts almost forever, this was the method of choice. It was slow-going to take hammer and chisel and carve out pictures and letters, and one could only

The Literature of the New Testament

fit so much on a large stone before having to continue on another stone. But it was so durable that we still have stone tablets that were carved thousands of years ago.

By the way, one theory about why Hebrew was written from right to left is this: imagine that you have a stone tablet to carve, and you have a hammer and chisel to do it with. It is much easier to use the hammer in your right hand and chisel to the left than the other way around (unless you are left-handed, which few people are!). Since writing started out this way, it's probable that this accounts for the direction of early alphabets.

But the disadvantages of carving in stone forced creative people to find new ways of writing. One popular method was **cuneiform** writing, in which one uses a stick with a wedge-shaped tip to press marks into soft clay. Then when the tablet is complete, bake it in an oven to make it almost as hard as stone. Cuneiform looks something like this:

𒀭𒂗𒆠𒈾𒁯

Another way of writing was with **papyrus** (*pronounced*: pa-PIE-rus), a plant that grew along marshes and rivers. They would slit the stems and lay them down in rows, then glue on another layer crossways to the first layer. It was actually the beginnings of the paper industry. Then they made a black ink with water and charcoal and used a pointed stick to write on the papyrus sheets. The sheets didn't last as long as clay tablets, but they were much easier to handle and were, of course, much lighter. They could also store more of them in a smaller space.

A third way of writing was to use scraped sheep-skin as a sort of paper. Another name for this material was **parchment**.

In order to solve the problem of storing their writings, they invented two ways of putting the material together. One was the **scroll**, in which the sheepskin or papyrus was made into a long strip, the message written on it, and then (starting at one end) they rolled the strip into a tight roll. With a scroll they could store a lot of information in a small space, and it was easy to carry around. The major problem was finding the text they wanted — they had to unroll most or all of the scroll to locate the spot!

A second way to assemble the material was in a **codex** — what we call a book. They cut sheets out of papyrus or sheepskin and glued or sewed them together along one edge, so that it formed individual pages. This was the most efficient way to do it, since all the information was easily found (not like a scroll). The only drawbacks were that it was a little bulkier to handle, and the pages could come apart over time.

Until the invention of the printing press around 1450 AD, making books was an extremely tedious affair: they were all copied by hand. This means that one person could make only one book at a time. "Libraries", therefore, in the old days were small and very rare.

The Jews were almost paranoid about how they copied their Scriptures. The text was so sacred to them that they did everything they could think of to keep mistakes from happening. In God's providence, this was so helpful for preserving the Hebrew Bible, since it had to survive the hand of man for twice the time that the New Testament did. Remember that the first books of Moses were penned about 1500 BC! Thus we have a book that is 3500 years old. It's a good thing that the Jews took their copying so seriously.

For example, each scribe had to check his work against the original copy during the entire copying process. When he was done, he had additional checks to do in order to insure its accuracy. They knew how many words and how many letters were supposed to be in each book of the Old Testament. They knew how many times each letter of the alphabet was used in each book. They even knew where the middle word and the middle *letter* of the Old Testament was! If a copy checked out to this degree of perfection, then they allowed its use; otherwise they either corrected it or threw it away and started over.

They were jealous for the integrity of the Scriptures, and sometimes their zealousness frustrates us who would like to see some of those ancient documents. One thing that they did was this: when they were done making a new copy of the Bible, they would destroy the old copy so that it wouldn't suffer from unholy wear and tear from continued use. It's this that accounts for the fact that we have very few ancient manuscripts of the Old Testament now. There are only a few hundred full and partial copies of the Old Testament in existence; in comparison, there are thousands of full and partial manuscripts of the New Testament in existence.

Another characteristic of Old Testament manuscripts is that they used no vowels at all. When everyone spoke Hebrew this was no problem, since Hebrew doesn't rely on vowels as heavily as English does. But sometimes it is a bit confusing to someone who doesn't know Hebrew well; and by the time of Jesus, when only the scholars knew it well, people were a little worried about those vowels — they were beginning to forget what they were!

The New Testament, written in Greek, had vowels in it — it resembles English much more than Hebrew does. One bothersome characteristic (to us, anyway!) of many of their early manuscripts was that they wrote everything in capital letters only — these copies were called "uncials." In "minuscule" manuscripts they at least used small letters as we do. But the major problem of early Greek manuscripts is that they used no punctuation! No periods, commas, question marks, quotes —

nothing. And some of them didn't even put spaces between the words! Sometimes it's nearly impossible to determine how to break up a sentence, or even where one sentence stops and the next one starts! A well-known example of this is in John 1:3-4 —

Here? *or* Here?
| | |

καί χωρίς αὐτοῦ ἐγένετο οὐδέ ἕν ὃ γέγονεν ἐν αὐτῷ ζωή ἦν,

You can translate this in one of two ways, and both ways make sense:

"and without him nothing was made. That which came to be in him was life,"

<u>or</u>

"and without him nothing was made that has been made. In him was life."

Most modern translations choose the second option, but it could just as easily be translated the first way too. (The Greek Bible that most people now use, for example, prefers to punctuate it the first way.) Without punctuation there is no way we can be certain of how the original manuscript read.

One more thing you should know. The system of verse numbers and chapter numbers is a (relatively) modern invention. The books were not at first written with the verses numbered. They were letters and histories, and of course the writers never thought to break up the text like we do. The verse numbers were added to the Old Testament about 900 AD by Masorete scholars, and later to the New Testament by a Catholic scholar (some say that he did it while he was on horseback during his travels, which may account for the uneven and strange way he assigned some of the verses!).

We moderns take our handy inventions for granted. When we want a copy of something, all we have to do is use a copier and we get an exact image (spots and all!) of the original in seconds. People in ancient times would have loved to own a copier! They, unfortunately, had to do it the old-fashioned way: by hand.

There were several ways to attack the problem. One was to assign someone the job of making a duplicate of a particular manuscript. He would work for months, painstakingly copying every letter and mark, producing a single exact duplicate from the original. As you can imagine, it was too easy to make a mistake. The sheer tedium of that much copying would likely produce errors. For example, these are the kinds of errors that can happen:

- *Duplicate words* — After copying for hours, one can get pretty tired and the words start blurring together in weary eyes. It's easy to get distracted and then, coming back to your work, think that you haven't yet copied the last word that you read in the original — when really you have already copied it.

- *Missing words* — The opposite problem from the last one and also easy to do. You may think that you already copied the word and go on, when really you are skipping it.

- *Duplicate lines* — If you follow along in the original by keeping your finger on the line that you are copying, it's easy to imagine forgetting to move your finger down a line — which means that you will end up copying the same line twice.

- *Missing lines* — The opposite problem from the last one and even easier to do, since you could move your finger down the page too far and miss an entire line in the process.

- *Misspelled words* — Instead of writing the word exactly as it is spelled, someone could read the word and then unthinkingly write the word with a different spelling — especially if the writer has always misspelled that word in the past.

- *Switched letters* — This happened a lot. The writer simply swapped two letters around. It's as if we would write "owe" instead of "woe." The trouble is that in Hebrew there are a lot of words that turn into other valid words simply by switching letters around. So this kind of mistake is hard to catch.

The point is that these mistakes aren't things that *could* have happened, they *did* happen. We can see many examples of them in old manuscripts. You would think that they are so obvious that a good copyist would have avoided them; but remember that not all copyists were good at their work, and in the middle of a tedious task you aren't thinking about whether what you are writing makes sense — you are just writing the letters in a mechanical way.

Another way to produce a copy is to gather a team of copyists into a room and have one person read the original out loud. Then each copyist would write down what he heard. If you have ten copyists, you would have ten copies made at the same time. This is a much more efficient way of producing many copies! The problem is that it leads to a new set of errors that can and often did happen:

- ***Homonyms*** — A homonym is a word that sounds like another word, but it's spelled differently because it's a different word. For instance, the words "reign" and "rain" are homonyms. You can easily imagine how a copyist would hear one word and write another by mistake.

- ***Missed words*** — If you aren't looking at the original copy yourself, it may be difficult to catch all the words that the reader speaks. It would be easy to leave out a word or two.

There were two more problems that came up during copying that led to errors in manuscripts. The first was that, especially while copying the New Testament books, sometimes the copyist himself was not a Christian and therefore wasn't very concerned with the accuracy of what he was doing. A Christian has a keener sense of the importance of God's Word and being faithful in its transmission; to an unbeliever, it was just a job, and accuracy wasn't a matter of faith to him.

The second problem was that sometimes a later editor would "fix" what he thought was certainly an error in the text, when really there was nothing wrong with it. He thought that an earlier copyist made a mistake, and he would insert the "correction" into the text itself or write it in the margin for the benefit of future copyists. Thus a new error was born. The most famous example of this was 1 John 5:7-8. For a long time the text read like this:

> For there are three that testify in Heaven: the Father, the Word, and the Holy Spirit, and

> these three are one. And there are three that testify on earth: the Spirit, the water and the blood; and the three are in agreement.

In most modern translations, however, it reads like this:

> For there are three that testify: the Spirit, the water and the blood; and the three are in agreement.

The difference is due to the manuscripts used. In our time we use older manuscripts, which means more reliable sources – and none of the older manuscripts have this extra material in them. The King James, however, didn't have access to those older manuscripts – it used manuscripts from the eighth century and newer. But even the manuscripts that the King James relied on don't have this extra verse in them! When scholars investigated the problem, they found a manuscript that had been made in the sixteenth century first had this verse added into it by a "pious" priest, and so all the following copies of that one had it in them as well. So when it came to translating the King James, the translators decided to add the verse into the English version even though their older manuscripts didn't include the verse – it sounded appropriate to them, considering the context!

When someone made a mistake that nobody caught, you can easily see what would happen. If, in the future, someone made another copy of that one, the second would have the same error in it that the first one had. For example, we can imagine something like the following happening in a chain of copies:

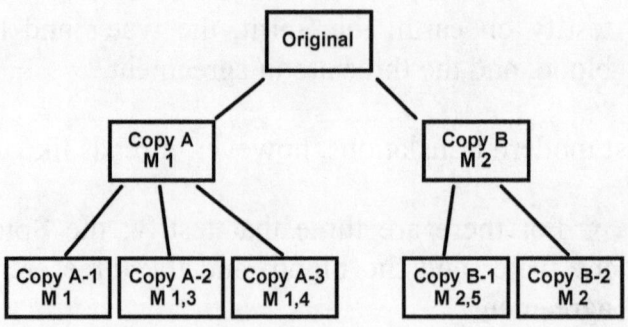

Let's say that someone made two copies of the **Original** and sent them to two different cities: **Copy A** and **Copy B**. The problem is that **Copy A** had a mistake in it — **M1** — and **Copy B** had a different mistake in it — **M2**. Then each church in each city decided to make additional copies. From **Copy A** came **Copy A-1**, **Copy A-2**, and **Copy A-3** — all of which have the same mistake **M1** in them. And in the process of copying, **Copy A-2** picked up an additional mistake **M3** and **Copy A-3** has a mistake **M4**. Meanwhile, in the second church, they made **Copy B-1** and **Copy B-2** from their copy. And **Copy B-1** got a new error **M5**.

As more copies were made, you can see how each "family" of copies developed new errors and preserved the old errors that were distinctive to that family. Pretty soon you could tell where a copy was made simply by checking what kind of errors were in the text!

To give you an idea of the kinds of problems that translators have to consider, here is a sample of what's at the bottom of a particular page in our Greek Bible:

[7] **33** {D} αὐτων ἡμιν C^3 E P 049 056 0142 33 81 88 104 181 326 330 436 451 614 630 945 1241 1505 1739 1877 2127 2412 2492 2495 Byz $Lect^m$ l^{1443} it^e ($syr^{p,h}$) arm geo Chrysostom Cosmas Greek$^{acc.to\ Bede}$ Theophylact // ἡμιν 142 // ἡμων p^{74} ℵ A

The Literature of the New Testament

B C* D it^{ar,c,d,t} vg eth Hilary Ambrose Cosmas // *ὑμων* Ψ it^p // *αὐτων* 629 it^{gig} cop^{sa,bo.mss} Ambrose // omit cop^{bo.mss}

It's a footnote for Acts 13:33. The problem is whether to translate it "… he has fulfilled for us, **their** children" or "… he has fulfilled for us, **the** children". The first set of manuscripts (up to the first // marks) *do* have the word "their", and the rest of them *don't* — they just have various forms of the word "for us." The last one omits the entire phrase and makes it read "for the children". (The numbers represent individual manuscripts — they can keep track of them better that way.) Which manuscripts are right? The "D" at the beginning is the scale of difficulty in trying to decide what the correct reading is. Since there are *very* dependable manuscripts that disagree here, the scholars could only make an educated guess about which one to use. If they would have put "A", this means that all the good manuscripts agree on a certain reading and the less dependable manuscripts disagree. "B" and "C" would mean there is more doubt about it.

This should give you an idea about how difficult it is for translators and Greek scholars to discover how the original manuscripts really read. But it also shows you the nature of the problem: none of the variations are about points of doctrine, or things that should divide Christians. Fortunately, the Bible is the best preserved document in all of history; in comparison, other ancient books, like Homer's stories, vary so widely from copy to copy that you would think that they were almost two different stories!

The "civilized world" at the time of the apostles was the Roman Empire, stretching all the way around the Mediterranean Sea. Christian teachers and preachers found it easy to use Rome's roads and communication network to spread the Gospel all over the Empire. Churches sprang up all over the place, but there were certain churches that were in major metropolitan areas and therefore drew the most Christians and — important to our discussion here — potential scholars.

Here is a map of the eastern end of the Empire, with major centers of learning:

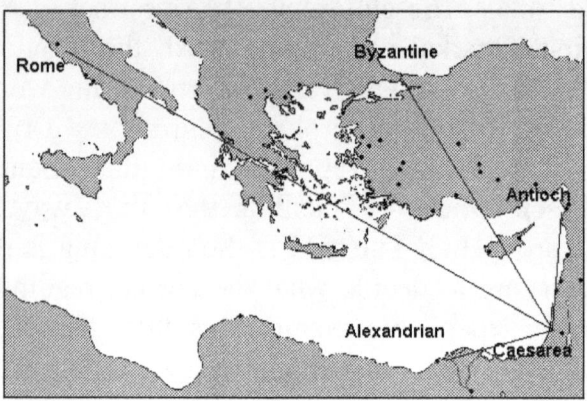

The apostles worked originally from Jerusalem, and spread out from there to other cities. Their letters spread out too, and as each church received an apostolic letter they got busy producing copies for everyone who wanted one. Soon there were large collections of letters in each city, laboriously but lovingly copied from the original. We call these collections (found in major cities) **families of manuscripts**.

We have already seen, however, that these copies were inevitably going to have copying errors in them. The thing to remember is this: each family has its own distinctive set of errors. A scholar who knows, for example, the errors of the Byzantine family can quickly tell whether a newly discovered manuscript belongs to that family. In fact, he will sometimes know the name of the scribe who introduced a certain error into the family!

Scholars know a lot about the history of each family of manuscripts, and they keep that in mind when judging which ones to use for translating. Manuscripts that prove to be full of errors will get only a passing glance during translating; but they rely heavily on manuscripts that consistently show a dependability for accuracy. Not only is this true for individual manuscripts, it goes in a general way for the families themselves. For example, we know some of the history and the dates of the Byzantine family (the one that the KJV uses exclusively). Unfortunately these manuscripts have obvious problems in them and are dated much later than the other families, so they aren't as dependable as the others. On the other hand, the Alexandrian and Roman families are older and have proved to be more accurate — there are less errors in the texts.

And there is one more thing to consider. Scholars will often use an early *translation* of the Bible as a clue for how the original manuscript that those early translators had must have read. This is a case of detective work, and can produce some solid results. For example, they can look at a Syriac translation made in 600 AD and, reasoning backwards, figure out what the translator's Hebrew and Greek originals must have read like. Sometimes they come up with different readings than *our* existing manuscripts which date much later — therefore ours probably have an error. But the scholar must also keep in mind the *family* of originals that the Syriac translator would have been using! The translator would not have known about that family's distinctive set of errors, and they naturally would have ended up in his Syriac translation. All this is to show how complicated the business of translating and manuscript research can be.

The History of the New Testament

Whereas the Old Testament covers a period of history of at least 2000 years (and more, since it also includes Creation), the New Testament records events across no more than a hundred years at the most. From the ministry of John the Baptist to the writing of the book of the Revelation by the apostle John, the entire book covers no more than the first century of the modern age. But what happened in that short century was nothing less than the pivot point of all of human history! The Old Testament system was changed from a physical to a spiritual reality. The world finally got an explanation of how God intends to fix the damage done by sin. And the Church was born, laid down on eternal foundations, and destined to be the future Kingdom that will completely replace the existing heavens and earth. The events of the New Testament shed a bright light of understanding and purpose on all the other events of history, before and after the time of Christ.

What we want to do is quickly sketch the main events of the New Testament to get an idea of what God was doing in that century – and why it was so pivotal in human history.

Pre-New Testament situation

First we need to look at the state of things in Israel when Jesus arrived. The last prophet to minister in Israel before John the Baptist was Malachi, who prophesied around 433 BC. He and two other prophets – Haggai and Zechariah – were "Post-Exilic" prophets, which means that their ministries took place after the Israelites returned from captivity in Babylon around 458 BC.

The History of the New Testament

The Israelites had learned their lesson well. God sent them into exile because of idolatry – God decided that they had played games long enough, worshiping false gods and living in immorality. During the 70-year captivity, while Jerusalem lay in ruins, they had plenty of time to think things over. When the Lord brought them back to Judah to rebuild the Temple, they decided that never again would they worship false gods. From now on, they said, we are going to learn the Law of God and keep it with all of our hearts. And they got busy learning and memorizing the Law (the first five books of Moses – Genesis through Deuteronomy) – which in Hebrew is the "Torah."

The problem is that they took the Law *too* seriously – as usual, when trying to fix a problem, they swung to the opposite extreme instead of finding a healthy balance. They felt that there were many new ways of applying God's Law to everyday life that the Bible didn't include, so they wrote supplementary works that told the Jew how to apply the Law to different circumstances. These additional works of law – called the **Mishnah** – took the Law to an extreme. They found creative ways to apply the basic Law of God to everything in life.

For example, they took seriously the Law against working on the Sabbath. They decided that in order to keep this Law, they had to find out what "work" might be – and then forbid people to do that. They decided, for instance, that paring your fingernails is "work," and so they wrote in the Mishnah that it's forbidden to cut your fingernails on the Sabbath. Their zeal knew no bounds.

The problem is that when you get so focused on outward actions – and think that God is primarily pleased with them – you forget about your soul and the shape that it's in. It's easy enough for a person to get his actions right (if he can learn what all the rules are!); it's quite another matter to change the heart from its inclination to evil. So by the time Jesus came, there were many experts in the Law – Pharisees and Sadducees and teachers of the Law – who could tell you anything you wanted to know about keeping the Law on the outside. But they missed the point about the Law entirely: that the Lord primarily is concerned with the *heart*. The Kingdom of God isn't outward and physical; it's a spiritual Kingdom, and only someone who gets his soul raised from its dead state into the light and life of God's presence can have a hope of being righteous to God's expectations.

The fortunes of the Jews had risen and fallen with the politics of the surrounding nations. For a while, under the Maccabean family, the Jews managed to throw off the yoke of Greek rule (imposed by the meteoric career of Alexander the Great) in 166 BC and rule themselves while the Greeks and Persians fought for control of the Middle East. But when Rome swept through and claimed the entire Mediterranean coastline as its empire, Jerusalem also fell to the hated victors and became a vassal state of the Caesars in 63 BC.

But what God was doing through these political and economic upheavals was creating a perfect environment for the birth and spread of the Gospel – and the Church. Greek became the universal language – the Koine Greek of the common man on the street. Most everyone in the Roman empire knew it. Plus, the Roman political and military juggernaut created peace throughout the Mediterranean area, and they built roads for its army and commerce. The result was that the circumstances were perfect for a peaceful and efficient way of carrying the Gospel to the entire empire. When the apostles were ready to evangelize, the lines of communication and travel were ready for their use.

The History of the New Testament
John the Baptist

The New Testament starts with the ministry of John the Baptist. He was born to a priest (Zechariah) who ministered in the Temple at Jerusalem. He was also a "miracle baby," since Zechariah's wife Elizabeth was along in years and unable to bear children.

John played a critical role in the events of the ministry of Christ. He was the Prophet whom the Old Testament prophets said would be sent out ahead of the King, to announce the coming of the Kingdom of God. In order to understand his role, we first have to review what the role of a prophet was in the Bible.

In old days, when two kings and their armies would meet for battle, each side would send out an emissary to discuss terms first. Usually they would trade insults, and threaten dire consequences if the other side didn't surrender on the spot. Then when the parley ended they would return to their respective sides and the battle would begin.

The prophets of the Old Testament were God's emissaries sent out ahead of his army. Their job was to announce the coming of the King with his host. God's intention was to destroy the kingdoms of this earth – because of their wickedness and rebellion – and to set up a righteous kingdom where he would rule. If you go back to those prophecies you will see these same elements in every one of their writings.

The prophet's job was to warn the enemy of what was coming. Repent now, they said, before the King gets here with his army and destroys you. Lay down your arms *now* and he will take you as one of his own. Those who ignore the warning will be destroyed without mercy. It was nothing less than a message of war.

True to form, John the Baptist did that very thing. He was the front-runner to the King himself. His job was to announce the coming King, and the kind of kingdom that Jesus was coming to set up. His message was one of war: repent *now* before it's too late. This King, he said, baptizes with *fire* and the *Holy Spirit* – you don't want to get on his bad side!

> I baptize you with water for repentance. But after me will come one who is more powerful than I, whose sandals I am not fit to carry. He will baptize you with the Holy Spirit and with fire. His winnowing fork is in his hand, and he will clear his threshing floor, gathering his wheat into the barn and burning up the chaff with unquenchable fire." (Matthew 3:11-12)

And when the King finally arrived, John pointed him out to the people. Now his job was over: he warned them of what was coming, and what they had to do. He had done his job.

> To this John replied, "A man can receive only what is given him from heaven. You yourselves can testify that I said, 'I am not the Christ but am sent ahead of him.' The bride belongs to the bridegroom. The friend who attends the bridegroom waits and listens for him, and is full of joy when he hears the bridegroom's voice. That joy is mine, and it is now complete. He must become greater; I must become less. (John 3:27-30)

The ministry of Christ

From here the Gospels take up the history of the King himself, Jesus Christ. We learn about his birth, and a few details of his childhood. But the history of Jesus starts getting detailed

The History of the New Testament

when he begins his actual ministry, starting with his baptism at John's hands.

From there we read about his approximately three-year ministry during which he "went through all the towns and villages, teaching in their synagogues, preaching the good news of the kingdom and healing every disease and sickness." (Matthew 9:35) He traveled all over the region where the Jews lived – from the area around Tyre and Sidon (north of the Sea of Galilee) down to Jerusalem itself. He worked mainly with the Jews, though occasionally he dealt with Gentiles (when circumstances allowed for it).

Another job he took on was the training of the twelve disciples. Not only did he come to announce the Kingdom of God, and teach the Jews what was about to happen to God's people, he laid the foundation for the future growth of this Kingdom – and the apostles were the key to that future.

We won't get into the details of what he taught and did during his ministry, since we will look at those things later. But when he felt that he had accomplished what he came to do, he *then* allowed the Jews to take him prisoner. The Jews, since they weren't allowed to put even their own prisoners to death, talked the Romans into doing the job for them. Even though Jesus had gotten a large public following over that three years, the hatred of the Jewish leaders was so intense that they whipped up the crowd into supporting their treacherous and unjust judgment against Jesus.

He was crucified according to Roman fashion. Only when he was determined to be dead by the Roman soldiers on the scene was his body removed from the cross and put in a borrowed tomb. His disciples returned disappointed to their former jobs. Everyone thought that the Kingdom that Jesus came to set up had come to an abrupt and disastrous end.

They little knew the Scriptures that predicted the power of that coming Kingdom! God raised Jesus from the dead after three days – this time with a body that could not be destroyed. The disciples saw him. Paul claims that over 500 people saw him over the next forty days. Finally, there was a last farewell when Jesus gave them some last minute instructions and he returned to Heaven in full view of hundreds of witnesses.

The birth of the Church

Even then the disciples knew almost nothing of what to expect next. They were together in an "upper room" (perhaps the same one where Jesus ate his last Passover meal with them). Suddenly the Spirit of God came down on them and they were enabled to speak in a score of foreign languages. They praised God in languages that none of them previously knew – a miraculous event.

At that same moment, there were thousands of pilgrims in Jerusalem for the Pentecost feast at the Temple. They overheard the disciples in the house declaring the Gospel in their own tongue – these pilgrims had come from all over the Roman empire for the feast – and naturally were amazed at what was happening. When Peter explained to them what was going on, and challenged them to repent and believe in the Gospel themselves, thousands did so on the spot and the Christian Church was born.

They grouped themselves together and "devoted themselves to the apostles' teaching and to the fellowship, to the breaking of bread and to prayer." (Acts 2:42). They quickly realized that the Spirit was leading them to form a brotherhood for the mutual benefit of all and the worship of God in Christ. They also learned about the job that Christ brought them together for: to spread the Gospel to all nations and peoples, and to make disciples of men and women everywhere. The Church was to grow and become universal.

One of the first things they learned was that the covenant wasn't just for Jews anymore. During the Old Testament the Lord kept things strictly within the Jewish circle; the covenant was limited to Abraham and his children. That left Gentiles out in the cold. But Peter and Paul were instructed to take the Gospel of Christ to Gentiles, and the Church learned that the old Jewish system of Law was superseded by a life of faith in Christ and following the Spirit. The door to salvation was now open to *any* who will believe.

The result was that the Jews as a group became offended with this upstart religion that seemingly had such a low view of the Law – especially the extra law that the Pharisees had come up with. So the Church leaders decided the Jews weren't going to be a fruitful field to work in, and they took their message almost exclusively to the Gentiles.

The Spread of the Gospel

The apostles took their message all over the Roman Empire, and if rumors had any basis in fact, some of them went outside of the Empire with the Gospel. Thomas, for example, was supposed to have visited India. Almost all of them were persecuted and killed for their faith.

Paul was the apostle who was given the job of opening up the Gentile field, for the most part. He made three missionary journeys through Asia Minor, covering many of the major cities and planting new churches wherever he went. He was the epitome of the apostle: always preaching Christ, always confronting the enemies of the Gospel, always starting and encouraging new churches, always being persecuted, always doing good to his enemies, always on the move.

The History of the New Testament

The apostles knew that they could touch only a few lives along the way, and they therefore made written records of their message and spread them around. The Gospels were written at this time, plus the various letters that Paul, Peter, James and some others wrote. These letters were treasured by the churches that received them. In order that others could get spiritual benefit from the letters, copyists made copies of them and gave them out to other churches – often two churches would trade copies of the letters that they had each received from apostles. In this way the letters of the New Testament quickly ended up all around the Empire – all written in Greek.

As for the extent of the apostolic travels, all we have are hints. Even Paul's travels, as well-attested as they are in Acts and in his letters, don't give us any certainty about his last days. Rumor has it that he either died in Rome at the hands of Caesar, or he was let out of prison and managed to travel as far as Spain.

Leaving it to run on its own

What the apostles did, when they did church planting, was to arrive in town and preach to the crowds wherever they could find them – in a synagogue, in the market square, in town halls, wherever they could. Then when a few people believed the message and were saved, the apostles would gather them together in homes and instruct them further in the faith.

They showed them how to conduct a Christian worship service. Acts 2 shows us the early church at work and what kinds of things they did when they got together. Paul in Corinthians gives us hints about how they conducted meetings, and when. The apostles also trained them on matters that would make them self-sufficient: for example, choosing and training leaders, exercising church discipline, dealing with sin, money matters, and so on.

The History of the New Testament

At a certain point the apostles would move on and let the church continue on its own. This was essential, because in every true church is the life and resources to exist – not only just to carry on, but to prosper spiritually. Like a baby that's born, the church has all the essential parts to grow and do its work under God. Apostles aren't necessary for the church to continue. But their work remains as the foundation of the church: just as in those early days when the new Christians soaked up the Word from the apostles' teaching, now in our day the churches still feed and grow on the testimony that the apostles left behind – the New Testament.

Apocalypse

God's history doesn't end with the New Testament. The apostle John was given visions of the end times, when Christ would return and set up his completed spiritual Kingdom for eternity. That day hasn't arrived yet, though it's been 2000 years since the original prophecies.

The apostles basically finished their part of the plan by the year 100 AD. By then the church was alive and growing, and the second generation of church leaders was continuing to guide the church in the apostolic teaching.

But many things are left unfinished. This is the day for preaching the Gospel and calling sinners to repentance; when they do repent, they join the spiritual church of Christ and join a fellowship of believers somewhere for their mutual benefit and growth. But the wicked still go on in their sins, there is little or no justice, there is still war and famine, there is still ignorance and rebellion in the world. Satan still holds sway over billions of human beings. The church right now is a small minority: they can be found all over the world, but in themselves they are a small flock of sheep trying to maintain their witness in a "howling wilderness."

The day has to come yet when God puts everything to rights. On that day, the wicked will get what they deserve and the righteous what they were promised in Christ. Then the world as we know it will be destroyed – completely, instantly, miraculously – and a "new heavens and a new earth" will be set in its place. Then the history of the world will come to an end, and we will begin a new chapter in the book of God's works.

When the books were written

There has been a constant and heated debate over when the books of the New Testament were written. It seems to me that if it were essential for our faith, we would have been told when they were written! But we don't know; we don't even have the originals that the apostles themselves wrote. But there are a few basic principles that we must believe about the books.

First, every one of these books were the product of a genuine apostle – or they came under the influence of one. Matthew obviously was an apostle, and so was John. Mark was written by a companion of Peter, and Luke was the personal physician of Paul. Hebrews, however, is more difficult. Many Christians feel that Paul wrote the book, while others think that it just doesn't have his style – that perhaps Apollos or Barnabas wrote it. In any case, either of these men were personally trained by one or more of the apostles.

Second, the books are eyewitness testimonies of the life of Christ. They are telling us the truth about Jesus, things that we need for our faith. God considers them to be legal documents that will

The History of the New Testament

convict us on Judgment Day. This is the truth, not the opinions of men or religious feelings that certain people developed on their own. We will be saved if we believe them, and condemned if we don't.

Now as far as when they were written, all we can do here is look at some likely options:

Matthew: Matthew may very well have been the first Gospel written, somewhere around 50 AD. He was the "publican" or "tax collector" mentioned in Matthew 9:9. Tradition says that Matthew first wrote his Gospel in Hebrew, because he primarily targeted a Jewish audience – and then it was later translated into Greek for the entire Church.

Mark: This book was written probably around 64 AD by John Mark, the young man that was perhaps the one mentioned in Mark 14:51-52. Modern scholars say that Mark was the first Gospel written, but the early Church believed that Matthew was first. Mark got his information mainly from the apostle Peter.

Luke: Luke was the Gentile doctor who accompanied Paul on some of his missionary journeys. His Gospel was written probably about 58 AD, and was specifically addressed to his patron Theophilus. His information about Jesus, although coming from many sources, also depended heavily on Paul's insights and knowledge.

John: The apostle whom Jesus specially loved – John – wrote his Gospel later than the others,

The History of the New Testament

probably between 70-80 AD. It adds new material that the first three Gospels (they're called the "Synoptic" Gospels – from "syn" which means "the same", and "optic" which means "to see") didn't mention or say little about.

Acts: Luke wrote this letter too, as a sort of "part two" after his Gospel. Obviously it was written – or at least finished – *after* Paul's last journey to Rome where he spent two years waiting for judgment from Caesar (unfortunately we don't get to find out how it turned out!). That would date it approximately 63 AD.

Paul's letters: Paul came late into the program. His conversion dates around 35 AD. His letters – from the earliest one to Thessalonians to the latest one sent to Timothy – date about 52 to 67 AD. They were written under many circumstances: on the road, in prison, and in-between missionary journeys.

Hebrews: This letter is anonymous; nobody signed it, so we don't really know who wrote it. Some think that Paul wrote it (but it doesn't have his characteristic style) and some think that Apollos wrote it. It might probably have been written before the destruction of the Temple, since it seems to assume that his readers currently enjoy a familiarity with the Temple and its workings. It's date, therefore, would be sometime before 70 AD.

The History of the New Testament

James: The half-brother of Jesus, James became a leader in the church of Jerusalem before the destruction of the Temple. He wrote his letter probably around 45 AD, and it has a decidedly Judaic character that doesn't even mention the Gentile influence in the fledgling church.

Peter's letters: The apostle Peter wrote two letters to the churches probably around 65 AD. He shows an evident familiarity with the other letters of the New Testament, including Paul's.

John's letters: The apostle John also wrote several letters to churches and particular individuals. They also would date later, sometime around 85 AD.

Jude: Jude – the brother of the apostle James – wrote a short note to the church about apostasy in the ranks. This dates it probably later in the growth of the church, around 66 AD.

Revelation: The apostle John's last letter to the churches in Asia Minor (now Turkey). John was in exile on the isle of Patmos when he wrote of his vision of the Lord Jesus and his Kingdom. It dates probably around 90 AD.

These weren't the only letters being sent to and from churches, however. There were many other letters sent by apostolic pretenders, letters that claimed to have some mysterious, formerly unknown information about Jesus and his ministry – and people believed in them. It got so bad, with hundreds of epistles getting sent all over the place, that the church decided something had to be done about it before it got to be ridiculous. They worked on the problem for quite some

The History of the New Testament

time, and finally by 400 AD they accepted a list of what they considered to be true and genuine apostolic letters – which forms our New Testament today. Their list is called the **canon** of Scripture.

Their criteria was that the letter had to have external evidences – a good history of where it had come from, and that it could be shown to be a work of the original apostles or at least under their direct supervision. It also had to show internal evidence as being the work of an apostle. James, for instance, gave them real problems because its message seemed to contradict the apostolic teaching of living by faith, not by works. Hebrews too was a problem because there wasn't any clear evidence that an apostle wrote it. But its message was so plainly apostolic that they included it in the canon.

Geography and Culture

As soon as we open the pages of the New Testament we realize that we are in a different world. Even though we now have this book in English, it seems to be a world all of its own that no amount of translating will make any plainer. And even when we have studied its customs and language we still don't understand certain things in it.

As a matter of fact, it *is* a different world, and the only way we can possibly understand it is to go back in time and live in it ourselves. That's true of any culture; you have to "walk in their shoes" if you really want to know why they live like they did and if you want to appreciate what they loved and feared.

Culture is a funny thing: everyone grows up in a culture, and you would think that you could explain your culture to someone from another country; but that isn't always true. The reasons why we value some things and not others, why we work for certain goals and not others, why we arrange our lives in certain ways and not in other ways, make sense to us until we try to explain them to someone who doesn't share our outlook on life.

And that's also true about the world of the Bible. Their culture was much different from ours, which is why we have trouble understanding it. But they weren't trying to explain their culture to us – they assumed that we wouldn't need to know

Geography and Culture

about that, so they spent their time explaining the things that transcend culture.

We don't have time here to get into a full-blown discussion on "culture" and how it relates to God's work in this world, but we do have to define some terms before we go on. "Culture" is the way a people live their daily lives. It could be a very low, "primitive" culture, or it could be a very complex and "advanced" culture. It consists of everything from what we wear and what we eat to how we run our government and how we educate our children. Cultures vary widely over the world; every "people group" (a local group tied together by language or geographic area or economic system or political system, sometimes as small as a local tribe or clan) has a distinguishing culture that makes it different from everyone else.

Much of culture is neither good nor bad. It doesn't make any difference, morally speaking, whether someone wears shoes or sandals, speaks Spanish or Japanese, eats rice or snakes, works in a factory or skins alligators. Sometimes, however, a cultural practice can be either very good or very bad. For example, Christian missionaries have had a difficult time persuading African chiefs that polygamy – a practice that has been passed down in their tribes for generations and that they stoutly claim is their "culture" – is wrong and against God's will. And we also have our own "sacred cows" in our culture that the Bible says are immoral – though we hate to give them up.

All this is to say that the people in the New Testament had a culture of their own, and much of it was perfectly legitimate. Of course we aren't going to understand it, because we didn't grow up in their world and it often takes years to break through some cultural practices and see the unspoken assumptions behind them.

Geography and Culture

But the point is this: *their particular culture is not the point that the Scripture is making*. God used their culture as a medium (a fitting one, to be sure, and not something to be taken lightly and still less to be ignored) for the *eternal* message. God's Truth is the one thing that is *not* cultural; it's beyond culture, above man's ways of doing things, guaranteed to be the same across any culture and across all time. God's Truth never changes; and it's the same truth to a tribal African as it is to an American businessman.

The beauty of reading the New Testament stories is that we get to see a real example of when God's Truth got worked out in a particular culture. It's as if the Lord were saying, "Here – this is an example of how I want you to use this truth." We don't necessarily have to do it exactly like the Jews and early Christians did it. For example, to think that one has to dress oneself in a plain robe and sandals, and travel from city to city on foot, make tents, and eat goat meat, in order to preach – just because that's how Paul did it – is entirely missing the point! We have our own ways to live out these truths.

On the other hand, we mustn't ignore the way that God used that particular Biblical culture. In his providence he used the Christians in *their* world, at that point in history, because no other culture would have done the job so well for his purposes of making the New Testament. Just because we have different ways of living nowadays doesn't mean that our ways of applying God's Truth are just as good as the Bible's examples – often we have far inferior ways of applying his Truth, and we would do well to take some lessons from the older saints. Newer is often worse, not better; it doesn't have the benefit of experience.

Basically speaking, whatever the Scripture *specifically* says to do or believe, we have no option or right to reinterpret in our own way; that's precisely what God wants us to do, and how

Geography and Culture

he wants us to do it. But where it says to apply a principle and it doesn't give us specific instructions on how to apply it, then it's our job to find a way to apply it in the context of our own culture.

In any case, studying the early Christians' world is both interesting and instructive. What we want to do here is take a quick look at the land they lived in and the way they lived. If you want a more complete study on this subject there are many good books that can go into more detail; here we will just paint a broad picture in order to appreciate the fact that the world of the New Testament is more important than we may have thought.

Geography

The story of the Bible is set in Canaan, a strip of land on the eastern shore of the Mediterranean Sea. (For maps of Palestine, please consult those in the back of your Bible – most editions of the Bible will have excellent maps showing the geography of Israel, and the ministries of Christ and Paul.) The land itself isn't very big – about 130 miles north to south, 35 miles across the top from west to east, and 90 miles across the bottom. On the larger scale it sits on the western edge of what is called the Middle East, a large area of land that was home to some of the world's most powerful empires in history. As a matter of fact, aside from the history of the Jews and the ministry of Christ and the apostles, Canaan was a small pawn in the never-ending shuffle of power between such kingdoms as Assyria, Egypt, Babylon, Persia, Syria, Turkey, and modern day Iran and Iraq.

Being a coastal country, Canaan naturally changes in geography as it moves away from the Mediterranean toward the desert behind it. It has four types of land area, each type running north and south like long strips through Canaan: *first*, the flat coastal plain on the edge of the sea; *second*, the abruptly rising mountains; *third*, the mountains fall off sharply into the trough

Geography and Culture

where the Jordan River runs from the Sea of Galilee down to the Dead Sea; *fourth,* a plain rises out of that trough and extends into the desert.

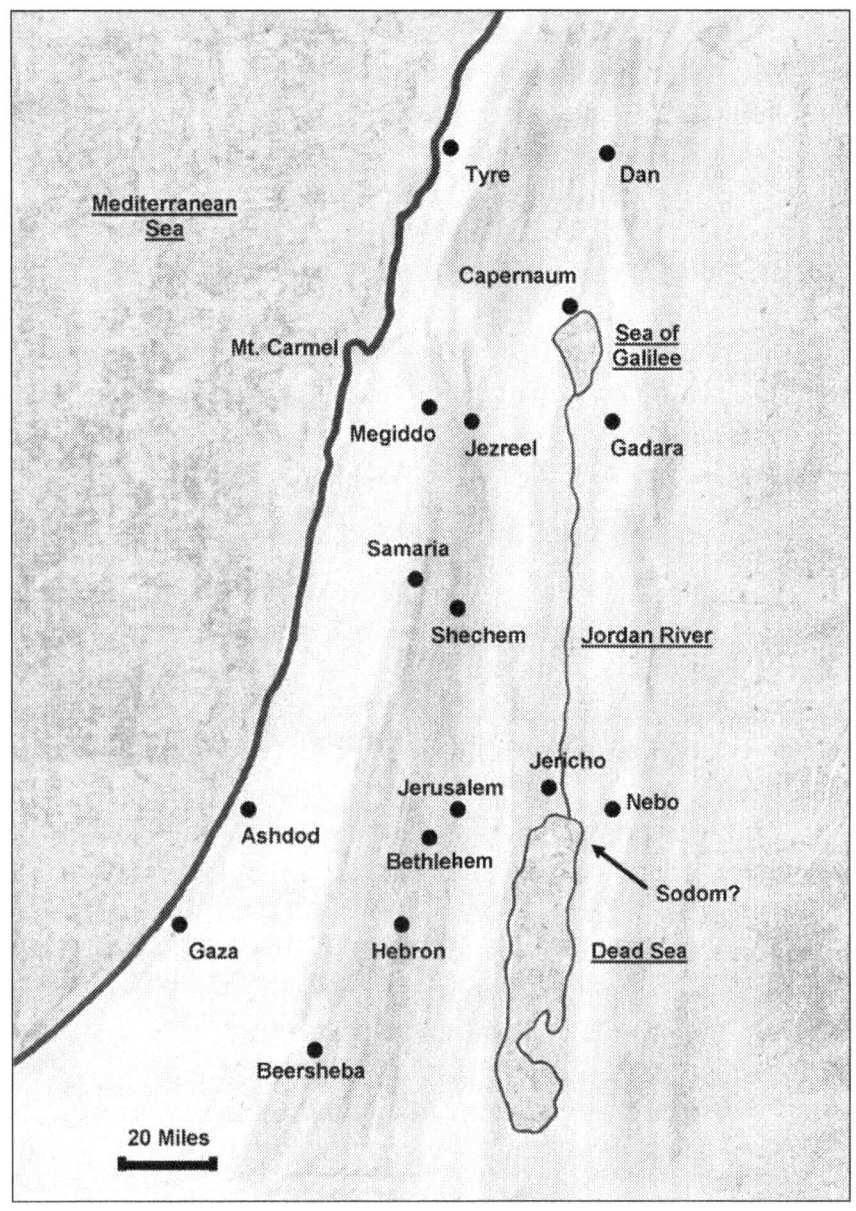

A Map of Palestine

Geography and Culture

Rainfall varies widely over Canaan. Most of the rain falls in the northern part of the land, mostly around Dan and Mt. Hermon in the north and gradually tapering off as you move south to Jerusalem. By the time you get to Beersheba in the far south there is very little rain during the year. Almost all of the rain falls in the winter months, from December to February. The rest of the year is usually exceptionally dry and very hot.

Over thousands of years the amount of forestation in Canaan has dramatically changed. There used to be thick forests covering the mountains of Israel. Man's inexhaustible needs for wood and grazing land took a heavy toll on Israel's greenery. Because of the need for wood for housing and heating and shipping and iron smelting, and clearing out pastures for herds and areas for towns, and the inevitable erosion that took over, the land today is in very different shape than it was 1000-2000 years before Christ.

Canaan was a natural crossroads for the Middle East. Because travelers didn't want to risk the dangers of desert journeys, they moved through Palestine on their way south to Egypt or north and east to Mesopotamia There were well-traveled roads that ran the length of Israel, both along the shore of the Mediterranean and along the mountain ridge from Dan to Beersheba. Merchants and armies and kings and slavers all traveled these roads – which means that the Jews had a wonderful view of how the rest of the world lived. They heard all the gossip from distant lands, they saw the customs of other peoples, they bought and sold to these travelers, and – more importantly – they were constantly in danger of being attacked by traveling bands or armies. It was just too easy, without natural defenses, for a powerful neighbor to march in along the roads and lay siege to Israelite towns and cities. Enemies could pick them off like shooting fish in a barrel.

Geography and Culture

On a map you will notice the two cities Megiddo and Jezreel. They lie in a trough between a triangle of mountain ranges – Mt. Carmel to the west, the range on the south that extends down to Jerusalem, and the range on the north reaching up from Dan to Turkey. That trough is a valley that lies at the crossing of roads going north, south and east – the perfect place for a meeting of armies. As a matter of fact, it was the site of some terrible battles between Israel and other nations, and the Scripture uses this place as the picture of the final battle between nations at the end of time – Armageddon, the "mountain (the Hebrew word for mountain is *har*, which loses its initial "h" when it moves into English) of Megiddo."

There was a main road that branched away from the road that runs alongside the Mediterranean Sea. It crossed the mountains in the area of Jerusalem and Bethlehem, plunged down into the Jordan River valley, and then ran north along the river past the Sea of Galilee and up into northern Mesopotamia. It was on this road, the place where it leaves the high mountains east of Jerusalem and overlooks the Jordan River below, that the Good Samaritan found a Jew lying helplessly on the road – a victim of the ever-present robbers that hid among the rocks and crags along the roads in those days.

The Dead Sea is the lowest spot on earth. It lies in the southern part of the Jordan River valley and is the lowest spot of that valley. One can look down from the edge of the mountains just ten miles east of Jerusalem and see over much of that lower valley – the Jordan River running into the Dead Sea and the northern section of the Sea. In fact, scholars think that Sodom and Gomorrah, long thought to lie on the southern edge of the Dead Sea, actually were on the northern edge; their reasoning is that the Bible states that:

> Early the next morning Abraham got up and returned to the place where he had stood before the

Geography and Culture

Lord. He looked down toward Sodom and Gomorrah, toward all the land of the plain, and he saw dense smoke rising from the land, like smoke from a furnace. (Genesis 19:27-28)

Jerusalem lies along the top of the central mountain range of Israel, nestled among some peaks that provided a natural barrier against enemies. One peak formed part of the city itself – Mt. Zion. As you read some of the Psalms you will notice that they are called "songs of ascent" – this is literally true. Jews came from all over Israel to worship at the Temple in Jerusalem at proscribed feasts, and as they came close to the city they had to climb *up* to the city in the mountains, and especially up to the Temple on Mt. Zion in the middle of the city. As they traveled up to Jerusalem on festival occasions they sang these songs in anticipation of the worship ceremony on the Temple Mount.

Lifestyles

Even within the pages of the Bible itself there were widely different customs that the different peoples of those days practiced. Without getting into the more obvious details – clothing, food, weapons, means of travel, shelter, etc. – we will look at some of the broader elements of their culture that explain much of what we may find puzzling in the stories of the New Testament.

One of the biggest differences between their world and ours was the way the local community operated. We are individuals at heart; it doesn't really matter to us what the rest of the community does as long as it doesn't interfere with what *we* want to do. We are willing to help out in some community matters – we raise money for a new fire truck or mow an elderly person's yard for them – but then we retreat to the shelter of our own homes where nobody can interfere with us.

Geography and Culture

But the culture of the Middle East was centered on the local community. The good of the group took precedence over the good of the individual. This was out of sheer necessity, because those were the days when there was no local police force to handle social problems; the men of a town had to decide what was good for everyone, and then everyone was expected to follow their instructions or people would inevitably die. Such basic necessities that we take for granted, like water and food, were community resources that everyone had to work for and share if all would have enough. Their work was for each other: instead of our way of traveling 10-20 miles to a factory or office where we do impersonal work to accomplish things that benefit people we will probably never meet, those people shoed each other's horses and built each other's furniture and traded milk and meat with each other in order to make a living. In other words, everyone's destiny depended on each other; each man's life could succeed only if the community itself succeeded.

So there were many times when the desires of the individual had to take second place to the desires of the community, simply because rugged individualism was not only unwise but it was dangerous to the good of the whole. We stand aghast at the law in the Old Testament which said that parents of a rebellious son had to bring him to the community leaders and themselves throw the first stones at him to kill him. (Deuteronomy 21:18-21) How could the Law expect parents to treat their son like this, even if he *were* rebellious? But considered in the context of the community there was no other safe recourse for everyone involved. A man who proved to be rebellious to his parents was only going to cause trouble for the whole town, and they didn't need that. He just may be the downfall of the town! At the very least he wouldn't carry his share of the load of work and responsibility, which meant that everyone else had to work extra hard to make up for his laziness or destructive habits. That would be like having an enemy within the ranks; many a town had fallen to the rape and slaughter and destruction of alien armies because of one man's sin. So rather than saddling the community with a problem like that and causing everyone pain and trouble, the parents were expected to themselves deal with the problem before it got to that stage. Their individual needs were second in importance to the needs of the community. Besides, by letting him live they were only postponing the inevitable (if it was inevitable – I'm sure that *every* "rebellious son" was not put to death, simply because we *all* have sin in our hearts! This was only for hard-core cases, such as we have in our society); the community would later find it necessary to put him to death for worse crimes if he were allowed to live, and then the shame would never leave his parents' household.

The community's success meant success for the individual. If there was plenty of rain and the bugs and birds didn't eat all of the harvest, the whole town benefited from the harvest; then the people would celebrate together with festivals. But if danger or famine struck the town, everyone suffered; there was no such thing as insurance in those days, and one family couldn't go out on their own to avoid the hazards of the community – it was do or die for all of the people together. If life was good, they all enjoyed it; if life was bad, they died together.

The family itself was also different from our modern family, and the reason was again because of survival and efficiency. We are individualists to the core, and usually we don't think twice about making the family serve our own personal purposes. But with them it was the other way around; each member served the purposes of the family. They put aside any thoughts of doing things that they wanted if it didn't fit in with the family's immediate needs.

In the first place, "family" was usually much larger than Mom and Dad and brother and sister. It wasn't unusual for uncles and aunts and grandparents and cousins to share a house together – the family was actually a small community in itself! They had to do it this way because life was rough, and trying to make it on your own meant certain failure. One needs lots of labor to manage flocks of sheep or cattle; one needs many hands to harvest a field of grain when the only tools were sickle and fork! Gathering and storing and preparing food, and making clothing, were jobs that lasted the year round; and that took up all the time available from sun-up to sundown, since they lacked the fast efficiency of modern technology that we have today. So it made much more sense to stick together rather than to separate, and newlyweds would take their place in their parents' homes and farms rather than go off by themselves to pursue their own "careers."

In the family, Dad was boss. He had that right in the eyes of the community, and he also had the responsibility that went with the job. He plowed the fields, he tended the herds, he attended community meetings and shouldered his share of the community work. When it came time to defend the town against their enemies, he took sword in hand and risked his life for his family. The average life expectancy of men in those days wasn't very long, given their hard labor and high death rate in battle. So nobody questioned his authority; in fact, respect for Father ran much deeper in that society than it does in ours. We think nothing of doing our own thing even if it runs against the wishes of our parents; they wouldn't have dared to think that way. The father had years of experience that the children needed if they hoped to make it in life as well as he had. If they got on his good side, they were assured of his inheritance and therefore of a secure future. And he bought the right – with his hard labor and protection and respect from his peers in the community – to be held in honor by his children. A man who had rebellious and self-willed children hid his head in shame when he went about the town.

Geography and Culture

Women never strayed from the home by themselves; not only was it not safe, but there was nothing in town for them to do like there is in our society. A woman who wandered the streets alone on her own business was considered a prostitute, because there wasn't any other reason she would be out there unless it was on family business. Women had plenty to do at home without wandering around doing their own thing: preparing meals (which took up a large part of the day), taking care of the children, carrying water (a small detail to us but a major chore in those days), planting and hoeing fields, making and mending clothing (again a long, involved process with the primitive tools that they had). If the women didn't pull their weight in this way, the family would literally starve or go in rags!

Children were extremely important in those days. In our own time children seem to be more of a nuisance than a blessing; they get in the way of our careers or whatever we want to enjoy in life. To many in our day, children are a curse! But to the Israelites, children were a blessing from God: it meant ready hands (if not willing!) in the fields and family business. They also served as a retirement plan: when the parents were too old to carry on, the children took over the family business and cared for Mom and Pop as long as they lived. That seems unfair to us that the children would be so bound by their family ties like this. But the day was coming when those children would need the same help from *their* children – the system worked. Nobody minded when everyone benefited.

A word about work in those days. Unless one was rich (and there were very few who were) one could expect to work as long as there was daylight. That meant that there was almost no time for leisure or hobbies or taking it easy. In our culture we think ourselves ill-used if we work more than eight hours a day. In their day, they felt that they had a chance to survive – and therefore were blessed by God – if they had strength and health

Geography and Culture

to work for 14-18 hours a day. There was no such thing as a vacation for them. They worked all their lives, and usually had only a place to live, a field to plow, perhaps some pasture land, maybe some flocks of sheep, to show for their hard work when they died. One's inheritance in those days would have made us laugh at its pitiful scarcity; but it meant the success of the children if they used it as wisely as their parents did.

The military life of those ancient people was also much different than we experience in our culture. Because of the necessity placed on them by their circumstances, nobody was exempt from service unless they were physically unable to take sword in hand. Young and old helped to defend the town from attackers; nobody argued about such matters when the town was liable to be burned to the ground and all the men and children inside murdered and the women carried off to grace the beds of their enemies! It was a hard world, and they did whatever was necessary to protect themselves and their families. And there were many times when the men were called out to travel across country to help other towns against their enemies. They did it willingly for a couple of reasons: first, those enemies, if successful against one town, would probably be at their own doorstep someday; and second, their community spirit extended to the whole race, and they were willing to die to help the entire Jewish nation succeed. The good of the nation outweighed the good of the local town and the individual.

Social agreements were fascinating in those days. Remember that they had no police force. When two men made an agreement with each other, they were expected to make sure *themselves* that the other man kept to the agreement. If one reneged on the deal, the other man had the right, in the community's eyes, to take whatever action that would be necessary to get what was due him. Who else would do it for him? The community would support him in his struggle for justice, but it was up to him to get it; nobody else could do it for him. So if he was cheated and had no way to force the other man to make it right, he was just cheated, that's all. That's why there was a strange-sounding law in the Old Testament about accidental killings: if a man accidentally killed another, the victim's family had the right to pursue the killer and kill him – unless he found safety in a City of Refuge and convinced the elders of that town that he was really innocent. Otherwise the victim's family had the right to his life. And if they didn't kill him, nobody else would; it was *their* responsibility to take care of the matter because nobody else had the right to his life.

Greek influence

Since coming back from the Exile in Babylon the Jews were rarely left alone by other nations. For a time they came under Greek influence (from the conquering armies of Alexander the Great), and it showed in their culture. Many Jews absolutely refused to have anything to do with the foreigners; but some Jews, looking for new experiences and contacts (perhaps profitable ones!) with the outside world, took on Greek ways and dress. This was always a bone of contention in Jewish circles: there were those who were "liberal" and trained their children in the ways of the "world," and there were conservatives who fought to resist outside influences, and raised their children to be faithful, orthodox Jews.

One influence, as we've seen already, that laid a foundation for the future of the Church was the fact that the Greek language became part of everyday life. Even when the Romans conquered the area later, most people in Palestine knew Greek and communicated on paper with that language. The apostles all wrote their letters in Greek because their churches, that were found all over the Roman empire, all knew and spoke Greek fluently.

But Greek influence went deeper than just the language. Philo, for example, who was a Jewish philosopher, was as Greek in his thinking as he could be. He wrote a great deal about the "mysteries" of the universe, and even wrote about the Logos – the mystical principle of the Word of God that lay as a foundation underneath God's Creation. His teaching no doubt influenced the apostle John as he too wrote about the Logos – the Word that was with God in the beginning, through whom all things were created. (John 1:1-5)

Roman influence

The Romans, as we've seen, conquered Palestine also as they made their sweep around the Mediterranean. The country was carved up into sections, and the family of the Herods ruled during the time of Jesus and the apostles.

The Roman government imposed several things on the Jews: *first*, they stationed garrisons of soldiers all through the land to keep the peace and enforce the laws. *Second*, they had their own governor there in Jerusalem to rule over the land in Caesar's name. *Third*, they imposed taxes on the country, and used local Jewish officials to collect them and send them on to Rome.

Aside from this overwhelming political control, the Romans actually affected the Jewish state very little in the way of culture. The main outside cultural influence that the Jews had to contend with was the Greek culture.

Rabbinical influence

After the Exile to Babylon, the Jews were extremely sensitive about the Law. The reason they were punished in the first place was because they weren't taking certain laws seriously. So in order to avoid further displeasure from the

Geography and Culture

Judge of the earth, they resolved to do whatever they could to fulfill the Law as best they could.

Ezra was, according to tradition, the first of the great teachers of the Law that culminated in the rabbis of the New Testament. He supposedly began the Oral Law – a commentary and extension of the Mosaic Law that explored further how to carry out the Law of God in every imaginable circumstance in life. For a long time this Oral Law existed side by side with the written Mosaic Law – a rabbi, or teacher of the Law of God, would learn both systems.

In Jesus' day the Oral Law had reached epic proportions. They had devised thousands of case-law studies on how to please God in every aspect of life. For example, the Jews tried to list every form of work that might be prohibited by the Fourth Commandment –

> Remember the Sabbath day by keeping it holy. Six days you shall labor and do all your work, but the seventh day is a Sabbath to the LORD your God. On it you shall not do any work, neither you, nor your so or daughter, nor your manservant or maidservant, nor your animals, nor the alien within your gates. (Exodus 20:8-10)

They figured out, for instance, that paring your fingernails is work and therefore illegal to do on the Sabbath!

There were three main "parties" of Jews, so to speak, in Jesus' day. The **Pharisees** were the best known; they were the legal experts and the keepers of the Oral Law. They also believed in the resurrection of the dead and a future life. Jesus most often had religious arguments with the Pharisees. The **Sadducees** were less interested in the moral aspects of Judaism, certainly not interested in the world to come (they didn't believe in it!), and very interested in national and local politics. And the **Essenes** were a fringe group that believed in the coming of the Messiah. They mainly gathered in desert communities to separate themselves from the world and prepare themselves morally for the last days.

The Jews had a sensitive relationship with the Romans. Though the Romans maintained ultimate power in Palestine, they let the Jews keep their own ruling body to decide religious, moral, and some political issues. This body of elders was called the Sanhedrin and consisted usually of 70 leaders from around the nation. They were not allowed to put anybody to death – a capital offense was a crime against the state, and therefore came under Roman jurisdiction. Thus they themselves could find Jesus guilty, but they then had to convince the Romans that he had done something against the state – and therefore against Caesar – in order to have him executed.

The third Temple, built by Herod, was still the center of Jewish life. It was a massive structure and one of the marvels of the ancient world. And during the religious festivals, Jerusalem was a hub of multitudes who came from all over the land of Palestine as well as from Jewish communities from the civilized world. But the Jews also had the **synagogue**: a local body of Jews in each community who gathered weekly to read the Scripture and discuss points of Jewish law. It corresponded somewhat to the idea of the local Christian church, and served a tremendous influence in Judaism not only in Biblical days but throughout history into our time.

Probably the one apostle that came under the influence of the rabbis the most was Paul. He was trained to be a rabbi: he was –

> Circumcised on the eighth day, of the people of Israel, of the tribe of Benjamin, a Hebrew of

Hebrews; in regard to the law, a Pharisee; as for zeal, persecuting the church; as for legalistic righteousness, faultless. (Philippians 3:5-6)

And you can see that rigorous legal training in how he presents his theological arguments in his letters. But it's a rabbinical training that has been baptized by the Holy Spirit. He isn't arguing for petty legalistic issues anymore, but for the mystery of the Gospel in Christ.

The Ministry
of Christ

The Ministry of Christ

The ministry of Christ that's recorded in the Gospels was more than just a story or local history. There's a reason we have these four Gospels, even though it's been almost 2000 years since those events took place. People are continually convicted with the story of Christ because something happened there that affects all of God's people, all over the world, in every time and culture. What Jesus did, in fact, affects everyone in history – and we all need to know about it.

The things that Jesus did were things that only he could do. Millions of people before his time tried to address these issues and failed. Philosophers, psychologists, scientists, politicians, and educators have all offered solutions to man's problems and failed. The Jews worked for 2000 years before the arrival of Christ, and were spiritually bankrupt by the time he arrived to tackle the same job. The requirements that God set down for his Kingdom were so complex, so spiritual, so eternal, so huge, that no government or organization or movement of man had ever, and has never since, succeeded in working them out. What is astonishing, however, is that Jesus came and single-handedly did the entire thing in one lifetime! Surely this is the Son of God doing what only God can do!

What Jesus did was fulfill the Old Testament system. The Jews missed it, because they weren't reading "between the lines" – they missed the importance of Jesus' work because they didn't understand what God was really doing in Moses' and the prophets' day. But the Temple led to Jesus, the Exodus led to Jesus, the story of Joseph taught about Jesus, the covenant to Abraham was founded on Jesus, the kingdom of David led to Jesus – they were all building up to the final stage when Jesus would come and pull it all together. The wise Bible student will see the unbroken bond between the Old and New Testaments, with Jesus as the keystone between the two systems of God's Kingdom.

What Jesus did was to lay the foundation for the Church and Judgment Day. If we have eyes to see it, he worked at setting down the foundation, the basic principles, the goals, of the Church. He picked and trained apostles to spread the Gospel to other peoples so that the Church would grow. He showed us the way the Church has to work, the materials it has to be built from, and the reason for its existence.

What Jesus did clears up the fog about what Jews were confused about. You can ask a Jew even now about what certain Old Testament passages or concepts really mean, and he won't be able to tell you. But once a person studies the life and work of Christ, concepts like the Passover and the sacrificial lamb, the Exodus and receiving the Law at Sinai, the kingdom of David and Solomon, the Temple and the sacrificial system, all become easier to understand.

Faith alone can grasp the truth about Christ. He came in humility, he refused to publish himself and glorify himself, he spoke in parables deliberately to confuse people, he answered questions with questions, he challenged time-honored traditions – he was a constant enigma. And he still is. But faith is the ability to see the world of God, to see the reality behind the veil. Faith sees the truth about Jesus: that he's more than the eye of flesh can perceive. Faith can take hold of the power and wisdom of Christ and take advantage of the riches that God has put in him for us.

The Ministry of Christ

Christ quite literally put together Christianity for us. Without his hard work, we wouldn't have a faith or hope to live by. So what we want to do is look at some of the things that were on Christ's agenda when he came to earth for the first time.

Saves his people

Jesus' primary purpose in coming into this world was to save his people from their sin. But not only do few people know that, even Christians have little understanding of how important it is, or how extensive and complex a job it will be.

When Jesus was born, the angel came to Joseph and Mary and told them what they must name their new child:

> She will give birth to a son, and you are to give him the name Jesus, because he will save his people from their sins. (Matthew 1:21)

There's a good reason for this. Jesus was the Jewish God come in the flesh; he was also called "Immanuel" – which means "God with us." The same God of the Old Testament, in other words, had appeared among them. Who was this God? What was his name? In the Old Testament he had a special name that set him apart from all other gods. Moses learned this name from him:

> The LORD, the LORD, the compassionate and gracious God, slow to anger, abounding in love and faithfulness, maintaining love to thousands, and forgiving wickedness, rebellion and sin. Yet he does not leave the guilty unpunished; he punishes the children and their children for the sin of the fathers to the third and fourth generation. (Exodus 34:6-7)

The Ministry of Christ

The name **Yahweh** had this meaning, according to the God of Israel. This formula for his name became well known, and many of the prophets quoted it later in their writings many centuries later (for example, see Nehemiah 9:17; Psalm 86:15-16; Jonah 4:2). The point was that the Jews had to turn to *this* God when they had sinned. They knew, by his name, that he wanted to forgive them and restore them to righteousness. No matter what they had done, if they would just repent he would forgive them.

And the Jews needed this God badly. They seemed to be the epitome of sinners! Every time they turned around they were guilty of some sin. But they kept finding God there ready and waiting for them, gracious and merciful, more than they could hope for. For example, King David was called a "man after God's own heart." (1 Samuel 13:14) He set up the Kingdom according to God's will, and led the people back to God in worship and service. All other kings were measured against David and his work. But in a fit of passion he committed adultery with another man's wife and then murdered her husband to cover up his crime. According to the Law, such a man must be put to death! He at least should have expected to be deposed as king over God's people. But he found his God so merciful, so gracious, so amazingly forgiving, that he repented in full confidence that his God would receive him back and restore him to his rule. David plumbed the depths of God's forgiving love and found that it was deep enough to cover his awful sin (see Psalm 51).

Jesus came to show us even greater depths of God's love. He spent his time with "sinners," tax collectors, prostitutes, lepers, the sick and blind and deaf, the demon-possessed, the despised of society. He came, he said, to "call sinners to repentance." (Luke 5:32) He preached salvation to all those who would come to God and ask for it.

The Ministry of Christ

But the greatest act of God's love, the act that actually broke the back of sin and death and made it possible for God's people to get freedom from the power of sin, was Jesus' death on the cross. He didn't have to die that way. He had glory with God before his incarnation, and he didn't have to come in such humility and end up in such shame. But he laid his life down willingly for his people, that they might be saved from their sin and escape the wrath to come on sinners. He took their sin on his own back and suffered the punishment that was rightfully theirs.

What this accomplished was our delivery from the power of sin. *Now a Christian doesn't have to sin.* This isn't to say that he won't, because we still have the "flesh," the "old man," that hates to give up sin. But with our hearts made alive to God and made new, and the Spirit of God living in us, we are free from the oppressive power of sin – it's no longer our master. We *can* walk away from it now. Now any sinner can find a love without limits if they turn to Christ for salvation. If we follow the Spirit we can turn our backs on sin and please God with the way we live. Sin is no longer our master.

This means that we are finally going to get rid of the one thing that made us offensive to God. He's going to let us into his Heaven, and we're going to live with him in eternity. Sin was the one thing that kept us from getting close to God and ruined our chances of living forever; with that gone, there is now nothing separating us from God. And it's all due to Christ's work.

> For I am convinced that neither death nor life, neither angels nor demons, neither the present nor the future, nor any powers, neither height nor depth, nor anything else in all creation, will be able to separate us from the love of God that is in Christ Jesus our Lord. (Romans 8:38-39)

The Ministry of Christ
Fulfills the covenant

When God decided to solve the problem that sin and death introduced into his Creation, he started with Abraham. The covenant with Abraham is the beginning of the answer that we have all been looking for.

The Lord promised to do four things for Abraham and his descendants:

To give him a son: Abraham and Sarah had no children when they moved to Canaan in obedience to the Lord's command. They were advanced in years at the time, and had basically given up hope that they ever would have a natural-born son. But the Lord promised them that they would, in fact, have their own son — clearly an impossible thing.

> But Abram said, "O Sovereign Lord, what can you give me since I remain childless and the one who will inherit my estate is Eliezer of Damascus?" And Abram said, "You have given me no children; so a servant in my household will be my heir." Then the word of the Lord came to him: "This man will not be your heir, but a son coming from your own body will be your heir." (Genesis 15:2-4)

He was too old to have a son, and his wife was long past the child-bearing age for women. God was promising them the impossible — a miracle, which happens to be the very method he uses to build his kingdom. At one point they both laughed at the idea of having a son in their old age; when the boy was born, then, they named him

"Isaac" which means "he laughs" (perhaps because the Lord had the last laugh in this!).

The promise was fulfilled in Genesis 21:

> Now the Lord was gracious to Sarah as he had said, and the Lord did for Sarah what he had promised. Sarah became pregnant and bore a son to Abraham in his old age, at the very time God had promised him. (Genesis 21:1-2)

To give him the land: When the Lord brought Abraham to Canaan, it wasn't just for a sight-seeing tour! He had Abraham look around at this new place and promised him that one day, both he and his descendants would own this land.

> Lift up your eyes from where you are and look north and south, east and west. All the land that you see I will give to you and your offspring forever. (Genesis 13:14)

The problem was that this would have to be as much of a miracle as the first promise! The Canaanites who already lived there wouldn't take kindly to an alien with strange ways and accents settling down among them, taking their valuable pasture and resources — they especially wouldn't appreciate his notions of owning the whole place someday! So they no doubt kept their eye on him at all times and encouraged him to move on, not settle down. (You can see this very thing happen in the story of Isaac — Genesis 26:12-31.)

The fulfillment of this promise came about in a strange way, certainly not in the way that Abraham would have wanted. Sarah his wife eventually died, and after Abraham mourned over her he looked around for a place to bury her. Since he had no land of his own, he went to the Hittites (a Canaanite tribe living near Hebron) and asked to buy from them a field with a cave in it so that he could bury her. They agreed on a price and the deed was made out in Abraham's name; he became the legal owner of a piece of Canaanite property for the first time.

> So Ephron's field in Machpelah near Mamre — both the field and the cave in it, and all the trees within the borders of the field — was deeded to Abraham as his property in the presence of all the Hittites who had come to the gate of the city ... So the field and the cave in it were deeded to Abraham by the Hittites as a burial site. (Genesis 23:17-18, 20)

The remarkable thing about this transaction was that it was the beginning of the fulfillment of the second promise that God made with Abraham. He was to become owner of the entire land, in spite of the Canaanites already living there. This was the first step to that ownership. It happened in the midst of trial; certainly Abraham didn't want his wife to die. Nevertheless that trial was the means that the Lord used to bring about what otherwise would have never happened.

To make a great nation from him: The Lord promised Abraham that not only would he get a son, but his descendants would become so numerous that they would be a great nation that nobody could count.

> I will make you into a great nation. (Genesis 12:2)

> He took him outside and said, "Look up at the heavens and count the stars — if indeed you can count them." Then he said to him, "So shall your offspring be." (Genesis 15:5)

Now Abraham couldn't become a nation all by himself. And his son couldn't become a nation without getting married. So they had a problem on their hands: where to find a wife for Isaac? Abraham absolutely refused to get one of the local Canaanite girls for Isaac's wife; they were pagans, worshippers of idols and would lead his son into wickedness and away from the Lord. So Abraham had his servant go back home to Haran where his extended family still lived and find a wife there.

Most people use this story as an example of how to find a suitable marriage partner. But we miss the main point of the story if we limit ourselves to just that. Genesis 24 is really showing us the beginning of the fulfillment of the third promise — the making of a nation. He provided a wife (Rebekah) to be the mother of Jacob, who was the father of twelve sons, who were the fathers of the twelve tribes of Israel. The promise had begun to unfold!

The Ministry of Christ

> And they blessed Rebekah and said to her, "Our sister, may you increase to thousands upon thousands; may your offspring possess the gates of their enemies." (Genesis 24:60)

To bless the nations through him: When man first sinned in the Garden of Eden, he brought upon himself and the entire world a tremendous curse of misery and death. As far as God was concerned, this was the worst thing that could have happened to his beautiful creation. He didn't curse us because he liked to, but because he had to. He had to confront sin with the severity of the Law because justice is important to him.

But the Lord never did like that answer for the entire world. From the very beginning he set about putting together a new answer for the problem of sin and death. He hinted at what it might be in Genesis 3:15, but he didn't really say yet what he had in mind.

Now in Abraham's life he was ready to start putting the plan into action. The first step was to promise Abraham that he would be a blessing to the nations:

> And all peoples on earth will be blessed through you. (Genesis 12:3)

> And through your offspring all nations on earth will be blessed. (Genesis 22:18)

This blessing would overturn the original curse that fell on mankind. But what would it look

The Ministry of Christ

like? Again, Abraham got a "foretaste", a glimpse of what that would look like, in his own experience. The Lord told him one time to take his only son Isaac and sacrifice him to the Lord "on one of the mountains I will tell you about." (Genesis 22:2) So Abraham took Isaac there and started to draw the sacrificial knife across his son's throat. Immediately the Lord stopped him and commended him for his faith.

What went through Abraham's mind during this crisis? He was about to lose his only hope! Upon Isaac rested the future of the entire covenant; it didn't make sense to put him to death, even if it *was* in obedience to the Lord. But the Lord showed Abraham a truth there that strengthened him to go on with the act:

> Abraham reasoned that God could raise the dead, and figuratively speaking, he did receive Isaac back from death. (Hebrews 11:19)

Abraham learned about resurrection that day; he got the first sample himself when the Lord gave Isaac back to him. This was in fulfillment of the fourth promise — the blessing that God had in mind, eventually, for people all around the world: life from the dead, eternal life.

So in Abraham's own lifetime he saw the beginning of all four of the promises that God had made to him in the covenant. They weren't complete fulfillments; his descendants would see much more as God kept these promises of the covenant. But they were foretastes, glimpses, the first experiences of the reality that God had for him and his children.

The Ministry of Christ

We must move on, however. The Lord had much bigger things in mind for Abraham and his children. Not only was the first taste of the promises insufficient, but all that came after that for many centuries failed to exhaust what God had in mind for Abraham's family. "These were all commended for their faith, yet *none* of them received what had been promised. God had planned something better for us so that only together with us would they be made perfect." (Hebrews 11:39-40)

Imagine a huge mansion, and the front door leads into a small room. From there you can go on into the rest of the mansion and see the richness and vastness of the place, or you can stay there in the little front room and miss out on the rest. Abraham's taste of what God had in mind in the covenant was like that little first room. The covenant was actually referring to the huge spiritual realities that lay beyond the limitations of time and space; it speaks of the Kingdom of God, Heaven, the vast treasuries that lay in God's eternal vaults. The front room is part of the mansion, but it hardly begins to show us what lies beyond its doors.

Abraham himself knew that he was only tasting the first fruits of the Kingdom of God. We have proof of this from the inspired writers of the Bible, who knew for certain (through the Spirit who knows the thoughts and hearts of all men) what went through Abraham's mind during his life. In fact, without this testimony we would never know for sure what Abraham knew! But we *can* know with confidence what Abraham really believed about these things, now that we have the New Testament's testimony.

Let's go through each of the four promises in the covenant and see what Abraham knew then about it or would eventually come to know:

The Ministry of Christ

The promise of the son: Abraham knew that his son Isaac wasn't the full promise that God had in mind, when the Lord promised to give him a son. We have proof of this from Jesus himself:

> Your father Abraham rejoiced at the thought of seeing *my day*; he saw it and was glad. (John 8:56)

There were several things about the birth of Isaac that taught Abraham what Jesus himself would be like. *First*, Isaac was a miracle baby — his birth was biologically impossible. Sarah was long past her age of bearing children. So was Jesus a miracle baby: he was born with no earthly father, by the action of the Holy Spirit on his mother Mary. *Second*, the covenant that the Lord gave Abraham was to be passed on to Isaac, not to the other son Ishmael (who was born of the slave woman). Isaac was the rightful heir of all that Abraham owned, including the special promises of the Lord. In the same way, Jesus is the rightful heir of all the promises of God, since he is the only natural Son of God. *Third*, as we shall see in a minute, Isaac's life was all but lost by God's decree, and yet Abraham received him "back from the dead." Jesus actually went through that death (a sacrifice, by the way, like Isaac was supposed to be) and still came back from the dead.

So Abraham knew, in several important ways, what God had in mind for the Son who was to come in the future. How much more he knew about Jesus, we don't know; but we do know, on the testimony of Jesus himself, that he understood the basics of the Christ child.

The promise of the land: Abraham also knew that the dusty piece of real estate called Canaan wasn't all that God had in mind when he promised him and his seed the land. Again, we don't have to guess what was in his mind; we have testimony from someone who was certain about how much Abraham knew about this matter:

> By faith he made his home in the promised land like a stranger in a foreign country; he lived in tents, as did Isaac and Jacob, who were heirs with him of the same promise. For he was looking forward to the city with foundations, whose architect and builder is God. (Hebrews 11:9-10)

This is another amazing statement, something that we couldn't be sure of unless we had this testimony. Abraham was glad enough to see that his immediate posterity would have a place to live, but the Lord showed him that Canaan itself wasn't good enough for *all* the people of God who would end up coming into the Kingdom. In fact, he himself looked forward to a far better place to live than Palestine, as these verses assure us.

The city that this refers to is the New Jerusalem that the New Testament describes, especially in the book of Revelation. (See Revelation 21-22) Christians don't lay claim to the old Jerusalem like the Jews do; we know that God's Temple is in Heaven, that he lives among his people — the Church — and we are to set our eyes on things above, where Jesus is now, not on things below. (Colossians 3:1-3) This world will one day disappear in judgment, and all of God's faithful servants, including Abraham himself, will live with God in Heaven forever.

In fact, Abraham got there ahead of us! Jesus himself assures us that Abraham has gone to his reward — not to the land of Canaan that his earthly descendants inherited from him, but the land of glory that God originally planned to give him. You can see this testimony in the story about Lazarus and the rich man. (Luke 16:19-31)

The promise of the nation: Abraham saw the beginning of the promise of a great nation when he got his son Isaac a wife and they started their family. Whether he knew at the time what would come of this marriage, we don't know; we do know that Abraham knows *now* what came of it! Obviously, as we see in the story of Lazarus (Luke 16), after Abraham died he evidently went into the presence of God. Shortly after arriving, he started receiving visitors — his own "children", in fact! As each new generation of Jews came and went in Canaan, some of them at least went on to glory to join Abraham there in Heaven. But don't miss the significance of who these people are: they are heirs of the promise of Heaven, just as Abraham was, because they are *children* of Abraham.

We don't know how many people there are in Heaven now, but we do know that the number is growing. Lazarus obviously is one of them. But look again at the testimony of Jesus, who came from Heaven and is an eyewitness of what is going on there right now:

The Ministry of Christ

I say to you that many will come from the east and the west, and will take their places at the feast with Abraham, Isaac and Jacob in the kingdom of Heaven. (Matthew 8:11)

The family of Abraham is getting larger, and they are gathering in Heaven for the great feast that God has planned for them. Perhaps Abraham was surprised to see *so many* Gentiles there, and *so few* of the Jews there! "But the subjects of the kingdom will be thrown outside, into the darkness, where there will be weeping and gnashing of teeth." (Matthew 8:12) At any rate he knows now exactly what God had in mind when he promised that he would become the father of a great nation.

The nation, of course, is the Church of God — the body of Christ, which consists of all believers whether they are Jew or Gentile. There used to be strict regulations about letting Gentiles around holy things, especially the Temple. But in Christ the barrier was broken down and the two parties were made one body, one believing Church. (Ephesians 2:11-22) Not everyone who was born a Jew became part of the Church, which shows that God never had only the physical family of Abraham in mind when he made that promise at the beginning. Only those who had the faith of Abraham would be a part of the family of God.

The promise of the blessing: When Abraham came so close to sacrificing his son Isaac, he thought that death was certain. But he also knew

The Ministry of Christ

that God wouldn't leave it that way. We already saw the testimony of Hebrews about this:

> Abraham reasoned that God could raise the dead, and figuratively speaking, he did receive Isaac back from death. (Hebrews 11:19)

In other words, he learned something about God and his ways: the Lord intends to raise his promised children from the dead. Death will not be the end of us; we will live again, never to die again, to serve the Lord forever.

How much Abraham really knew about the resurrection that God has in mind for the Church of Christ, we don't know. Perhaps he didn't know the many details that we have now in the Scriptures — like the teachings of Thessalonians and 1 Corinthians 15. But he did understand the concept, and he knew the mind of the Lord about the matter. As far as God is concerned, death is *not* the last word over us: Abraham knew this for certain about his own son. There was just too much hanging in the balance, too much to happen in the coming kingdom, to let death be the end.

The resurrection of Christ is the great hope of the Church, and it's a hope that the unbelievers don't have. Nobody but Abraham and his children have the right to expect that God will raise them out of the grave into newness of life and give them eternity in Heaven. It's a special promise to the family of Abraham; it's going to overturn everything that sin and death has done to ruin us. Our resurrection will be much more than just a

The Ministry of Christ

physical reversal, however; it will be a new kind of life — as Paul carefully explains in 1 Corinthians 15. This life will defeat death forever; it will be a life to God, never to sin or darkness.

Now these promises are things that every Christian knows about and hopes for. What we may not have known, however, is that they were originally given to Abraham long ago! They aren't our property but his property. We have them only by inheritance; he had them given to him directly by God. Abraham has the signed covenant in his hand, so to speak; that's his hope. We, however, have to prove that we are actually his children if we want to share in his property.

Let's look at this another way. What could you possibly be hoping to get from God except these four things? Isn't **Christ** the very one you love the most, your only Friend and Savior, your "all in all?" Isn't **Heaven** your hope, the place that Jesus went to prepare for your coming, your only home? Isn't the **Church** the place where God meets with you through others and their ministry and good works for you, your real family when your earthly family is long gone? Isn't the **resurrection** going to be the end of all that is bad in this world and the start of an eternity of bliss and joy and holiness? What more could you want but these things? What else did you hear about in the Gospel and put your hope in?

My point is that *this is* your Christian faith; there isn't anything else important that you could want from God but these promises. So if these are what you want and expect because of your faith, you are wanting the *covenant promises* that the Lord gave Abraham long ago! These spiritual realities, as fully as you know them now, were what Abraham received from God's hand. And if you want Abraham's property, you must prove your relationship to him in order to legally get it. Only Abraham's heirs will get the promises of God.

Reveals God

One of the most important things that Jesus came to do was to reveal the true God to us. This was for two reasons: *first*, the Jews were laboring under a lot of misconceptions about God. They had the truth in their Bible, but they didn't understand it correctly. They read it superficially, not in its spiritual depth, and naturally missed its real meaning. As proof that they didn't know their God nearly as well as they thought they did, they completely missed the importance of the Son of God when he came – in fact, they didn't recognize him at all.

Second, the people of the rest of the world were almost completely in the dark about who God is. Their idolatry, rebellion, ignorance, and misery were the direct result of not knowing God or being able to get in touch with the God who forgives, heals, and gives life. And since the Gospel was to be for the entire world, the story of Jesus would have to teach the Gentiles who the "unknown God" was (Acts 17:23) that they needed to know.

So Jesus started a massive educational campaign. First, we learn that God put his fullness in Christ, so that we can know God when we look at Jesus:

> For God was pleased to have all his fullness dwell in him. (Colossians 1:19)

> For in Christ all the fullness of the Deity lives in bodily form. (Colossians 2:9)

Jesus, we are told, is the very image of God: though God himself is invisible, Jesus makes God's characteristics, personality, ways, works and thoughts visible to us.

> He is the image of the invisible God. (Colossians 1:15)

The Ministry of Christ

Jesus perfectly revealed the Father in everything he did. Not that those who were watching always got the point, however! Usually people are oblivious to Jesus' words and works, and they miss entirely the real point of what he's saying. His own disciples, who ought to have gotten the message about him, missed the point:

> Don't you know me, Philip, even after I have been among you such a long time? Anyone who has seen me has seen the Father. How can you say, 'Show us the Father'? (John 14:9)

Jesus best revealed the Father in what he did and what he said. His works, he told us, were God's own works.

> Don't you believe that I am in the Father, and that the Father is in me? The words I say to you are not just my own. Rather, it is the Father, living in me, who is doing his work. Believe me when I say that I am in the Father and the Father is in me; or at least believe on the evidence of the miracles themselves. (John 14:10-11)

> I have testimony weightier than that of John. For the very work that the Father has given me to finish, and which I am doing, testifies that the Father has sent me. (John 5:36)

The idea is that if we watch him closely, we will notice strong similarities between what he did and what God did in the Old Testament. If we missed the meaning of God's works then, we can see them up close in Jesus' works. We can study his works and find out what God wants to do, how he prefers to do it, and what goals he is after.

The Ministry of Christ

We also see in Jesus, to an extent that nobody had ever realized before he came, how much God loves his people. He will do anything for them! Jesus told his disciples to ask for anything:

> And I will do whatever you ask in my name, so that the Son may bring glory to the Father. You may ask me for anything in my name, and I will do it. (John 14:13-14)

> In that day you will no longer ask me anything. I tell you the truth, my Father will give you whatever you ask in my name. Until now you have not asked for anything in my name. Ask and you will receive, and your joy will be complete. (John 16:23-24)

The cross, however, was the most astonishing display of love that man has ever seen. That the Son of God would willingly lay aside his glory, take on a human form, and live with sinners was amazing enough; that he would die for such people is beyond imagination.

> You see, at just the right time, when we were still powerless, Christ died for the ungodly. Very rarely will anyone die for a righteous man, though for a good man someone might possibly dare to die. But God demonstrates his own love for us in this: While we were still sinners, Christ died for us. (Romans 5:6-8)

> It was just before the Passover Feast. Jesus knew that the time had come for him to leave this world and go to the Father. Having loved his own who were in the world, he now showed them the full extent of his love. (John 13:1)

Miracles

In our day, miracles are of little importance even to the Church – probably because science has pretty much talked us out of the possibility of a miracle. We don't think that such things happen anymore; whoever believes in miracles is scientifically naïve. The people in the Bible times weren't as sophisticated as we are, so naturally we think that they attributed strange events that they didn't understand to miracles.

But we're cutting ourselves off from one of the most powerful aspects of God's Kingdom when we downplay miracles like that. From the very beginning of the Bible we see God turning to miracles to do his work. Creation was done by miracles – the story says that plainly, and it's the best possible way to make a world like ours. Even though the scientists assure us that the world came about through physical laws and evolution, the believer knows that our God does his important work by way of miracles – because the natural laws that run our world as it stands now couldn't possibly have put together the world at the beginning in its physical and spiritual complexity.

The Old Testament events after the Creation also depend on miracles. The reason the Israelites needed those miracles is because their spiritual needs required them. There was no other way to answer the problems, or to fulfill the needs, without doing it by miracle. For example, when Sennacherib and his army surrounded Jerusalem, threatening to destroy it, King Hezekiah knew that there was only one way out of this problem: he needed the Creator God to come and deal with this enemy force *now*.

> O LORD, God of Israel, enthroned between the cherubim, you alone are God over all the kingdoms of the earth. *You have made heaven and earth.* Give ear, O LORD, and hear; open your

The Ministry of Christ

eyes, O LORD, and see; listen to the words Sennacherib has sent to insult the living God. It is true, O LORD, that the Assyrian kings have laid waste these nations and their lands. They have thrown their gods into the fire and destroyed them, for they were not gods but only wood and stone, fashioned by men's hands. Now, O LORD our God, deliver us from his hand, so that all kingdoms on earth may know that you alone, O LORD, are God. (2 Kings 19:15-19)

So we learn in the Old Testament that God turns to miracles when he has kingdom work to do. No other method will get the job done.

This is what we also see in the ministry of Christ. We are told that he went around –

… all the towns and villages, teaching in their synagogues, preaching the good news of the kingdom and healing every disease and sickness. (Matthew 9:35)

He raised the dead, he gave sight to the blind, he opened the ears of the deaf, he fed thousands with almost no food, he walked on water and stilled storms. He proved that he was the same God of the Old Testament, the Creator God who has come in the flesh, doing the same kind of works in the same way.

But we're supposed to take the lesson we learned from the Old Testament and apply it to Christ too. He resorted to miracles because nothing less but miracles can build his eternal kingdom. They weren't magic tricks to impress people; they were the means of putting together the house of God.

The Ministry of Christ

For a while Jesus did physical miracles to convince the Jews (who had just come through 2000 years of being trained by God about how the Kingdom works) that he really was their God. The period recorded in the Gospels was a transition time: he had to move them out of the system they'd been used to all this time, into a new system. They had to switch from a physical Kingdom to a spiritual Kingdom. Though he did physical miracles, the time would come when the Kingdom of God wouldn't be an outward physical reality but an inward, spiritual reality. This means, then, that the *kind* of miracle would also switch – from physical to spiritual.

Now, in the age of the Church, Jesus rules from Heaven and sends out his Spirit to make the Church grow. Now we see hardened, dead hearts being made alive and aware of God. We see sinners changed into saints. We see love replacing the old legal system (in which people were forced, under threat of punishment, to do things for others). We see a spiritual house where God the Spirit lives, instead of the old stone and wood Temple in Jerusalem. All these new things are just as much miracles as the physical ones recorded in the Gospels.

The point is that we can't do without the spiritual miracles of Christ any more than the Jews could do without his physical ones. He's still building his Kingdom by resorting to the only method that *can* build such a Kingdom – the miraculous.

Destroys the works of the devil

Since the beginning of the world, when Satan first tempted Eve with the fruit of the forbidden tree, he has been busy building a "counter-kingdom" opposite God's creation. It's a project that both Satan and man participate in, though man is definitely getting the short end of the deal. This is the "world" that God warns us of in John's letter:

The Ministry of Christ

> Do not love the world or anything in the world. If anyone loves the world, the love of the Father is not in him. For everything in the world — the cravings of sinful man, the lust of his eyes and the boasting of what he has and does — comes not from the Father but from the world. The world and its desires pass away, but the man who does the will of God lives forever. (1 John 2:15-17)

It's a world of lies, deceit, oppression, anti-God, anti-Bible, and misery and destruction everywhere. It's a world in which the principles and goals that God had when he made the world are being challenged, torn down and replaced with the works of man. It's a moral and physical wasteland that only the devil and those whom he has thoroughly deceived could be pleased with.

Kings and presidents, common laborers, scholars and philosophers, housewives and construction workers, field hands and computer programmers – we are all part of this world and we love it. At least we love the pleasures we can get from it. Whenever it backfires on us (and it often does, because the works of man aren't perfect and they usually hurt us in some way eventually) we try to change our circumstances. But whatever our circumstances may be, the world we are *least* interested in is a world where God is again the Ruler and whatever he says, is law. That's the world that Adam and Eve rejected, and we still reject it.

So one of the first things on the agenda for Christ when he came was to lay the ax to the root of this world system. He came to destroy the devil's kingdom:

> The reason the Son of God appeared was to destroy the devil's work. (1 John 3:8)

The Ministry of Christ

And the devil knew why he was here. The very first time Jesus appeared in public to start his ministry, the devil showed up personally to try to prevent what he knew was coming.

> Then Jesus was led by the Spirit into the desert to be tempted by the devil. After fasting forty days and forty nights, he was hungry. The tempter came to him and said, "If you are the Son of God, tell these stones to become bread." (Matthew 4:1-3)

And Jesus dealt with him decisively and characteristically: with the Word of God. From this point on it was war. He threw demons out of the possessed, he threatened the downfall of the "strong man's house," he spoke of the time when he saw Satan "fall like lightning" out of his former place in Heaven. The demons were terrified of him. He accused the Jews of being traitors and aiding the hand of the enemy – believing his lies instead of God's Word. Jesus also pinpointed the precise weapon that Satan uses to lead us away from God and into sin and death: **lies**. Satan is the father of lies:

> You belong to your father, the devil, and you want to carry out your father's desire. He was a murderer from the beginning, not holding to the truth, for there is no truth in him. When he lies, he speaks his native language, for he is a liar and the father of lies. (John 8:44)

Once we realize this, we can appreciate why Jesus emphasized the truth so much. The Word of God is a powerful weapon that will destroy the devil's complex work of deceit. Even in the hands of novices the truth can stop the enemy cold. Christ taught the truth to his disciples, and sent them out with a full understanding of the mysteries of the Gospel. They were armed with the truth so that they too could do battle with the enemy, who fills the entire world with his lies.

> Resist the devil, and he will flee from you.
> (James 4:7)

Fulfills the law

Christ stands in a unique position in regard to the Law of God. He alone was able to fulfill the Law perfectly; the Law has no complaint about the character and actions of Jesus Christ. This is an amazing record, in light of how complex and demanding the Law is. But it's also understandable, since Jesus is the Son of God and could do no other than keep his own Law to the letter!

Christ related to the Law on several levels. In order to understand our own relationship with the Law, we have to distinguish each of the things that Jesus did for us:

- *What he did with the Law:* Christ came to earth to do more than keep the Law for his own sake. He came to solve man's problem of sin, which is *lawlessness*. The Law's complaint is with us, not with him. So here is what Jesus did: he became man, like us except for our sin, so that he could be "under the Law" and accomplish his goal. Then *as man* he fulfilled the Law completely and perfectly. When he was done, the Law was forced to admit that *a man* had kept the Law to God's satisfaction! This was the first time that such a thing had happened. Even though the Israelites had the Law for almost 1500 years, nobody had ever kept it perfectly until Jesus came.

- ***What he did for us:*** Now for the final step in God's plan of salvation. Jesus sent his Spirit and made us *one with him* — we are in him, united to him in all ways, so that whatever happens to him will also happen to us. This means several things: *first*, since the Law is satisfied with him, it's also satisfied with us. There is nothing more to be done! This is what Hebrews means when it says that we *rest* in Christ; he rested from his labors (remember his last words on the cross? "It is finished." John 19:30) and now we rest in him. "Take my yoke upon you and learn from me, for I am gentle and humble in heart, and you will find rest for your souls." (Matthew 11:29) The work of satisfying the Law is over now, for him *and* for us. If there were any more to do on this score then salvation wouldn't be done yet!

Second, whatever rewards are in store for Christ as the perfect man, we also can expect to receive. If he was lifted on high, we will be too. (Colossians 3:1) If he sits at God's right hand, so will we. (Colossians 3:3) If he rules over the universe, so will we. (Colossians 3:4) Since we are one with him, we will share in his glory and receive the inheritance that Jesus bought for us.

Everything that happens *to us* must go *through him* first; he put himself between us and the Law for this reason. And since he did this, we never deal with the Law directly. There is no salvation for us in the Law! Our only hope is in what Christ, as the firstborn of many brethren, achieved for us and passes on to us.

Since Christ fulfilled the Law for us, what is left for us to do? Can we sin now and not have to worry about punishment since Christ took that burden upon himself? Paul tells us that such a thing is unthinkable! "By no means! We died to sin; how can we live in it any longer?" (Romans 6:2) Remember why Jesus came: he came to save us *from* our sin, not leave us in it. "You are to give him the name Jesus, because *he will save his people from their sins.*" (Matthew 1:21)

- **What he does in us:** He died to save us from condemnation, but that's only one thing he wanted to do. The other was to get us out of the moral mess that resulted in our condemnation in the first place.

So, right now the Lord Jesus is busy with our **sanctification** — the process of making us holy and set apart for the Lord's use. He is applying *his* righteousness to *our* souls so that we look more and more like him. "And so he condemned sin in sinful man, in order that *the righteous requirements of the Law might be fully met in us,* who do not live according to the sinful nature but according to the Spirit." (Romans 8:3-4) Did you catch that phrase about the Law? The Law of God hasn't gone away; it wasn't put away permanently when Jesus fulfilled it. The Law isn't going away because the God whom it describes isn't going away. Jesus is *making* us conform to what the Law says is a righteous man; only he can do that, of course, since only he lived that righteous life. But the fact remains that the Law is still in full force; the only difference now is *who* has to keep the Law. If we do it, the outcome is in serious question; if Christ does it, it's certain to succeed.

There's a prophecy in Ezekiel that shows us what God had in mind long before Jesus came to earth, but is exactly in line with what the New Testament teaches about our present relationship with the Law.

> I will give you a new heart and put a new spirit in you; I will remove from you your heart of stone and give you a heart of flesh. And I will put my Spirit in you and *move you* to follow my decrees and be careful to keep my laws. (Ezekiel 36:26-27)

This agrees with what Paul says about the subject. The Lord will put his Spirit into us, and the Spirit will make us conform to the requirements of the Law. Before this time the Israelites were doing their best to obey the Law — and failing at it. It just couldn't be done by sinners. God finally got tired of fooling with them and predicted the time when *he* would make them righteous; instead of waiting on them to do

The Ministry of Christ

what is right, he would change their hearts himself. When this happens, of course, he will get the credit for the job, because if the Spirit is making you conform to the requirements of the Law then *you* can't claim any credit for doing it! But that's what being part of the Church is all about; it's an entirely different thing from what the Israelites were living under.

- ***What he's doing right now:*** Christ is also doing something *right now* in respect to the Law. He fulfilled its requirements as far as living a righteous life; but he's also in the Heavenly Temple right now fulfilling his duties as our High Priest. The earthly Temple was a picture of the one in Heaven: if you want to know what it's like in God's eternal Temple, read the description in the Law of the Israelite Temple. You must realize, however, that none of that has disappeared from Heaven as the earthly one has. Though the Jews lost their Temple, God still lives in his! And there must still be a sacrifice on the altar to atone for the people's sins — but now it's Jesus' eternal sacrifice that was made "once for all" for our sake. (Hebrews 12:24) There must still be incense burning day and night — though in God's Temple that's the "prayers of the saints" that always go up to him. (Revelation 5:8) There must still be a Holy of Holies, because that's where God sits and rules over his people and gives them what they come to him and ask for. Now, however, the veil that used to separate us

The Ministry of Christ

from God is torn away and the way into the Holy of Holies is open to "whosoever will." (Hebrews 10:19-22) And the High Priest still lives to intercede for the people: Christ is always presenting our requests to the Father and getting answers for us. (Romans 8:34)

So the Law hasn't gone anywhere. It's still in full force, because that's still the way that God wants to run his kingdom. The difference now is that Jesus is doing all these legal requirements for us and sending us the benefits.

Sets up a new kingdom – on David's throne

The prophets taught us that David would one day have a son to sit on his throne – forever.

For this is what the LORD says: 'David will never fail to have a man to sit on the throne of the house of Israel.' (Jeremiah 33:17)

Though David had many sons – in fact all the kings of the southern tribes were descendants of David – none of them sat on his throne forever. Obviously the prophecy remained unfulfilled in the Old Testament. The prophecies were obviously about Christ.

But before we look at Jesus as the son of David, we first need to look at why David himself was so important in the history of Israel.

When David was crowned king over Israel, he had a tremendous job on his hands. Saul, the former king, had just died in battle, and left a moral and political disaster behind. The tribes of Israel were fighting among each other, there was no single leader strong enough to unite the people, they were being oppressed continuously by their pagan neighbors, and the worship of the true God was sporadic at best, even when done at all.

In order to fix the situation, David had to do five things:

First, he captured Jerusalem from the Jebusites. He knew that he needed a capital city to work from. He himself would live there, govern the nation from there, and set up the Temple worship for all the Israelites to come to and use.

Second, he turned on the enemies of Israel and beat them so thoroughly that they were no longer a nuisance. This too had to be done; the Philistines had been a thorn in their side for generations. God's people couldn't go on with their lives until this problem was solved once and for all.

Third, he set up a government there in Israel. He appointed government officials, and established a law that he used to rule from Dan in the north to Beersheba in the south. He drew the separate tribes together into one nation, instead of letting the people wallow in their bickering and division.

Fourth, he led the people back to God. He found where the ark of the Covenant was, planned for an elaborate ceremony, and himself led the priests, the ark, and the people back to Jerusalem to set it up for worship. He was the author of many of the Psalms of worship that we have in our Bibles. He felt responsible, as king, to lead the Israelites to God in a way that would please the Lord.

Fifth, he made plans for the Temple in Jerusalem. Though he himself didn't actually build the Temple – the Lord wouldn't let him since he was "a man of blood" (1 Chronicles 22:8) – he drew up complete plans and collected most of the materials for it. Most people think that his son Solomon did all the organizing for the Temple; actually *David* planned the entire thing out and instructed Solomon to do it exactly has he drew it out!

> Then David gave his son Solomon the plans for the portico of the temple, its buildings, its storerooms, its upper parts, its inner rooms and the place of atonement. He gave him the plans of all that the Spirit had put in his mind for the courts of the temple of the LORD and all the surrounding rooms, for the treasuries of the temple of God and for the treasuries for the dedicated things. He gave him instructions for the divisions of the priests and Levites, and for all the work of serving in the temple of the LORD, as well as for all the articles to be used in its service ... "All this," David said, "I have in writing from the hand of the LORD upon me, and he gave me understanding in all the details of the plan." (1 Chronicles 28:11-13,19)

We have to understand that David did these things because they were absolutely necessary for the plan of God for his people. He was, remember, a "man after God's own heart." (1 Samuel 13:14) He knew what had to be done to have a nation that would know God and serve him acceptably. He was careful to do things God's way. What he did was the will of God for God's people.

All the kings of Israel that came after David were compared with their father David. If they did as he did, they were commended; if they didn't do as their father David had done, they were censured.

> So Solomon did evil in the eyes of the LORD; he did not follow the LORD completely, as David his father had done. (1 Kings 11:6)

> Asa did what was right in the eyes of the LORD, as his father David had done. (1 Kings 15:11)

Now Jesus, as we've seen, was called the "son of David." (Matthew 1:1) We must see the significance of this name. He came to sit on David's throne – not the literal throne that used to be in the city of Jerusalem, but on the spiritual throne in Heaven that David's own throne symbolized. He came to set up a Kingdom like the one his father David set up. And if he is really like his father David, he's going to do it the same way that David did it:

> **First**, he will set up a capital city – the Heavenly Jerusalem. He has his throne there, from which he rules over all the earth.

> **Second**, he will finally destroy our enemies. Our enemies aren't flesh and blood, but principalities and powers – the forces of darkness led by Satan, using this rebellious world system, to deceive and coerce us into sinning against God.

> **Third**, he will unite the people of God into one nation. From all around the world he will make the Church, which will consist not of Jews or Gentiles but the "New Man."

Fourth, he will lead his people back to God. Jesus' mission is to reconcile us to God, to bring the prodigal son back to the Father. He gives us his Spirit so that we *can* come before God, and we'll know the right things to say and ask for. And God promises to give them to us when we ask him.

Fifth, he will draw up the plans of the Temple. He himself is the sacrifice on the altar; he is the high priest who offers the sacrifice to God. Everything in the Old Testament Temple is actually symbolic of the ministry of Jesus: in him, God put together the entire system that would fulfill the Law, cleanse us from our sin, and present us faultless before the presence of God.

Jesus as a prophet

Jesus talked a great deal about the Kingdom of God. The reason is obvious: he himself was the King, and he came to start setting it up. But the very fact that Jesus warned us so much about the coming Kingdom makes him a *prophet*.

We can best understand this if we use an example of early warfare. When two nations went to war against each other, the armies would move out into the field to fight each other – and then stop. Each side would send an emissary out to meet in the middle of the field. They would trade insults, show contempt for each other, and warn each other to give up or else. Then if they didn't manage to frighten the other side into submission, they would go back to their ranks and the fight would commence.

This is exactly what is happening with the prophets. The Kingdom of God is coming to make war upon the kingdoms of the earth, to destroy the works of the devil, and set up a new

The Ministry of Christ

Kingdom with Christ as the King. And the prophets are God's special messengers, sent to warn us — who are rebels on the enemy's side — that he is coming. The message is that we must give up now — repent — before he gets here, because he will show no mercy on the wicked on the Day of Judgment. The day of mercy is *now*.

This is what the prophets saw. They didn't just see God in Heaven, and report to us on how he's doing. The Lord was angry at the rebellion, wickedness, ignorance, and death in his world. He first formed Israel into a nation to rescue them from sin, and to give them the blessings of the covenant that he made with their father Abraham. He separated them from the nations, gave them their own land, gave them the Temple and the sacrificial system. They had everything they could ever want! Yet they continually rebelled against God; they exchanged the worship of God for idols, and learned the practices of their pagan neighbors. They thought the treasures of Heaven were of so little worth that they were willing to throw it all away for the pleasures of sin. So, God sent prophet after prophet with warnings: **repent**, before I come and destroy you.

Jesus' preaching was full of warnings of the coming Kingdom, and what we had to do to get ready for it. He uncovered, for example, the hearts of his hearers and proved that God had a rightful claim against them as rebels:

> Woe to you, teachers of the law and Pharisees, you hypocrites! You shut the kingdom of heaven in men's faces. You yourselves do not enter, nor will you let those enter who are trying to. (Matthew 23:13-14)

Jesus insisted that people get right with God before God comes to destroy them:

The Ministry of Christ

"I tell you, my friends, do not be afraid of those who kill the body and after that can do no more. But I will show you whom you should fear: Fear him who, after the killing of the body, has power to throw you into hell. Yes, I tell you, fear him. (Luke 12:4-5)

Jesus gave us fair warning of the kinds of things that the King will do when he comes to judge the nations:

> For everyone who has will be given more, and he will have an abundance. Whoever does not have, even what he has will be taken from him. And throw that worthless servant outside, into the darkness, where there will be weeping and gnashing of teeth. (Matthew 25:29-30)

> When the Son of Man comes in his glory, and all the angels with him, he will sit on his throne in heavenly glory. All the nations will be gathered before him, and he will separate the people one from another as a shepherd separates the sheep from the goats. He will put the sheep on his right and the goats on his left … Then they will go away to eternal punishment, but the righteous to eternal life. (Matthew 25:31-33, 46)

And he tells us that he is that King – and that people ought to take his message seriously:

> Then Jesus began to denounce the cities in which most of his miracles had been performed, because they did not repent. "Woe to you, Korazin! Woe to you, Bethsaida! If the miracles that were performed in you had been performed in Tyre and Sidon, they would have repented long ago in

The Ministry of Christ

sackcloth and ashes. But I tell you, it will be more bearable for Tyre and Sidon on the day of judgment than for you. And you, Capernaum, will you be lifted up to the skies? No, you will go down to the depths. If the miracles that were performed in you had been performed in Sodom, it would have remained to this day. But I tell you that it will be more bearable for Sodom on the day of judgment than for you." (Matthew 11:20-24)

Moses was the greatest prophet of the Old Testament, we are told (Deuteronomy 34:10-12), who saw and heard God. He had to be able to, because his job was the biggest of all: to implement God's Law among the new people of God. At Sinai the Israelites became the nation Israel, and Moses' work over the next forty years literally formed the foundation that generations of Israelites – even the Jews of our day – depend on for their religion.

Hebrews tells us that there were two great builders of God's house – not just Moses, but Jesus too.

> He was faithful to the one who appointed him, just as Moses was faithful in all God's house. Jesus has been found worthy of greater honor than Moses, just as the builder of a house has greater honor than the house itself. For every house is built by someone, but God is the builder of everything. Moses was faithful as a servant in all God's house, testifying to what would be said in the future. But Christ is faithful as a son over God's house. And we are his house, if we hold on to our courage and the hope of which we boast. (Hebrews 3:2-6)

In fact, Moses himself predicted that a second great Prophet like himself would appear among God's people.

> The LORD your God will raise up for you a prophet like me from among your own brothers. You must listen to him. (Deuteronomy 18:15)

His job was the same as Moses, only this time on a spiritual level instead of a physical level. He would bring together God's people out of slavery, make a nation out of them, write his Law into their hearts so that they would obey him willingly, and lead them to the Promised Land. Like Moses, Jesus would put together and operate the Kingdom of God.

Makes a New Man

In the Old Testament days, the Jews were the rightful heirs of the covenant with Abraham. They were the ones who received the Law from God. They were special and they knew it:

> He has revealed his word to Jacob, his laws and decrees to Israel. He has done this for no other nation; they do not know his laws. (Psalm 147:19-20)

The Gentiles were out of the picture. No other people on earth – and they lived around the globe even in those days – knew God or what kind of trouble they were in spiritually. They worshipped false gods, and all of their sacrifices were worthless as far as pleasing God or taking care of their sin.

But God had planned, even in Old Testament times, to eventually include the Gentiles in the plan of salvation. Right at the very beginning he promised Abraham that he would be a blessing to the nations:

> I will make you into a great nation and I will bless you; I will make your name great, and you

The Ministry of Christ

will be a blessing. I will bless those who bless you, and whoever curses you I will curse; and all peoples on earth will be blessed through you. (Genesis 12:2-3)

And as Old Testament history unfolded, there were more hints dropped about what God had planned for the Gentiles. But nothing serious was done about it until the New Testament and the time of the Church. Even Jesus pretty much avoided the Gentiles and had little to do with them.

These twelve Jesus sent out with the following instructions: "Do not go among the Gentiles or enter any town of the Samaritans. Go rather to the lost sheep of Israel." (Matthew 10:5-6)

But with the formation of the Church the situation changed completely. The Lord deliberately sent the apostles out to the *world* – they were to take the Gospel to all nations, not just to the Jews. Paul's ministry focused almost exclusively on the Gentiles, because the Jews quite simply rejected him in most synagogues he went to.

Therefore I want you to know that God's salvation has been sent to the Gentiles, and they will listen! (Acts 28:28)

But we see something else new in this spread of the Gospel to the whole world. God isn't satisfied with the way the Jews do things, and obviously the Gentiles have to be remade and retrained. What Jesus did, therefore, was make a **new man** and bring both sides into the middle, so to speak. The Jew will become a Christian, and the Gentile will become a child of the Jew's God. Both have to change, because the new man that Jesus became in himself is the real goal that God had in mind.

The Ministry of Christ

> For he himself is our peace, who has made the two one and has destroyed the barrier, the dividing wall of hostility, by abolishing in his flesh the law with its commandments and regulations. His purpose was to create in himself one new man out of the two, thus making peace, and in this one body to reconcile both of them to God through the cross, by which he put to death their hostility. He came and preached peace to you who were far away and peace to those who were near. For through him we both have access to the Father by one Spirit. (Ephesians 2:14-18)

This new man has certain characteristics that make it possible to live in the new Kingdom that Jesus is building.

First, he is filled with the Spirit, which means that he will now fulfill the righteous requirements of the Law without consciously trying to follow the Law! All he has to do is follow the leading of the Spirit.

> And so he condemned sin in sinful man, in order that the righteous requirements of the law might be fully met in us, who do not live according to the sinful nature but according to the Spirit. (Romans 8:3-4)

Second, this new man lives in the presence of God – a new thing for both Jew and Gentile. Instead of putting our eyes on things of this world, we now lift up our eyes and look at the Heavenly Kingdom where Jesus now sits and rules.

> Since, then, you have been raised with Christ, set your hearts on things above,

where Christ is seated at the right hand of God. Set your minds on things above, not on earthly things. For you died, and your life is now hidden with Christ in God. (Col. 3:1-3)

Third, we are one with Jesus himself now. We aren't living by ourselves – Jesus lives in us through his Spirit. Whatever happens to Jesus will also happen to us. If he is considered righteous by the Law, then so are we. If he rules from Heaven, then so will we. We identify so closely with Jesus that he's our Head, our Husband, and our Brother. In him we have everything, and as long as we stay in him we will live forever.

> To them God has chosen to make known among the Gentiles the glorious riches of this mystery, which is Christ in you, the hope of glory. (Colossians 1:27)

> I have been crucified with Christ and I no longer live, but Christ lives in me. The life I live in the body, I live by faith in the Son of God, who loved me and gave himself for me. (Galatians 2:20)

These three elements describe a Christian. Paul described us like this:

> For it is we who are the circumcision, we who worship by the Spirit of God, who glory in Christ Jesus, and who put no confidence in the flesh. (Phil. 3:3)

The Ministry of Christ

The reason God must remake us is twofold: *first*, what we are now is the result of sin and death. Our hearts became like stone, hardened to the voice of God, rebellious against his Law, and full of hatred for his works. We first have to be saved from this miserable spiritual state that we're in.

> There is no one righteous, not even one; there is no one who understands, no one who seeks God. All have turned away, they have together become worthless; there is no one who does good, not even one. Their throats are open graves; their tongues practice deceit. The poison of vipers is on their lips. Their mouths are full of cursing and bitterness. Their feet are swift to shed blood; ruin and misery mark their ways, and the way of peace they do not know. There is no fear of God before their eyes. (Romans 3:10-18)

Second, we can't inherit the next world until we are changed. Not only do we have to shed this body of sin and death, but we have to put on new selves – both spiritual and physical – that will be able to survive and work in the new world of Heaven.

> Put to death, therefore, whatever belongs to your earthly nature: sexual immorality, impurity, lust, evil desires and greed, which is idolatry. Because of these, the wrath of God is coming. You used to walk in these ways, in the life you once lived. But now you must rid yourselves of all such things as these: anger, rage, malice, slander, and filthy language from your lips. Do not lie to each other, since you have taken off your old self with its practices and have put on the new

self, which is being renewed in knowledge in the image of its Creator. (Col. 3:5-10)

> So will it be with the resurrection of the dead. The body that is sown is perishable, it is raised imperishable; it is sown in dishonor, it is raised in glory; it is sown in weakness, it is raised in power; it is sown a natural body, it is raised a spiritual body. If there is a natural body, there is also a spiritual body. So it is written: "The first man Adam became a living being"; the last Adam, a life-giving spirit. The spiritual did not come first, but the natural, and after that the spiritual. The first man was of the dust of the earth, the second man from heaven. As was the earthly man, so are those who are of the earth; and as is the man from heaven, so also are those who are of heaven. And just as we have borne the likeness of the earthly man, so shall we bear the likeness of the man from heaven. I declare to you, brothers, that flesh and blood cannot inherit the kingdom of God, nor does the perishable inherit the imperishable. (1 Corinthians 15:42-50)

Summary

At first glance we probably wouldn't see all of this in Jesus' ministry. Many Jews, who ought to have known much about the works of God and his plans for Israel, completely missed what Jesus was doing. It shouldn't be any surprise, then, that Gentiles (who didn't have the benefit of the Bible) would have been mystified by this strange man!

The Ministry of Christ

That's why we have the Spirit of God: to explain to us what Jesus was all about. It's his job to reveal the real work that Jesus was doing here, and its magnificent results in subsequent history.

> All this I have spoken while still with you. But the Counselor, the Holy Spirit, whom the Father will send in my name, will teach you all things and will remind you of everything I have said to you. (John 14:25-26)

The work that Jesus did was on a tremendous scope; it was so complex that nobody really can plumb the depth of its meaning. Only God could have attempted this kind of work and actually accomplished it in one lifetime. The fact that Jesus did it all so perfectly, so completely – that the Church as been able to live and grow from it for the last 2000 years – is testimony to his divine nature, power, and wisdom. Jesus did the impossible, because it had to be done so that his people could be saved.

*The Apostles –
Interpreters of Christ*

The Apostles – Interpreters of Christ

This may sound strange, but if we only had the Gospels and their account of Jesus Christ, we wouldn't get a full picture of who he really is. The Gospels focus on his earthly life and ministry. But Jesus purposely set aside his glory before being born a man – which means that there is a great deal more to be known about him than his biography! If we are to know about that bigger picture of Jesus, someone has to pull aside the veil and reveal him to us in his larger role as King, Prophet, Priest, and the Son of God.

That's the job of the apostles. They followed him for up to three years in Israel and learned as much from him as possible. They were selected for this job. Once he was done training them and he returned to Heaven, they were to go out and spread the news of his life to the whole world. This much is obvious, when you read the book of Acts and the apostles' travels. But they had another job too: to uncover the mystery of this man Jesus so that we can have faith in a spiritual King. The apostles saw Jesus as he really was – the Son of God who came to build a new Kingdom. It was *that* message that they spread around the world and passed on to us in the writings of the New Testament.

The Mystery

By means of the Old Testament, God taught his people the principles of his Kingdom. If the Jews had eyes to see it, they could see (as did their father Abraham) that the physical realities of the Temple, Canaan, King David, and so on were symbols of spiritual realities in God's eternal world. By the end of the Old Testament times, a wise Jew who knew his Scriptures could pretty well piece together the picture of God's system of salvation, Kingdom, righteousness and hope. A Jew *could* have done that, we know, because Jesus rebuked the "wise" Jews of his day for not knowing their Scriptures.

> You are in error because you do not know the Scriptures or the power of God. (Matthew 22:29)

But God didn't tell the Jews everything plainly. A lot of it was hidden in parables and history; it would have taken a spiritually-sharp Jew to work out some of the complexities of the New Testament doctrines. Jesus himself had to come and show people what those Old Testament stories were talking about. (For example, see Matthew 12:39-41; Luke 17:30-35) We can look back to the Old Testament now and understand what a lot of those passages meant, but we're after the fact: we have the benefit of seeing the fulfillment in Jesus.

What God wanted to do, with the coming of Christ, is make those old parables and hints plain and easy to see. He of course doesn't want us to miss the point! Our spiritual well being, our very salvation, depends on seeing Jesus as he really is and laying hold of our salvation in him.

So, the "mystery of the Gospel" has to be uncovered, made plain, made accessible to everyone who wants to see it. Paul refers to God's unveiling in our day – now is the day of salvation:

> Surely you have heard about the administration of God's grace that was given to me for you, that is, the mystery made known to me by revelation,

The Apostles – the Interpreters of Christ

as I have already written briefly. In reading this, then, you will be able to understand my insight into the mystery of Christ, which was not made known to men in other generations as it has now been revealed by the Spirit to God's holy apostles and prophets. This mystery is that through the gospel the Gentiles are heirs together with Israel, members together of one body, and sharers together in the promise in Christ Jesus. (Ephesians 3:2-6)

I have become its servant by the commission God gave me to present to you the word of God in its fullness — the mystery that has been kept hidden for ages and generations, but is now disclosed to the saints. To them God has chosen to make known among the Gentiles the glorious riches of this mystery, which is Christ in you, the hope of glory. (Colossians 1:25-27)

The Gospels, of course, tell us the actual events of Jesus' life, but they are more than simple histories. They show us Jesus from the eye of faith: the writers have been specially trained in the truths of the Old Testament so that they would show us Jesus from the right point of view. Call it propaganda if you wish, but God doesn't want us to read the story of Jesus from just any point of view. We have to see Jesus from *his* point of view; otherwise we won't be saved.

Historians know the value of interpretation. No historian just records actual events without putting his own spin on the facts. For one thing, he has to decide *which* facts to select – the process of selecting facts is itself a decision process that depends on one's personal value system, one's goals, one's cultural viewpoint, and so on. A lot of factors go into writing history.

The Apostles – the Interpreters of Christ

For example, if a newspaper reporter had covered the ministry of Christ, his story would have been much different than the Gospels we have now! He would have had different goals in mind, and would have selected his "facts" to please his particular audience. There's nothing wrong with that – every historian does it, *has* to do it, in fact. It's just that the reporter's story wouldn't have given us what we needed to know about Christ to be saved.

The apostles were specially trained to look for Kingdom realities in Christ's ministry. Their goal was to inform the Church about the Savior, about the King of God's new world. They were very selective about their facts. They didn't tell us, for example, much about Christ's personal life, because that has nothing to do with our souls. They did show us the miracle worker, the one who taught with authority, the man of humility who was despised by the Jews and Romans, the Son who pleased his Father.

So the Gospels themselves were carefully written historical accounts that tell us how to look at Jesus if we want to be saved, if we want to go to Heaven. It takes some wisdom and the help of the Spirit to be able to read the Gospels and get these things from them.

Uncover the mystery

The apostles went on to write other letters to the Church about Jesus Christ. If you read each of them, you will see them carefully studying and digging to reveal more of Jesus that we need to know. We learn things here that we couldn't see clearly in the Gospels.

- *Christ's nature* – The apostles show us that there's more to Jesus Christ than meets the physical eye. There were obvious clues in the

The Apostles – the Interpreters of Christ

Gospels about what kind of person Jesus was, but the New Testament epistles spell it out for us in case we missed the point.

One thing we are told about him is that he's the **Creator**. He was there in the beginning of the world, and the world was made through him, for him, and by him.

> In the beginning was the Word, and the Word was with God, and the Word was God. He was with God in the beginning. Through him all things were made; without him nothing was made that has been made. (John 1:1-3)

> For by him all things were created: things in heaven and on earth, visible and invisible, whether thrones or powers or rulers or authorities; all things were created by him and for him. He is before all things, and in him all things hold together. (Col. 1:16-17)

This explains a lot about what we saw him do in the Gospels! No wonder he had the power to control the wind and waves, to raise the dead to life, to heal the blind and deaf, and to create bread for thousands of people. He has all power to do whatever he needs to do to build his Kingdom.

We are told that Jesus is the **King**, and that too explains why he acted the way he did. He expected obedience from his subjects; he laid the Law down and surprised us with its spiritual depth. He spoke with authority, as if he intended for us to take him seriously and change our lives to suit his will.

> The people were amazed at his teaching, because he taught them as one who had authority, not as the teachers of the law. (Mark 1:22)

Jesus is also the **Sacrifice**, the Lamb slain from the foundation of the world. His death means that we don't have to die for our sins. To understand this, we have to go back to the Old Testament sacrificial system – the whole thing. Everything that God set up in the Temple symbolized the complex and enormous spiritual problem that Jesus solved in order to save us.

> It was necessary, then, for the copies of the heavenly things to be purified with these sacrifices, but the heavenly things themselves with better sacrifices than these. For Christ did not enter a man-made sanctuary that was only a copy of the true one; he entered heaven itself, now to appear for us in God's presence. Nor did he enter heaven to offer himself again and again, the way the high priest enters the Most Holy Place every year with blood that is not his own. Then Christ would have had to suffer many times since the creation of the world. But now he has appeared once for all at the end of the ages to do away with sin by the sacrifice of himself. Just as man is destined to die once, and after that to face judgment, so Christ was sacrificed once to take away the sins of many people; and he will appear

The Apostles – the Interpreters of Christ

a second time, not to bear sin, but to bring salvation to those who are waiting for him. (Hebrews 9:23-28)

Jesus is the **Word of God**. Since he's the Son of God, and since he's now here among us so that we can hear him, we can hear the very words of God. He has a lot to say to us! And what Jesus says is the truth, not the opinions and feelings of men. His perspective on things is the correct one. That's why he claimed that we have to believe what he teaches us, we have to accept what he says, or we will die in our sins.

> "No one ever spoke the way this man does," the guards declared. (John 7:46)

> Lord, to whom shall we go? You have the words of eternal life. (John 6:68)

> For I did not speak of my own accord, but the Father who sent me commanded me what to say and how to say it. (John 12:49)

Jesus is **Yahweh** of the Old Testament. God, in the Old Testament, revealed to Israel his special name – the name he wanted them to memorize, call on, and trust in. He tells us what this name means in Exodus:

> The LORD, the LORD, the compassionate and gracious God, slow to anger, abounding in love and faithfulness, maintaining love to thousands, and forgiving wickedness, rebellion and sin. Yet he does not leave the guilty unpunished; he

The Apostles – the Interpreters of Christ

punishes the children and their children for the sin of the fathers to the third and fourth generation. (Exodus 34:6-7)

When Jesus came, the angels instructed Joseph to call the new infant "Jesus, because he will save his people from their sins." (Matthew 1:21) The name Jesus is actually the Greek form of the Hebrew name Joshua – which means "the Lord (Yahweh) is salvation." In other words, Yahweh from the Old Testament showed up to save his people! We could go into great detail about this name and its significance, but we'll limit our discussion to two points: *first*, the Temple that Solomon built was to be the place where God's Name would dwell – the Israelites were to turn to the Temple, when they needed help, and call on his Name. So it is with Jesus. *Second*, the love of God shines out of that Name in Exodus! And that's what we find in the life and ministry of Jesus, so much so that the apostles were amazed at the depth of God's love in the way Jesus reached out to sinners to save them.

And everyone who calls on the name of the LORD will be saved. (Joel 2:32)

Salvation is found in no one else, for there is no other name under heaven given to men by which we must be saved. (Acts 4:12)

For this reason I kneel before the Father, from whom his whole family in heaven and on earth derives its name. I pray that out of his glorious riches he may strengthen you

The Apostles – the Interpreters of Christ

with power through his Spirit in your inner being, so that Christ may dwell in your hearts through faith. And I pray that you, being rooted and established in love, may have power, together with all the saints, to grasp how wide and long and high and deep is the love of Christ, and to know this love that surpasses knowledge — that you may be filled to the measure of all the fullness of God. (Ephesians 3:14-19)

- *Faith* – Faith is being able to see God's world, and live in it as if it's real and has real results in our lives.

And without faith it is impossible to please God, because anyone who comes to him must believe that he exists and that he rewards those who earnestly seek him. (Hebrews 11:6)

Faith is a spiritual gift that only the children of God have – because they need it. If any of us are going to get benefit out of knowing Jesus Christ, then we have to have the ability to sense his presence, come to him in confidence, and draw from his spiritual resources.

Jesus came as a humble servant. That one fact has thrown millions of people into confusion about him. The Jews were mystified by him because he didn't assume an earthly throne and challenge the Roman government. Pilate was mystified by him because he willingly went to the cross without defending himself, yet he claimed to be a king. Centuries of generations of people around the world have been, and still are, mystified by him because he's supposedly the Head of the Church yet he isn't here where people can see him. All this was for a reason: in order to grasp the point about Jesus, in order to actually touch the spiritual reality of Christ, it must be through faith and not through the physical senses.

The problem starts with us. We were born dead spiritually. We can't know God, because our sin deadens us to his presence. So the Spirit first wakes up the heart of the believer so that he's alive spiritually. Now he can know, hear, and see God. Now he can live in God's world and take advantage of spiritual treasures in it. We can actually enter into the throne room of God and see what's going on there!

> But you have come to Mount Zion, to the heavenly Jerusalem, the city of the living God. You have come to thousands upon thousands of angels in joyful assembly, to the church of the firstborn, whose names are written in heaven. You have come to God, the judge of all men, to the spirits of righteous men made perfect, to Jesus the mediator of a new covenant, and to the sprinkled blood that speaks a better word than the blood of Abel. (Hebrews 12:22-24)

When we live by faith, we see things that others can't see. We see that Jesus is a deep well, full of the treasures of Heaven, that we can ask for and receive. We see that he's the King, the Prophet, and the Priest who is interceding for us in

Heaven at the throne of Grace. We see the state of our sinful hearts and that we must repent and confess our sins. We see that holiness and righteousness is the order of the day – that's at the top of the agenda if we want to be considered for Heaven. We see the world around us as the enemy's dominion, in which millions are being deceived and led to death through immorality and ignorance. We learn to step around the spiritual dangers that others can't see. We see so much, because of our eyes of faith.

- *New creature* – In the Old Testament, only the Jews were included in the counsels of God. They alone had the privilege of coming close to God and getting salvation. The Gentiles – all the other nations of the world – had no right to get anything from God. Abraham was told that the covenant was for him and his seed – meaning his descendants. Nobody else had legal claim to the covenant besides the children of God.

> I will establish my covenant as an everlasting covenant between me and you and your descendants after you for the generations to come, to be your God and the God of your descendants after you. (Genesis 17:7)

But in the New Testament we find out that God actually had a different thing in mind than what the Israelites thought. When he said "to Abraham's Seed", he didn't mean just the Jewish race – he meant the *spiritual* children of Abraham. Some Jews qualify, but not all of them do!

The Apostles – the Interpreters of Christ

Understand, then, that those who believe are children of Abraham. The Scripture foresaw that God would justify the Gentiles by faith, and announced the gospel in advance to Abraham: "All nations will be blessed through you." So those who have faith are blessed along with Abraham, the man of faith ... He redeemed us in order that the blessing given to Abraham might come to the Gentiles through Christ Jesus, so that by faith we might receive the promise of the Spirit. (Galatians 3:7-9, 14)

A man is not a Jew if he is only one outwardly, nor is circumcision merely outward and physical. No, a man is a Jew if he is one inwardly; and circumcision is circumcision of the heart, by the Spirit, not by the written code. (Romans 2:28)

What we discover in the New Testament is that God had planned from the very beginning to make a *New Man* who was a Jew *inwardly*, not just outwardly. In fact, the New Man that God had in mind wouldn't be a Jew or a Gentile – he (or she, since there is neither male nor female in the Kingdom of God!) would be a *Christian*.

His purpose was to create in himself one new man out of the two, thus making peace, and in this one body to reconcile both of them to God through the cross, by which he put to death their hostility. He came and preached peace to you who were far away and peace to those who were near. For

The Apostles – the Interpreters of Christ

through him we both have access to the Father by one Spirit. (Ephesians 2:15-18)

The new man is going to inhabit God's eternal Jerusalem. People from all over the world will receive this citizenship, not just the Jews.

Jesus shows us in his own life what the New Man will be like. The Jews were often frustrated with him because he didn't abide by the Old Testament system of laws as they did. He repeatedly taught them, however, that he knew better than they did what the requirements for pleasing God are! He obeyed God from the heart, he knew the purpose of the Sabbath and lived by it, he loved and healed and rejoiced in God his Father. His life was perfection, as far as the Law was concerned. This is what all of God's people will be when they too are perfected.

But whenever anyone turns to the Lord, the veil is taken away. Now the Lord is the Spirit, and where the Spirit of the Lord is, there is freedom. And we, who with unveiled faces all reflect the Lord's glory, are being transformed into his likeness with ever-increasing glory, which comes from the Lord, who is the Spirit. (2 Corinthians 3:16-18)

… since you have taken off your old self with its practices and have put on the new self, which is being renewed in knowledge in the image of its Creator. (Colossians 3:9-10)

The Apostles – the Interpreters of Christ

How will Jesus do this? This is the amazing part: Jesus, who made the first heavens and earth (we're told that God made all things through him and by him) is in the process of making a new Heaven and new earth. And to get us there, he became a man, died, and himself rose from the dead into that new world. *He the Creator himself led the way to the new Creation.* There's no better answer to our problem of how to get to Heaven than to have the One with all power and authority blaze the trail open for us to follow him in.

• *One with him* – Though Jesus was perfect, there's little hope in that for us unless there's a way to spill some of that perfection over to us! If we hope to be saved, somehow we have to look like Jesus looked. Is that possible? Does God in fact expect that kind of perfection from us too?

The answer to the second question is undeniably **yes**. God expects perfection from anybody who wishes to spend eternity living with him in his house. Jesus told us this:

> Be perfect, therefore, as your Heavenly Father is perfect. (Matthew 5:48)

The first question, then, as to how we will become this perfect, is answered in an amazing way. We become *one with Christ* – so that whatever happens to him, happens to us as well.

We can use an example (though it's imperfect, it does show the point somewhat). When a woman becomes pregnant, she and the baby form a single system to some extent. Though each one is an

The Apostles – the Interpreters of Christ

individual (each has their own heart, mind, soul, etc.), they share certain things, like the food that the mother eats which also feeds the baby in her. And where the mother goes, the baby (naturally!) goes too. They act as one unit, yet they are really two people. If the mother abuses herself or suffers, the baby suffers too; if the mother is healthy, the baby shares in that health.

This is a picture of what life is like for Christ and his people. He brings them into himself – makes them one with him (closer than a baby is with its mother) so that they go where he goes, and experienced what he experiences. So, when he satisfied the Law, the Law was also satisfied with us – since we are part of him. When he returned to Heaven, we also find ourselves coming into the presence of God with the same right of access as the Son of God. Since he lives, we also live. Since he was raised above all principalities and powers, we too are no longer dominated by them, since we are with him in Heaven spiritually.

Paul says that this is the heart of the mystery of the Gospel. While there are many other things about Christ that need to be unveiled and shown us for our life of faith, this is the most important principle that we must learn. We have what we have, and we are what we are, only because we have been made one with Christ – that's the key behind our getting anything from God. When God looks at Christ, he sees us there too. Christ and we are united and cannot be separated now, like a husband and bride. The two shall become one.

The Apostles – the Interpreters of Christ

After all, no one ever hated his own body, but he feeds and cares for it, just as Christ does the church — for we are members of his body. "For this reason a man will leave his father and mother and be united to his wife, and the two will become one flesh." This is a profound mystery — but I am talking about Christ and the church. (Ephesians 5:29-32)

- *The House of God* – Heaven is going to be the family reunion of all of God's people – a reunion that will last forever. We will live with each other, and with God, in unbroken, fervent, perfect fellowship. If we can't imagine doing such a thing for so long and enjoying it (!), we *will* understand it then. Love here is often imperfect, but love there will be perfect because God is perfect, and his house is perfect.

To get ready for the occasion, God has been putting together a house for us all to live in. We have to understand that such a house isn't made from earthly materials. God wants something that will last forever, and gold and stone can't last forever, even in the best of circumstances. So he will use living stones to build his house:

As you come to him, the living Stone— rejected by men but chosen by God and precious to him — you also, like living stones, are being built into a spiritual house to be a holy priesthood, offering spiritual sacrifices acceptable to God through Jesus Christ. (1 Peter 2:4-5)

The Apostles – the Interpreters of Christ

Jesus told us that he was going away to work on this house:

> In my Father's house are many rooms; if it were not so, I would have told you. I am going there to prepare a place for you. And if I go and prepare a place for you, I will come back and take you to be with me that you also may be where I am. You know the way to the place where I am going. (John 14:2-4)

What we may not realize, though, is what he meant by that. Every person who believes and becomes a Christian is another "living stone" being laid in the walls of God's house. We are being built *now* into a Temple where the Spirit lives and works among us. He grafts another person, when they believe, into the living Tree which feeds, supports, and protects God's people as well as causing them to bear fruit pleasing to God.

> I am the vine; you are the branches. If a man remains in me and I in him, he will bear much fruit; apart from me you can do nothing. If anyone does not remain in me, he is like a branch that is thrown away and withers; such branches are picked up, thrown into the fire and burned. If you remain in me and my words remain in you, ask whatever you wish, and it will be given you. This is to my Father's glory, that you bear much fruit, showing yourselves to be my disciples. (John 15:5-8)

The Apostles – the Interpreters of Christ

The reason we need this house is that there, in Heaven, we will live in such close proximity with God the Father that we won't need anything physical anymore to exist. He himself will be our sun, our light, our food, our clothing – he will be everything we need, so that we will need nothing else. That's why the apostles were so eager to point out the fullness of Christ: if we can see it, we can discover so much in him that we can use that this should encourage us to depend on him alone. We may as well get good at doing that now, because we will be doing it all the time in Heaven! He is our "all in all." (Colossians 3:11)

- ***Spiritual kingdom*** – Christ once confused Pilate when he claimed to be a King, yet he did nothing to protect himself from crucifixion. A king would naturally try to preserve his life, because his life means the well-being of his kingdom. As long as he lives, the kingdom continues in peace. But Jesus was willingly going to his death!

> When Pilate heard this, he was even more afraid, and he went back inside the palace. "Where do you come from?" he asked Jesus, but Jesus gave him no answer. "Do you refuse to speak to me?" Pilate said. "Don't you realize I have power either to free you or to crucify you?" Jesus answered, "You would have no power over me if it were not given to you from above." (John 19:8-11)

The secret was that his kingdom wasn't physical – it wasn't a kingdom of *this* world. It's a spiritual kingdom, and its throne is in Heaven, not on earth. It's made up of the "spirits of righteous men made perfect." There will be thrones for all of Jesus' "mighty men" who fought with him in the wars against Satan.

> I tell you the truth, at the renewal of all things, when the Son of Man sits on his glorious throne, you who have followed me will also sit on twelve thrones, judging the twelve tribes of Israel. (Matthew 19:28)

> Do you not know that we will judge angels? (1 Corinthians 6:3)

The kingdom of Christ is a place where the servants of God are righteous and holy – perfectly so. There will be no sinners or rebels there. God's Word will be Law, and perfectly obeyed. King will love subject, and subject will love King. There will be no more tears of pain or sickness or death, because the King works miracles and will heal and restore and give life to all. The man we saw in the Gospels who healed and spoke with authority is the one who will rule over this spiritual Kingdom and restore all things to its rightful place and nature.

We would be surprised, at first, at what we see in this new kingdom. Imagine going to a foreign country and not being used to anything that you see there. The language is strange, the food is strange, the natives are strange, the laws and customs are strange – we need a guidebook to help us figure out how to get around in it without getting hurt or lost or embarrassed. The same

The Apostles – the Interpreters of Christ

holds true for Christ's kingdom: the people in it do things a certain way (because the King demands it of them), they talk about certain things, they speak in spiritual words, they work for spiritual goals, they use spiritual supplies to build a spiritual kingdom – the whole thing seems strange and contrary to common sense until we begin to see for ourselves the nature and reality of the Kingdom that we're in.

- *Life in the Spirit* – When Jesus returned to Heaven, his disciples were devastated. They were devastated by his crucifixion, but when he rose from the dead they had hopes that he would at last set up his kingdom on earth and fulfill the things he had been promising. Now he was gone again, apparently for good. They forgot what he had told them about the Holy Spirit.

> But the Counselor, the Holy Spirit, whom the Father will send in my name, will teach you all things and will remind you of everything I have said to you. (John 14:26)

> When the Counselor comes, whom I will send to you from the Father, the Spirit of truth who goes out from the Father, he will testify about me. (John 15:26)

> Because I have said these things, you are filled with grief. But I tell you the truth: It is for your good that I am going away. Unless I go away, the Counselor will not come to you; but if I go, I will send him to you. (John 16:6-7)

The Apostles – the Interpreters of Christ

The reason we have the Spirit now is so that we don't miss anything that Jesus has for his people. Though he isn't with us in person, his Spirit now brings us his life – and all the treasures that we could hope to have from him, whether he was here in person or not. In other words, we aren't missing a thing as long as we have his Spirit in us.

> I pray that out of his glorious riches he may strengthen you with power through his Spirit in your inner being, so that Christ may dwell in your hearts through faith. (Ephesians 3:16-17)

The important thing, though, is that we walk in the Spirit. The Spirit's job is twofold: to save us from our sin (remember the reason behind Jesus' name in Matthew 1:21?) and to get us ready for Heaven. He will lead us into life and away from sin and death. He will take Christ's righteousness and work it into our hearts (remember that we are one with him – what he gets, we also get). The Spirit will reveal the things of Heaven to us and help us pray for those things that we see.

> For you did not receive a spirit that makes you a slave again to fear, but you received the Spirit of sonship. And by him we cry, "Abba, Father." The Spirit himself testifies with our spirit that we are God's children. Now if we are children, then we are heirs — heirs of God and co-heirs with Christ, if indeed we share in his sufferings in order that we may also share in his glory. (Romans 8:15-17)

The Apostles – the Interpreters of Christ

In fact, the one characteristic of a Christian, something that the Old Testament saints didn't know much about and only experienced off and on in special occasions, is that we live continually in the power of the Spirit of God. He controls our lives completely: he brings us continually into the presence of God, he guides our steps into righteousness, he gives us hope by revealing Heaven to us, he puts the hatred and loathing for sin in our hearts, he strengthens us in our fight against the enemy, and he makes it possible for us to actually help with the building of God's Kingdom.

> We have not received the spirit of the world but the Spirit who is from God, that we may understand what God has freely given us. This is what we speak, not in words taught us by human wisdom but in words taught by the Spirit, expressing spiritual truths in spiritual words. (1 Corinthians 2:12-13)

That last point is especially important in the life of the Church. The Church couldn't exist without the working of the Spirit among us. He gives us the gifts that we need to minister the grace of God to each other. We have unity, the same faith and doctrine, peace, holiness, love for the brethren, the same work, the same goal of God's glory among us, all because of the working of the Spirit of Christ among the believers.

> There is one body and one Spirit — just as you were called to one hope when you were called — one Lord, one faith, one

baptism; one God and Father of all, who is over all and through all and in all. (Ephesians 4:4-6)

These are the things that the Apostles saw in Christ. They didn't make these things up; what they saw was due to the Spirit enlightening them, revealing the foundations in the Old Testament and the connection, the fulfillment that's in Christ.

Eyewitnesses

The apostles lived with Jesus for up to three years during his ministry on earth. They saw what he did – the miracles, his confrontation with the Pharisees and Sadducees, the travels to Jerusalem and around Galilee. They heard his teaching and his explanation for the parables. They witnessed everything. God particularly wanted eyewitnesses there on the scene because, unfortunately, nobody would have believed the truth about Jesus unless there *were* eyewitnesses.

Eyewitnesses serve a critical function in the search for truth. In a court of law, the accused has to prove that he didn't do the crime in question, and the prosecutor has to prove that he did. Both can bring evidence to prove their point, but what will really clinch the argument is if one of them can provide an eyewitness who was there on the scene. The witness testifies that he saw what happened. To the judge that's a near-perfect argument, since physical evidence can often be interpreted in different ways according to one's point of view!

God provided eyewitnesses who saw Jesus do the things that the Gospels record:

> The man who saw it has given testimony, and his testimony is true. He knows that he tells the

The Apostles – the Interpreters of Christ

truth, and he testifies so that you also may believe. (John 19:35)

Jesus did many other miraculous signs in the presence of his disciples, which are not recorded in this book. But these are written that you may believe that Jesus is the Christ, the Son of God, and that by believing you may have life in his name. (John 20:30-31)

Now *those* are the men who wrote the New Testament. When they recorded the actual events of Jesus' life, they were writing a testimony of what they knew to be true. We have no freedom to doubt their word; in a court of law, their testimony would stand as written until someone could provide absolute proof (like another eyewitness) that they were *lying*. There is no room for personal opinions here, or offense taken because the story doesn't fit with one's personal beliefs. These men saw Jesus' works.

We did not follow cleverly invented stories when we told you about the power and coming of our Lord Jesus Christ, but we were eyewitnesses of his majesty. For he received honor and glory from God the Father when the voice came to him from the Majestic Glory, saying, "This is my Son, whom I love; with him I am well pleased." We ourselves heard this voice that came from Heaven when we were with him on the sacred mountain. (2 Peter 1:16-18)

When they wrote the Epistles of the New Testament, they went even further and told us about the spiritual depth that they saw in Jesus. Again, the Spirit is helping them see these things; the deep mysteries of Heaven unfolded before them, and that's

The Apostles – the Interpreters of Christ

what they're passing on to us. They can no more deny the reality of what they have seen than doubt their own existence.

> Surely you have heard about the administration of God's grace that was given to me for you, that is, the mystery made known to me by revelation, as I have already written briefly. In reading this, then, you will be able to understand my insight into the mystery of Christ, which was not made known to men in other generations as it has now been revealed by the Spirit to God's holy apostles and prophets. (Ephesians 3:2-5)

The point is that the type of literature we have here is a *legal document*. We are obligated to believe it. God has already proceeded to judge people's hearts over this material. We will be judged to be fit for Heaven or for Hell based on how we have received this testimony of the New Testament writers about Christ.

> Anyone who believes in the Son of God has this testimony in his heart. Anyone who does not believe God has made him out to be a liar, because he has not believed the testimony God has given about his Son. And this is the testimony: God has given us eternal life, and this life is in his Son. He who has the Son has life; he who does not have the Son of God does not have life. (1 John 5:10-12)

Just as in a court of law, which proceeds to make a ruling based on the evidence and testimony provided in court under sworn oath, God is taking action for or against us based on the realities that the apostles tell us about in the New Testament. It doesn't help us, either, to ignore it, because we all know that ignorance of the law is no excuse! This was written that all might hear and believe, and come to the knowledge of the truth.

If some don't, then so much the worse for them on Judgment Day.

Our Foundation

The fact that Jesus chose the disciples to carry out his message to the world was no accident of history, nor was it just a clever political move on his part. It was planned long before any of them were born. The success of the Church depends quite literally on the special role and work of the Apostles.

The Apostles tell us that the Church of Christ is a great spiritual house, and the cornerstone is Christ himself. He is laid down first, to provide direction for the rest of the house. Then the rest of us are laid like "living stones" into the walls of God's eternal house.

> As you come to him, the living Stone— rejected by men but chosen by God and precious to him — you also, like living stones, are being built into a spiritual house to be a holy priesthood, offering spiritual sacrifices acceptable to God through Jesus Christ. For in Scripture it says: "See, I lay a stone in Zion, a chosen and precious cornerstone, and the one who trusts in him will never be put to shame." (1 Peter 2:4-6)

But every building needs a foundation. The foundation is the solid strength beneath that holds up the walls. It's what the entire building rests upon, and it keeps the walls straight. And the foundation for God's Church is the testimony of the Apostles and Prophets:

> Consequently, you are no longer foreigners and aliens, but fellow citizens with God's people and members of God's household, *built on the*

The Apostles – the Interpreters of Christ

foundation of the apostles and prophets, with Christ Jesus himself as the chief cornerstone. In him the whole building is joined together and rises to become a holy temple in the Lord. And in him you too are being built together to become a dwelling in which God lives by his Spirit. (Ephesians 2:19-22)

In other words, what the Apostles tell us about Jesus is the foundation of our faith. *That's* what keeps the Church going. And their testimony is, of course, the Bible. The Church can no more live without the truth of the Bible than a building can stand without a foundation. As Jesus so graphically pointed out in the Sermon on the Mount, a building with a poor or no foundation will collapse. (Matthew 7:24-27) And any Christian or church that tries to set aside the Bible and live without it in any way will also collapse when the trials of life and the warfare with the enemy threaten them.

There's a revealing story in the New Testament about the role of the Apostles in Christ's project. When he was out in the countryside with thousands of people, teaching them and healing the sick, he had compassion on them because they had gone for several days without food. So he put the problem to his disciples. They thought he ought to send them back to town to buy food for themselves. He had something else in mind, however:

As evening approached, the disciples came to him and said, "This is a remote place, and it's already getting late. Send the crowds away, so they can go to the villages and buy themselves some food." Jesus replied, "They do not need to go away. ***You give them something to eat.***" "We have here only five loaves of bread and two fish," they answered. "Bring them here to me," he said. And

The Apostles – the Interpreters of Christ

he directed the people to sit down on the grass. Taking the five loaves and the two fish and looking up to heaven, he gave thanks and broke the loaves. Then he gave them to the disciples, and the disciples gave them to the people. They all ate and were satisfied, and the disciples picked up twelve basketfuls of broken pieces that were left over. The number of those who ate was about five thousand men, besides women and children. (Matthew 14:15-21)

Notice what he told them to do: *You give them something to eat.* They of course didn't know what he meant by that, but he proceeded to show them. Then Jesus took the bread that his Father in Heaven gave him, and he put it in the hands of the disciples to give to the crowd. That's the dynamic principle behind the ministry of the Apostles. They took the truth from Jesus and faithfully passed it out to the people, which we now have as the New Testament. They didn't change the message in the process, nor did they withhold anything that they were given. Their job was to pass on what they saw and heard to the rest of the Church as it stands. How *could* they do anything to the message without ruining it? Jesus had the words of eternal life! (John 6:68) We can, therefore, accept everything they told us about Jesus as the absolute truth.

The Old Testament and the New Testament

The Old Testament and the New Testament

The relationship between the Old and New Testaments is a difficult and yet interesting subject. The difficulty is that, during the Old Testament times, the Jews didn't think that there was going to be such a thing as a "New Testament" – as far as they were concerned, this was God's only and last Word. And the Gentile Christians were handed a *new* book (the New Testament) which focused on Christ, apparently fulfilling all of their needs – which seemed to encourage a break from the Jews and all those "old" ways.

The interesting part is that in each Testament there are clear statements to the effect that we need the other one. The Old keeps pointing us to the New, and the New keeps assuming the Old. We aren't permitted to forget either one; in fact, they both teach that we won't know the whole truth – our understanding of Scripture will be dangerously off balance – if we ignore either one. So our job is to become master of both.

What we want to do now is look at exactly how the two relate to each other. But first there are some compelling reasons to consider for pursuing this subject.

Why both?

Probably the basic reason why we need to know just as much about the Old Testament as the New is because God gave *both of them* to us. Here we are, arguing about whether or not we

The Old Testament and the New Testament

should study the Old Testament and wondering what use it is to us, in light of the fact that the Lord preserved it for 4000 years through fire and war and miracle so that we could have it! And he plainly says in the New Testament, in many ways, that the Old Testament is useful to us. If God himself has gone to so much trouble to put it in our hands and even personally recommends it to us, then the least we can do is give it a try!

There are some other compelling reasons for studying the Old Testament along with the New. For one thing, you'll be in good company if you do. Both Christ and the apostles considered the Old Testament to be God's Word – long before the New was written down. Second, the Lord had some design considerations in mind when he put together the Old Testament – it needs the New to complete the total picture of the Kingdom of God.

- **Christ fulfilled the Old Testament.** Jesus was always aware that he lived in the shadow of the Old Testament. His mission was to fulfill the old Scriptural promises, to make sure that everything that God had said in the Old Testament would come to pass. "In order that the Scriptures might be fulfilled ..." occurs in several places in the Gospels. When he started his ministry, he read from Isaiah and claimed that it was speaking of him.

> He went to Nazareth, where he had been brought up, and on the Sabbath day he went into the synagogue, as was his custom. And he stood up to read. The scroll of the prophet Isaiah was handed to him. Unrolling it, he found the place where it is written: "The Spirit of the Lord is on me, because he has anointed me to preach good

The Old Testament and the New Testament

news to the poor. He has sent me to proclaim freedom for the prisoners and recovery of sight for the blind, to release the oppressed, to proclaim the year of the Lord's favor." Then he rolled up the scroll, gave it back to the attendant and sat down. The eyes of everyone in the synagogue were fastened on him, and he began by saying to them, "Today this scripture is fulfilled in your hearing." (Luke 4:16-21)

He applied the Law in a much more forceful way than the people were used to, saying that his stricter interpretation was what it really meant. (Matthew 5:17-20) He found his own ministry summarized in the Old Testament commandments which he called the "greatest of the commandments." (Mark 12:28-34) He knew that the Old Testament saints looked forward to his ministry for their own spiritual needs:

> Your father Abraham rejoiced at the thought of seeing my day; he saw it and was glad. (John 8:56)

There are many other passages that prove that Christ worked hand in hand with the Old Testament.

- ***The apostles only had the Old Testament.*** We usually don't think of the fact that the only Scriptures that the early Church had was the Old Testament. Of course, it wasn't called the "Old" Testament – to them it was the "Holy Scriptures." They must have used their Bibles constantly because they knew it quite well. For instance, the

The Old Testament and the New Testament

New Testament writers quote extensively from the Old Testament in their books: one count gives over 380 direct quotations from the Old in the New, and there are over 2500 other places where the writer obviously has an Old Testament passage in mind.

They always referred to the Old Testament with the greatest reverence. Peter says that the New Testament message simply confirms what God had already spoken in the Old; he tells us that the old prophets were inspired by the Spirit when they wrote their books and we would do well to heed their message.

> And we have the word of the prophets made more certain, and you will do well to pay attention to it, as to a light shining in a dark place, until the day dawns and the morning star rises in your hearts. Above all, you must understand that no prophecy of Scripture came about by the prophet's own interpretation. For prophecy never had its origin in the will of man, but men spoke from God as they were carried along by the Holy Spirit. (2 Peter 1:19-21)

Paul, in the middle of an argument, quoted an Old Testament passage and said "Surely he [God] says this for us, doesn't he? Yes, this was written for us ..." (1 Corinthians 9:10) The thought would never have occurred to them to set aside their Scriptures because of new books coming on the scene; the Old Testament did the job quite well for them.

The Old Testament and the New Testament

- ***Gentiles need more than the Old Testament.*** Not only does the Church need the Old Testament, but it needs the New as well. While we are attempting to bring the OT back into the limelight, we don't mean to overlook the fact that it doesn't have the complete picture – the New finishes it out perfectly. Remember that the Gentiles weren't really part of the plan in the Old Testament. It was a Jewish nation then, and the blessings were given to the Jews alone for the time being. Although the deeper level of the promise given to Abraham had the Gentiles in mind, the stories of the Old Testament centered solely around the Israelites and *their* relationship with God.

So we need a definitive statement on where the Gentiles fit into God's scheme, and the New Testament gives us that statement. Now, in the NT era, we understand God's purpose when he made the promise to Abraham about blessing the entire world through his Seed. Peter's experience with Cornelius (Acts 10-11) and Paul carrying the Gospel to the Gentiles (Acts 15) were necessary steps in the historical progress of the Church. Without these spiritual milestones we would still be confused about how the Gentiles fit into God's plans.

- ***Old Testament shadows became New Testament realities.*** Although almost all the points of the doctrine of God's grace are in the Old Testament, they were physical lessons for the spiritual realities to come. Everyone who had spiritual eyes to see the truth realized that the blood of bulls and goats couldn't take away sins.

The Old Testament and the New Testament

And when they sent the goat out into the wilderness with the sin of the Israelites on its head, they would know that it was a symbolic act – there was still sin in the camp. When Solomon built the Temple for God to live in, he said ...

> But will God really dwell on earth with men? The heavens, even the highest heavens, cannot contain you. How much less this Temple I have built! (2 Chronicles 6:18)

Only in the New Testament do we find out what God had in mind for a satisfactory dwelling place – the spiritual Temple of the body of Christ, the body of believers. Without the New Testament we wouldn't know God's ultimate purposes for the Old Testament shadows. We would be like the Jews were – they knew that God had something real going on in the background, but they didn't know exactly what it was.

What did the Old Testament anticipate?

An astute reader of the Old Testament will pick up on some interesting hints of things to come. The old writers knew that this wasn't to be God's last word; they knew that the Lord was only mixing the necessary ingredients, so to speak, for the final Bread of Heaven to be revealed later. For one thing, the measures that God took to deal with the people back then were obviously temporary measures at best. Something eternal and spiritually solid had to come someday or none of this was going to work. So the Old Testament looks forward to the New in several important ways.

The Old Testament and the New Testament

- ***Inclusion of the Gentiles.*** From the very beginning we get clues that God was interested in more than the Jewish nation. For example, the first eleven chapters of Genesis deal with men everywhere, not just the Jews. God created all men, all men are fallen into sin, all men are subject to God's judgment, and God is displeased with this problem that all men have – he wants to solve the problem on a world-wide scale.

Another clue is the covenant with Abraham, in which God promises that he will use Abraham's Seed to bless all nations. Although he doesn't tell Abraham the details of how he will do this, something is in the air and we can expect to see great blessings for the Gentiles as well as the Jews.

The Israelites were supposed to treat the alien with respect and care, since they were once aliens themselves. (Exodus 23:9) But a Gentile wasn't a Jew, after all, and there were strict regulations about keeping uncircumcised Gentiles out of the Jewish sacred places. However, there were instances when Canaanites married into the Jewish people – for example, Tamar, Joseph's wife, Rahab, and Ruth. Even some of the ancestors of Christ were non-Jews by birth!

There were many prophecies about the Gentiles coming into the Church of God; here are some of the references:

Genesis 49:10	Isaiah 55:5
Psalm 2:8	Isaiah 56:3-8
Psalm 22:27-31	Isaiah 60:1-14
Psalm 46:4,10	Isaiah 65:1
Psalm 65:2,5	Is. 66:12,19,23
Psalm 66:4	Jeremiah 3:17
Psalm 68:31-32	Jeremiah 4:2
Psalm 72:8-19	Jer.16:l9-21
Psalm 86:9	Ezekiel 47:3-5
Psalm 102:5-22	Daniel 2:35,44
Psalm 145:10-11	Daniel 7:13-14
Isaiah 2:2-5	Hosea 2:23
Isaiah 9:2-7	Joel 2:28-32
Isaiah 11:6-10	Amos 9:11-12
Isaiah 18:7	Micah 4:3-4
Isaiah 24:16	Haggai 2:7
Isaiah 35:1-7	Zech. 2:10-11
Isaiah 40:5	Zechariah 6:15
Isaiah 42:1,4	Zech. 8:20-23
Is. 45:8,22-24	Zechariah 9:1,10
Isaiah 49:1-23	Zech.14:8-9,16
Isaiah 54:l-3	Malachi 1:1

Is this proof enough that the Old Testament was looking forward to the Gentiles coming into God's plan? The theme runs through the entire Scriptures!

- ***Solving man's basic problem.*** Another hint of things to come concerns the final solution of man's basic problem: sin. From the beginning of the Bible we see that man labors under his burden and pays a heavy price for it. No one can rebel against God and succeed, though men have tried for thousands of years. But God has never been satisfied with allowing men to continue to sin. A solution has to be

The Old Testament and the New Testament

found – an effective and far-reaching solution that will put sin to death forever in any person, no matter what time or place they may come from.

From the very first book we see God's intent to do something formidable about sin. In Genesis we read this promise:

> And I will put enmity between you and the woman, and between your offspring and hers; he will crush your head, and you will strike his heel. (Genesis 3:15)

What exactly he has in mind here we don't know, if we just go by the words themselves. His solution in chapter six of Genesis (the Flood in Noah's day) obviously wasn't the answer that he was looking for, although he wasn't unwilling to use severe judgment against sinners over and over again in history. But Leviticus 4-5 and 16 get us closer to God's intentions: here we read that a sacrifice – someone's death – will satisfy God's need for justice. When the people sin, let someone (or something, in the case of an animal sacrifice) die in their place and then God will forgive their sins.

The problem with this solution was that the people went home, after offering their sacrifice, only to sin again; the animal sacrifice didn't do anything to their *hearts* to make them more holy. Furthermore, what were sacrifices of bulls and goats to God when men and women rebel against him? Did they think that forgiveness could be bought that easily? Does the death of an animal really satisfy God's justice when men have sinned against him? David realized the truth of the matter when he said ...

> Sacrifice and offering you did not desire, but my ears you have pierced; burnt offerings and sin offerings you did not require. (Psalm 40:6)

And in Isaiah 1:11 God says very explicitly: I have no pleasure in the blood of bulls and goats.

What he wanted was their hearts – but he wasn't getting them. Something had to be done. In Isaiah 53 we get a glimpse of what he intends to do to purify his people, a stunning solution that will forever solve the problem. And in Ezekiel we find another piece to the puzzle.

> For I will take you out of the nations; I will gather you from all the countries and bring you back into your own land. I will sprinkle clean water on you, and you will be clean; I will cleanse you from all your impurities and from all your idols. I will give you a new heart and put a new spirit in you; I will remove from you your heart of stone and give you a heart of flesh. And I will put my Spirit in you and move you to follow my decrees and be careful to

keep my laws. You will live in the land I gave your forefathers; you will be my people, and I will be your God. I will save you from all your uncleanness. (Ezekiel 36:24-29)

But even with these clues, the details for the final solution aren't really clear, and not until we arrive at the New Testament do we find out the Lord's hidden purposes.

- ***The Heavenly patterns.*** In Exodus 26:30 we read that Moses saw a pattern for the tabernacle that he was to build – it was the Heavenly Temple in which God lives. He was instructed to build the earthly copy exactly after the Heavenly model.

> They serve at a sanctuary that is a copy and shadow of what is in Heaven. This is why Moses was warned when he was about to build the tabernacle: "See to it that you make everything according to the pattern shown you on the mountain." (Hebrews 8:5)

God wanted the tabernacle to be as close as possible to the one in Heaven, because he wants things here to be like they are there.

> Your Kingdom come, your will be done on earth as it is in Heaven. (Matthew 6:10)

When we compare the earthly copies with the realities that we finally get to see in the

The Old Testament and the New Testament

New Testament, we find that the Jews *could* have had a fair idea of God's spiritual Kingdom if they would have had eyes to see it. Consider these Old Testament concepts:

Worship: The Israelites had to be careful to approach God in holiness, in the prescribed manner, cleansing themselves with sacrifices and washings. This corresponds to what we find in Jesus who provides the necessary cleansings for us – so that we can now come "boldly to the throne of grace." (Hebrews 4:16)

Kingdom: David's reign was the picture of God's kingdom on earth; he ruled in righteousness, executed justice, led the people to God in the Temple, and protected the people from their enemies. That's the kind of king that God is to his people – which we see plainly when we watch Jesus rule his Church.

Law: The Law that the Israelites received on Mt. Sinai carefully outlined the will of God for their entire lives, from eating to working to worship to public justice. Was the Law simply to order their outward lives? Wasn't the purpose of the Law to give them an opportunity to obey the Lord from their hearts, and not just when someone was looking? The New Testament teaches that this was precisely its purpose, even

The Old Testament and the New Testament

for the Jews. See Jesus' interpretations of the Law in Matthew 5-7 in this regard.

Deliverance: From Lot's deliverance from Sodom, to Israel's deliverance from Egypt, to the constant deliverances during the time of the Judges, to David delivering the Israelites from the Philistines – and so on throughout their history – God showed himself a Deliverer of his people But where was the deliverance from the most deadly enemy – the burden of sin that people carry in their own hearts? These stories show us that God can and will deliver his people from whatever trouble they are in, even if they got themselves into it. We are well prepared, in other words, to move to the New Testament's story of Jesus who delivers people from their greatest spiritual enemies.

- *The missing answer.* As we have seen all along, the Old Testament keeps us on the edge of our seats with the drama of God working with his people. Sin and death loom over the nation, and their lives are always in the balance. What will God do? What will be his solution? We must confess that the answers given are temporary – they don't answer the real problem. But it's not as if God doesn't have the power to solve the problems of sin and death, or that he doesn't know how. His temporary answers are like picture puzzles that are almost done: we can see the picture forming, but the heart of it is still missing. When he gets to the New Testament, all he will need is one more critical piece, because he has already spent a lot of time getting things in place in the Old Testament. So the Old Testament keeps us waiting for the final steps in God's plan yet to come.

What does the New Testament rely on?

The New Testament would be indecipherable without the Old Testament. In fact, the New just doesn't go over the same ground that the Old does. There are many things in the New Testament that, if we want to understand them better, we have to stop reading the Gospels and Epistles for the time being and turn back to the Old Testament stories for a while.

The New Testament picks up where the Old leaves off. If we read only the New, that's like starting a book near the end somewhere – if we want to know how things got to where they were by the end of the book then we'll just have to go back to the beginning and follow the plot as it builds up. If we do, then we will find, by the time we finish the Old Testament, that there are many threads left hanging in God's overall plan. The Lord purposely left them hanging, though: the New Testament will finish what the Old started; it will take up these threads and finish the tapestry of God's plan of salvation for all men. The Old Testament stories aren't going to be retold in the New, nor will the New rehash the important concepts of the Old. The New Testament is only going to tell how God took the final step.

So there's an unfinished story in the Old Testament, a plot taking shape that the New will finish. Like a master story teller, however, the Lord takes great care laying the foundations in the beginning so that the message of the New will have the greatest effect when it is finally told. It's like running a relay race. If the first runner has done a good job, the second runner has a better chance to win. If the Old Testament gives us a dependable revelation of God and man, and tells us the truth, and accurately describes the problem, then the New Testament can go ahead and apply the solution to the problem with great success.

What is it in the Old Testament that prepares the way for the New?

- *Our understanding of God* – The Old Testament teaches us about God. And this Old Testament witness is vitally important for the preparation of the message of the New Testament.

    The Old Testament reveals God. "Revelation" means uncovering the truth, making something plain that used to be mysterious and unknown. The Old Testament was the first written witness in the history of mankind that told something true and accurate about God. Outside of Jewish circles there were many religions and many explanations of the Divine world, but none of them were true enough to base one's life on. None of them were God's self-revelation – and unless God reveals himself we will never know what he's like! The Lord revealed himself to the Israelites, however, and that cleared up a lot about who God really was. Now man could offer an acceptable worship to a God who really exists, a God whom we know.

The Old Testament and the New Testament

If there are still many mysteries of God in the Old Testament, that's not a problem – it doesn't put the lie on the whole business. After all, even the New Testament doesn't tell us everything about God! Paul himself said that there were things he saw in Heaven that aren't to be revealed to man right now, "inexpressible things, things that man is not permitted to tell." (2 Corinthians 12:4) But that doesn't make the rest of the revelation of God in the New Testament inaccurate, does it? The Old Testament is the same way: we don't see some of the details there that we find in the New Testament, but that doesn't mean that what it does show us is wrong or unusable.

First impressions count. The reason that the Old Testament comes first in the Bible is because it wants to get us acquainted with the true God; we may as well get the facts straight about him before we go any further.

- ***The ways that God does things*** – God has ways of doing things. "Ways" can mean two things; *first*, the route that God takes to get from point A to point B; *second*, peculiar things about his personality that make him unique from everyone else. In both these respects the Old Testament reveals God's ways to us.

If it's true that God has certain ways of doing things, then we must learn those ways. For one thing, if we can learn how God does something then we can easily identify it when it happens – we won't confuse it with the works of man, or vice-versa. Another reason that it's

The Old Testament and the New Testament

important to know his ways is so that we can work *with* him instead of *against* him. It's no use claiming to be partners in the Lord's work if we are busy undoing what he put together!

The Old Testament is a rich source for the ways of the Lord. In fact, if we learn his ways well in the Old Testament, we are going to better appreciate certain things in the New Testament when we read them. Ah yes, we will say, this is very characteristic of the way God does things. We will recognize him from having read the Old Testament accounts.

But the ways of the Lord aren't immediately obvious. God must open our eyes to see them and train our spiritual senses to detect them.

> As the heavens are higher than the earth, so are my ways higher than your ways and my thoughts than your thoughts. (Isaiah 55:9)

> Show me your ways, O Lord, teach me your paths; guide me in your truth and teach me ... Good and upright is the Lord; therefore he instructs sinners in his ways. (Psalm 25:4-5,8)

If we don't know the ways of the Lord, some disastrous things may happen! For example, the Lord swore that the Israelites who came out of Egypt would never enter the Promised Land – why?

The Old Testament and the New Testament

> Your fathers tested and tried me and for forty years saw what I did. That is why I was angry with that generation, and I said, "Their hearts are always going astray, and *they have not known my ways*." So I declared on oath in my anger, "They shall never enter my rest." (Hebrews 3 9-11)

What are some of the ways of the Lord? **First**, we have seen many times he refuses to do anything that will allow you to sin. He is not the author of sin, nor will he put up with sin in your life.

Second, he often uses the underdog to do his greatest works. David was considered the runt of Jesse's family; even Samuel, prophet of God though he was, was surprised at God's choice of a king in David. This characteristic way of God appears over and over again in the Old Testament stories. We shouldn't be surprised, then, when we read in the New Testament that Christ bypassed the religious leaders of his day and used a pitiful bunch of nobodies to build his Church.

Third, he often uses failure to achieve lasting success. What the world considers a disaster, the Lord calls an opportunity. Moses, for example, was hardly the man to pick to face Pharaoh and lead the Israelites out of Egypt; he rejected his upbringing in Pharaoh's house, he murdered one of the Egyptians, and he was eighty years old before the Lord called him! In spite of the overwhelming disadvantages, however, the Lord used him to pull off a

The Old Testament and the New Testament

stunning success. In the same way, the Jews and the Romans shouldn't have written Jesus off so quickly when they watched him die on the cross. They should have waited at least another three days before closing the book on this wandering Teacher.

- ***The role of history*** – History is the essence of the Old Testament, and the New Testament gets a lot of mileage out of that. History a very picturesque way of getting across God's lessons to us – reading stories of others' experiences gets us involved emotionally as well as intellectually, so that it has a better chance of reaching the heart and making a difference in our lives.

But it serves several other purposes as well: for instance, it's a record of what God has done. Has God ever listened to his people? Has he ever disciplined them? Did he ever deliver them from their troubles? Did he lead them and provide for them? If he did these things for Israel, his chosen people, he certainly is able to do them any time he pleases for us too. The history shows us what he *can* do and what he *wants* to do for his people. Now all we need is the faith that the Israelites had, so that he will do these things for us. If God was willing to save and provide and rebuke in those days, then we can be assured that he's willing to do the same with us. God hasn't changed at all over the centuries. Maybe some think that he has changed (maybe they are hoping he *has* changed, if they have something to hide!) but that's not true: he is the same God.

The Old Testament and the New Testament

The way he treated the Israelites shows his intentions for the Church now.

History is a way of seeing God's overall plan; it progresses from one goal to another. Some nations have progressed from bad to worse; some nations have stepped into history and made their mark, only to disappear again, leaving their legacy to following generations. But Israel's history was different: it was designed to teach the people of God some important things about what God wants to do with man. The Lord had something in mind when he led the Israelites out of Egypt, when he raised David up to be their king, when he sent them away to Babylon and then brought them back again. A discerning eye will follow the story line and come to some conclusions about where God is going with all this. Then with the events that the New Testament gives him, he can peer far into the future and understand where God is taking the entire world in the end.

- *The preparing of the Messiah* – The New Testament depends heavily on the Old Testament for the story of the Messiah. All the prophets contributed in some degree to the theme. There are no surprises when we get to the story of the life of Christ; the Jews should have known about him when he arrived, and welcomed the fulfillment of their Scriptures. And what Jesus *did* was no surprise either, when one knows the prophecies of his ministry that are found in the pages of the Old Testament.

The Old Testament and the New Testament

The Lord progressively revealed the picture of his Messiah to the Israelites through the Prophets and types (which we'll see more about in a minute). At each step they got another piece to the puzzle, the "mystery" that God was preparing for his people.

But what we might miss, even though it's just as important, is the fact that God was *preparing his people* for the Messiah. One has to be a humble, obedient servant to believe in the Christ. The Lord spent centuries breaking their wills, teaching them about sin and deliverance, and showing his utter determination to love them. If you can read the Old Testament's stories with this in mind then you will appreciate the fact that Christ came to a people whom God prepared. They didn't accept him, but that wasn't God's fault: he was faithful in doing his preparatory work even though they were unfaithful to him in the end. Besides, all that preparation wasn't wasted; eventually there were twins born in God's family, the Jews and the Gentiles, and the hard work that God did in their day is for our benefit now.

> "... their transgression means riches for the world, and their loss means riches for the Gentiles ..." (Romans 11:12)

- ***The people of God*** – The New Testament is also obliged to look to the Old Testament for an explanation of the phrase, "the people of God" – or, the Church. What does it mean, to be "chosen by God"? Abraham was chosen from the heathen to receive God's promises – why? Nobody knows why. Though he was obligated to respond to God in faith, it's still a fact that God graciously chose Abraham and his descendants from among the nations to be his special people. We would never have chosen God if it were up to us; Abraham didn't even know God! It was a mercy that God introduced himself to him and made a covenant that included even us.

A family. The one thing that is common among all Christians is that we are children of Abraham. Our main family characteristic is what made Abraham stand out from the rest of the world: *his faith*. Just as he trusted God to do the impossible, we also trust God to do what he promised for us in Christ. Jew and Gentile both must trace their spiritual ancestry back to their father Abraham, if they want to prove that they have the right to Abraham's inheritance; and God – through Christ – makes us all into one family.

A holy priesthood. The privilege of being God's people brings some responsibility with it as well as blessing. The Israelites were to worship the Lord according to the prescribed ceremony in the Temple, and they were to testify to God's power and glory among the nations. They were witnesses of God in the world. They had access to God, they had his ear and his heart, and their prayers could move him when nothing else would.

The Old Testament and the New Testament

The Lord gave them amazing power and privilege!

Separate from the world. God called the Israelites to separate themselves from their sinful neighbors and walk in righteousness instead. He warned them that the native Canaanites would be their undoing if they didn't kill every one of them. He expected them to look to him for help and not to the Egyptians. He told them not to live like the heathen nations, to avoid them and their sins.

Now these pictures in the Old Testament give us a better idea of what the Church should look like. It's true that the OT saints experienced physical blessings and Christians experience spiritual blessings; but nevertheless the same principles hold from one to the other.

Where is Christ in the Old Testament?

One of the questions often asked of the Old Testament is this: does Christ appear in its pages anywhere? It would help a lot if we could see him there; this would strengthen our faith that the Old Testament is, indeed, a book for Christians.

Well, although he didn't appear in those days in the flesh like he did in the New Testament, he does fill the entire Old Testament – in various ways. You just have to keep a sharp eye out for him. For example, he told the Jews that Abraham knew about him – 2000 years before Christ was born!

Your father Abraham rejoiced at the thought of seeing my day; he saw it and was glad. (John 8:56)

The Old Testament and the New Testament

Here are some of the ways that he shows up in the Old Testament Scriptures:

- ***Theophanies*** – A "theophany" is when Christ made an actual appearance in Old Testament times. This is by no means something that every Christian is agreed about; some think that it really was Christ that appeared then, and others think that it must have been an angel or the triune God in the form of a man – in other words a vision.

  But if you believe that Christ could certainly have shown himself on earth before his actual Incarnation, you may be interested in looking up the following passages; these are the times that seem like he could have actually appeared to men: – Melchizedek Genesis 14:18-20; Hebrews 4) – the "man" who wrestled with Jacob (Genesis 30:22-32) – the fourth man in Nebuchadnezzar's furnace (Daniel 3) – the "son of man" in Daniel's vision. (Daniel 10)

- ***Predictions*** – There was certainly an abundance of predictions of Christ in the Old Testament. They range from mere hints of his coming to outright detailed descriptions of his person and work. Some of them were amazing in their accuracy. But all of them directed the attention of the Israelites to the One who would come and make everything right – who would set up God's eternal Kingdom on earth.

  These predictions served to strengthen the faith of the Israelites in their God who keeps his promises. For example, the Messiah would rule

The Old Testament and the New Testament

in such a way that justice would at last find full expression. The Lamb of God, they said, would take away the sins of his people. The Deliverer would rescue his people from their enemies. The great High Priest would bring his people before the throne of God to worship him. In other words, they looked past the shadows in their own times and saw the bright light shining in Christ who lives in eternity. Whoever held out for that more certain reality would find what their hearts were looking for.

- *Types* – A "type" is a kind of symbol. It's an object or person or situation that teaches, in a symbolic way, an eternal truth. When the type itself appeared, people may not have realized that it represented something far bigger in importance; it takes spiritual insight to understand the lesson of a type.

The idea of a type is not new; they go way back in Biblical history. For example, Paul said that the situation between Sarah and Hagar was a type of the situation between the Jews and the Church of God. The situation was this: Abraham was waiting on God to fulfill a promise that he would have an heir. At one point Abraham grew tired of waiting, and had a son through his wife's servant girl (a legal custom in those days), hoping that Hagar's son would be his heir. But it was not to be: Sarah's son, not Hagar's, would be the heir. In his day there was an argument about who would be the legal heir of Abraham; Sarah was trying to protect her son's inheritance. What God meant by it, though, was to teach the Church that Christians are the sole heir to

The Old Testament and the New Testament

Abraham's promises – which are the spiritual riches in Christ. The unbelieving Jews have no right to claim the inheritance of Abraham. (Galatians 4:21- 31)

There are many types of Christ in the Old Testament. Joseph was a type of Christ, because he typified the Deliverer that God raised up from the dead to deliver his people. The Tabernacle and Temple were both types of Christ, because they showed God living with man and providing a sacrifice to deliver their souls from sin and death. David was a type of Christ because he showed the way Christ himself would rule over his people and the benefits from living in a Kingdom like that.

One must be careful of types, however. It isn't necessary or wise to see types everywhere in the Old Testament. The Old Testament is rich enough without reducing the whole thing to types of Christ. Some of the "types" that people have discovered in the Old Testament are ridiculous and not necessary. It's safer to appeal to the Scriptures for proofs of types, or the sound judgment of the Church over the centuries.

- ***By faith*** – What this means is that God gives us the faith to see Christ in the Old Testament stories. In order to please God, we need to live by faith; if we read the Bible without faith then we won't see the Lord's glory in it.

Jesus rebuked the Pharisees and teachers of the Law for not understanding their Scriptures (Old Testament) when it spoke of him. (Matthew

The Old Testament and the New Testament

21:42) He had to explain to his disciples the meaning of the prophecies about him; they didn't see it at first. (Matthew 26:54) Jesus claimed that the Scriptures (Old Testament) spoke mainly about him. (John 5:39) The disciples who were walking to Emmaus after the crucifixion had to have the Scriptures (Old Testament) explained to them before they saw Christ there. (Luke 24:13-35)

Christianity is a tough business because the "realities" of this world work against it. We are called to believe things that the world laughs at; we are called to dedicate our lives to values that the world despises. The natural mind will never see Christ in the Old Testament, and unfortunately it isn't easy for God's people to see him there either. It takes the Spirit of God to open up the Bible to us and open our eyes to see the truth. If we don't see it, we will be as blind and as hopeless as the Pharisees were.

- *Anything of grace* – Whenever the Old Testament talks about God's love and grace and mercy, there is Christ. There's no reason to limit the influence of Christ to theophanies and predictions and types. The love of God for the world, that is spelled out so clearly in the New Testament, is what motivated God to prepare for that great event way back in the Old Testament. So it's no wonder that the Jews began to hear the sweet strains of God's love in Christ long before he actually came in person.

If it's true that Christ is "the radiance of God's glory and the exact representation of his being" (Hebrews 1:3) then whenever we see the glory of God in the Old Testament, we see Christ.

If it's true that "by him all things were created ... and in him all things hold together" (Colossians 1:16-17) then we can assume that he appears in the Genesis account of Creation, and he shows up again and again when God provides for, and cares for, the whole world and especially his people – both physical and spiritual care. It's because of Christ that Israel was preserved!

If it's true that he has a "power that enables him to bring everything under his control" (Philippians 3:21) then we can assume that the power that God used upon his enemies in the Old Testament was Christ working, and the power that God used on behalf of his people for their deliverance and care was Christ working.

If it's true that Christ is "the wisdom of God" (1 Corinthians 1:24) then we can assume that Proverbs was a work of Christ, that Ecclesiastes was a work of Christ, and that any passage that deals with God's wisdom is a testimony of Christ himself.

What do we do with the shadows in the Old Testament?

Many Christians stumble over the parts of the Old Testament that don't seem to pertain to us. For instance, what are we supposed to do with the laws about cleanness, and about sending the defiled and diseased outside of the camp? Or what

The Old Testament and the New Testament

about the sacrifices for praise, and atonement, and fellowship? What about Mt. Sinai – doesn't Hebrews tell us that we aren't supposed to worry about that, now that we have a new way to approach God? How about David and the kingdom of Israel? Now that Christ has come, do we have to worry about those old shadows of the realities? Aren't these things gone now? Do Christians have to pay any attention to them?

We have to be very careful here. There is nothing unnecessary in the Old Testament. Those old laws were given to the Israelites for a reason: if a man didn't follow them to the letter, he would never gain access to the throne of grace. Mt. Sinai was a critical stop for the Israelites; it helped make them into a nation. David's kingdom was the pattern for all the kings to follow – indeed, it's the very pattern that Christ uses to rule his Kingdom.

But neither are we Jews, nor are we Old Testament Christians alone. Christ has indeed done a work that frees us from the terrors of the Law. His life, death and resurrection take all these "shadows" into account and satisfies the spiritual requirements that we now have. When we hide in him, we receive all the benefits of an Israelite who was supposed to follow the Law perfectly. When we hide in him, we find that he has undergone the terrors of Mt. Sinai, and fulfilled the whole Law to the letter, and got us access to God's throne of grace. When we hide in him, he rules over us in the same way that David ruled over the Israelites.

We can take advantage of the truth of the Old Testament by living by faith in Christ. All these shadows were, after all, an explanation in physical terms of the spiritual realities of Heaven. If the Jews were obligated to faithfully perform the "shadow" ceremonies, then we are much more obligated to be just as faithful to the corresponding spiritual realities! The difference between the Israelites and us isn't *what* they were obligated to do, but *who* was responsible for doing it:

- ***Christ has answered the requirements of the Law.*** The Law required a certain ceremony from those who wanted to approach God; Christ accomplished this for us perfectly. So perfectly, in fact, that we need not worry about that anymore. Even when there is sin in our hearts, we can come to God knowing that he will accept us and Christ will cleanse us with the blood of his sacrifice. All the purity laws are also taken care of, since Christ's life has made us acceptable and clean in God's sight.

- ***Christ is the reality of the Old Testament types.*** What God did for Israel, Christ does for us. He is our Deliverer, our Provider, our High Priest, our Redeemer, our Shepherd, our King, our Prophet – we have no need for someone else to take care of these necessities for us. But it's important that we depend on him for these things, because God still works with his people in these ways. It's just that Christ has taken over the job for our benefit.

- ***Christ is the assurance of our salvation.*** While risking the chance of a misunderstanding here, the fact remains that Christ makes up whatever is lacking in his people. By the fact that he rose from the dead and ascended into Heaven to God's right hand, we can know that our salvation is sure. Since he lives forever, we will live forever. Our future is in as much "doubt" as his future – in other words, there is *no* doubt now. He has taken care of the whole thing for us. When once we are fully united to him, there will be a "Sabbath rest" for all of us to enjoy. This doesn't allow us to sin, though; we can't think – "well, I'm saved and Christ has taken care of everything for me." Only to someone who repents of his sin will God show his perfect love in Christ; anybody who presumes on God's love while still holding on to his sin is fooling himself.

Of what use is the Old Testament to Christians?

I hope that it isn't necessary to answer that question by now. We've seen that the Old Testament is rich with truth, full of the knowledge of God and his eternal purposes. If it doesn't have the full picture that the New Testament gives us, it still paints that picture to the point where the New Testament could finish it.

Christians should respect and use the Old Testament. There are some guidelines in using it; one should be aware of what he is working with and become skilled in using it. The Old Testament can be difficult sometimes, and misguided zeal will make it say things that it doesn't say. But its difficulty is no argument for ignoring it, because we will definitely not understand God's truth if we don't use it. The task is before us, there are effective tools for studying it, and when we ask God to help us he will show us what the book means. Besides, our Lord is glorified there, and studying it will be an answer to his prayer:

> Father, the time has come. Glorify your Son,
> that your Son may glorify you. (John 17:1)

The Old Testament and the New Testament

Step Three

Step Three

The first great phase of the plan of salvation was from the time that God made a covenant with Abraham to the time of John the Baptist. The second great phase was from John the Baptist, through the birth and ministry of Christ, and the beginnings of the Christian Church. The first phase worked out all the details of salvation (in an easy-to-understand physical level), and the second phase put the plan into action (on the spiritual level, where it really counts).

There remains yet the third step of the plan. God isn't done yet in the plan of salvation. If he would have worked only with the Jews in the Old Testament, not only would we have not known about the spiritual fulfillment of the covenant with Abraham, but we Gentiles would be left out in the cold. And if God doesn't bring the current Church age to a close, there wouldn't be a final victory over sin and death, and there would be a lot of unanswered problems strewn through history.

We need this final third step of the plan. God always did intend to wrap up what he started, even from the beginning. Everything in history has been proceeding exactly as he always planned for it. "I make known the end from the beginning, from ancient times, what is still to come." (Isaiah 46:10) Our salvation wouldn't be complete without it. And although during the era of the New Testament the third step wasn't ready to put into action, we find there a good description of what's *going* to happen and *why* it has to happen. There is just too much unfinished business left to leave things the way they are now.

Let's look at how God intends to wrap things up for the third and final phase of earth's history.

The Second Coming

The first time that Jesus came, he put aside his glory as the Son of God and took on a humble form. The second time won't be that way. Then we will see him as he is in Heaven, glorious, full of power, ready to do battle against God's enemies. John saw Jesus in his glory as he is now:

> I turned around to see the voice that was speaking to me. And when I turned I saw seven golden lampstands, and among the lampstands was someone "like a son of man," dressed in a robe reaching down to his feet and with a golden sash around his chest. His head and hair were white like wool, as white as snow, and his eyes were like blazing fire. His feet were like bronze glowing in a furnace, and his voice was like the sound of rushing waters. In his right hand he held seven stars, and out of his mouth came a sharp double-edged sword. His face was like the sun shining in all its brilliance. When I saw him, I fell at his feet as though dead. (Revelation 1:12-17)

But to the rest of the world, the change in Jesus' appearance on that day will be startling. Jesus warned the people in his day that even those who rejected his earthly ministry would be terrified of him when he came back the second time:

Step Three

O Jerusalem, Jerusalem, you who kill the prophets and stone those sent to you, how often I have longed to gather your children together, as a hen gathers her chicks under her wings, but you were not willing! Look, your house is left to you desolate. I tell you, you will not see me again until you say, 'Blessed is he who comes in the name of the Lord.' (Luke 13:34-35)

This reminds us of the old prophecy in Zechariah:

And I will pour out on the house of David and the inhabitants of Jerusalem a spirit of grace and supplication. They will look on me, the one they have pierced, and they will mourn for him as one mourns for an only child, and grieve bitterly for him as one grieves for a firstborn son. (Zechariah 12:10)

Jesus' ministry can actually be divided up into three sections:

- **First**, he came as a humble servant. The first time Jesus came, he brought news of the kingdom of God and the need to repent. He didn't come in his divine glory, because he wanted to identify with man, not destroy him. His ministry then set the pace for the ministry of the entire Church after that. The idea was that *now is the time for salvation*, not punishment. The day to change this world forever hadn't come yet. He worked among the Jews, and the Church works among the Gentiles, to save people from sin and death – while there's still time.

The Lord is not slow in keeping his promise, as some understand slowness. He is

Step Three

patient with you, not wanting anyone to perish, but everyone to come to repentance. (2 Peter 3:9)

• **Second**, he rules as Head of the Church. That confuses people now – this historic pause when the Lord sends out his representatives to call all nations to repentance. Why isn't he making himself known? Why doesn't he just fix what's wrong with the human heart and condition and set up his Kingdom now? The reason is that there are many sheep yet who have to hear the call of the Gospel and come into the fold. When that phase is done, then Jesus will come a second time to set up the new Heavens and the new earth, and do away with the old.

When his disciples, for example, resented the fact that people rejected Jesus and his teaching, Jesus rejected their solution. They wanted God to send down fire from Heaven and destroy the rebels! But that's not the program right now:

> And he sent messengers on ahead, who went into a Samaritan village to get things ready for him; but the people there did not welcome him, because he was heading for Jerusalem. When the disciples James and John saw this, they asked, "Lord, do you want us to call fire down from heaven to destroy them?" But Jesus turned and rebuked them, and they went to another village. (Luke 9:52-56)

• **Third**, he will return as the King to finish setting up his Kingdom. But the day of mercy and

Step Three

forgiveness won't last forever. The King is coming to straighten things out! One day the Lord will decide that he has accomplished all that he wants to do in history, and the last soul has entered the ranks of the Church. Then the sky will open up and Jesus will appear to the entire world as the Lord and King that he is. Then he will destroy the principalities and powers that have controlled this world, and set up his own kingdom in their place.

His second coming is necessary as the final step in God's overall plan. During the Old Testament times, God wrote out the blueprints for his Kingdom that Jesus would rule over. During the times of Jesus' ministry on earth, and during this Church age, God is drawing people over to Christ from around the world – preparing the Nation over which he intends to rule in eternity. The third step has to happen to finish what God has been working on. The King himself must come back to claim the Kingdom that his Father has been preparing for him all these centuries.

> Then the end will come, when he hands over the kingdom to God the Father after he has destroyed all dominion, authority and power. For he must reign until he has put all his enemies under his feet. The last enemy to be destroyed is death. For he "has put everything under his feet." Now when it says that "everything" has been put under him, it is clear that this does not include God himself, who put everything under Christ. When he has done this, then the Son himself will be made subject to him who put

Step Three

everything under him, so that God may be all in all. (1 Corinthians 15:24-28)

The New Jerusalem

Jesus promised us once that he was leaving to prepare a place for us:

> In my Father's house are many rooms; if it were not so, I would have told you. I am going there to prepare a place for you. And if I go and prepare a place for you, I will come back and take you to be with me that you also may be where I am. You know the way to the place where I am going." (John 14:2-4)

Perhaps you haven't seen yet what he was doing in his ministry, but Jesus was actually doing what his father David had done before him. Remember that the first thing that David did as King over Israel was to capture Jerusalem and set up the city for his own capital. From there he went on to rule over God's people, and set up the Temple worship and its sacrificial system. He had to have a center to work from, a place which everyone identified as the home of the King, the government, and the worship of God.

Jesus is doing the same thing. As King over God's kingdom, he is setting up his capital, his center of operations from which he will rule over his people. He is also building a house in which he plans to live – the new Temple:

> Consequently, you are no longer foreigners and aliens, but fellow citizens with God's people and members of God's household, built on the foundation of the apostles and prophets, with

Step Three

Christ Jesus himself as the chief cornerstone. In him the whole building is joined together and rises to become a holy temple in the Lord. And in him you too are being built together to become a dwelling in which God lives by his Spirit. (Ephesians 2:19-22)

> As you come to him, the living Stone—rejected by men but chosen by God and precious to him — you also, like living stones, are being built into a spiritual house to be a holy priesthood, offering spiritual sacrifices acceptable to God through Jesus Christ. (1 Peter 2:4)

To some people the Bible can be a bit confusing at this point, because Jesus' goal is to make us one with *him*, and that's not a matter of a physical Temple made of stones and mortar. He's making a spiritual house: *we* are the stones of that house. He's making a spiritual Temple: *we* are that Temple, in which we will be always in the presence of God. And he's putting the thing together *now*, not waiting to do the whole thing after Judgment Day.

> There remains, then, a Sabbath-rest for the people of God; for anyone who enters God's rest also rests from his own work, just as God did from his. Let us, therefore, make every effort to enter that rest, so that no one will fall by following their example of disobedience. (Hebrews 4:9-11)

Do you see the importance of getting into this Kingdom *now*? On Judgment Day his work will be revealed as complete – he won't be just starting on it then! He started on it during Abraham's day, and he did a lot more work on it when he was born a man himself. The Second Coming will be the day of unveiling the great work that's been going on for thousands of

Step Three

years – it will finally be finished. It's absolutely essential, therefore, that we get placed into that spiritual house now, *before* we die.

> But you have come to Mount Zion, to the heavenly Jerusalem, the city of the living God. You have come to thousands upon thousands of angels in joyful assembly, to the church of the firstborn, whose names are written in heaven. You have come to God, the judge of all men, to the spirits of righteous men made perfect, to Jesus the mediator of a new covenant, and to the sprinkled blood that speaks a better word than the blood of Abel. (Hebrews 12:22-24)

Many people think that this new city will be made of earthly gems, real silver and gold. But if God rewards us only with the riches of *this* world – the very things that he's been warning us against setting our hearts on all this time – that would be a cheap, empty victory. When the Bible describes the new city as having streets of gold, and gates of precious gems, that symbolizes the tremendous value in the city of God. Just like the other symbols of apocalyptic literature, it's using pictures to represent realities. If we want to know what the gold of Heaven represents, all we have to do is refer back to the Scriptures that teach us about gold – and what's more valuable than gold:

> And the words of the LORD are flawless, like silver refined in a furnace of clay, purified seven times. (Psalm 12:6)

> How much better to get wisdom than gold, to choose understanding rather than silver! (Proverbs 16:16)

Step Three

We do know that when we are in Heaven, we will have a perfect knowledge about God that we don't have in this world.

> For we know in part and we prophesy in part, but when perfection comes, the imperfect disappears. When I was a child, I talked like a child, I thought like a child, I reasoned like a child. When I became a man, I put childish ways behind me. Now we see but a poor reflection as in a mirror; then we shall see face to face. Now I know in part; then I shall know fully, even as I am fully known. (1 Corinthians 13:9-12)

Now put those two facts together – the wisdom of Proverbs, and the knowledge of Corinthians – and we begin to understand why Heaven is such a precious treasure chest. This is what God's people are looking forward to, and the lack of earthly riches will be disappointing only to unbelievers who love this world's wealth.

Destroy this world

Another item on Christ's agenda when he comes back, during the third phase of earth's history, is to destroy this world. This is bad news for unbelievers, and good news for those who long for a better world.

Ever since Adam and Eve sinned against God and turned God's creation into their own perverted system, God has been laying the groundwork for a replacement world. He has been planning a "new Heavens and a new earth" (Isaiah 65:17) because the first one is corrupted by sin and death.

What people don't realize, however, is that this old world won't be of any use to him once the new one is finished. When

Step Three

Christ comes to get his people and move them into the new house, so to speak, he's going to get rid of the old world. *There is nothing here in this physical world that would be of any use to him in eternity.* No riches, no earthly power, no physical body, nothing can provide anything useful for God's eternal house. The house that Jesus is building is spiritual, perfect, eternal, and it glorifies him. Nothing in this world fits that description. It accomplished God's purposes the first time around, at the first Creation, but it's all useless to him for the second Creation.

Therefore he plans to destroy it all, without leaving a single trace:

> By the same word the present heavens and earth are reserved for fire, being kept for the day of judgment and destruction of ungodly men ... But the day of the Lord will come like a thief. The heavens will disappear with a roar; the elements will be destroyed by fire, and the earth and everything in it will be laid bare. (2 Peter 3:7,10)

Notice that the prophecy includes what will happen to the wicked as well on that day. People don't like to think in these terms, but the wicked have cast their lot with this physical world and don't want anything to do with the new Creation. Like Lot's wife, they look back at what God wants them to leave and can't bear to put it behind them. The warning, however, holds for us just as it did with the ancient Sodomites:

> Woe to you, Korazin! Woe to you, Bethsaida! If the miracles that were performed in you had been performed in Tyre and Sidon, they would have repented long ago in sackcloth and ashes. But I tell you, it will be more bearable for Tyre and Sidon on the day of judgment than for you. And you, Capernaum, will you be lifted up to the skies? No,

Step Three

you will go down to the depths. If the miracles that were performed in you had been performed in Sodom, it would have remained to this day. But I tell you that it will be more bearable for Sodom on the day of judgment than for you. (Matthew 11:21-24)

Jesus predicted the coming destruction too. He also warned that the wicked would get caught up in the general destruction:

The master of that servant will come on a day when he does not expect him and at an hour he is not aware of. He will cut him to pieces and assign him a place with the hypocrites, where there will be weeping and gnashing of teeth. (Matthew 24:50-51)

The warning, then is this: get out now while you can. You don't want to get caught on the wrong side of the river when the King comes to destroy this world. That day won't be a day of bargaining, there won't be time to hold an interview with him, he won't have time to do any last-minute apologies or excuses. He will have sword in hand, and so will his Heavenly host. There will be blood and war, not peace and second chances. We can see the King on his way now in John's prophecy:

I saw Heaven standing open and there before me was a white horse, whose rider is called Faithful and True. With justice he judges and makes war. His eyes are like blazing fire, and on his head are many crowns. He has a name written on him that no one knows but he himself. He is dressed in a robe dipped in blood, and his name is the Word of God. The armies of Heaven were following him, riding on white horses and dressed in fine linen,

Step Three

white and clean. Out of his mouth comes a sharp sword with which to strike down the nations. "He will rule them with an iron scepter." He treads the winepress of the fury of the wrath of God Almighty. On his robe and on his thigh he has this name written: KING OF KINGS AND LORD OF LORDS. (Revelation 19:11-16)

The New Testament shows us these things to alarm us – to make us serious about our present condition. We have to make our peace with this King before he comes. When he comes, if we haven't done anything before then to save ourselves from the coming destruction, then we will die with the rest of God's enemies at the hand of a relentless warrior who will listen to nobody's excuses. His mission here will be total war.

There's a reason that Jesus intends to destroy this world, besides the fact that it won't be of any more use to him. The devil has made it his own stronghold of darkness, ignorance, lies, rebellion, misery, wickedness and death. The "principalities and powers of the air" have twisted God's beautiful creation into an ugly zone of death and destruction. For the most part, God's truth doesn't hold sway here – the devil's lies do. It's a world of deception and ignorance. People believe anything but the Bible, and they suffer greatly as a result. In our age we've seen innumerable examples of the powers and authorities that promote every kind of god and religion except the Bible. The result is a world that can't continue to go on – it's a stench in God's nostrils, it offends him in its every aspect. Destruction is the only option.

Now if that's God's intentions for this world, it would be a mistake to invest in anything here. Putting your heart, your whole life, into a world that will soon be done away with is foolish. Jesus told the story of a man who decided to spend his

Step Three

time accumulating his physical wealth instead of looking to the state of his soul:

> The ground of a certain rich man produced a good crop. He thought to himself, 'What shall I do? I have no place to store my crops.' "Then he said, 'This is what I'll do. I will tear down my barns and build bigger ones, and there I will store all my grain and my goods. And I'll say to myself, "You have plenty of good things laid up for many years. Take life easy; eat, drink and be merry."' "But God said to him, 'You fool! This very night your life will be demanded from you. Then who will get what you have prepared for yourself?' "This is how it will be with anyone who stores up things for himself but is not rich toward God." (Luke 12:16-21)

He counseled us to store up treasures in Heaven, not on earth, because it's a wiser investment – Heavenly treasures don't disappear, but earth's treasures will.

> Do not store up for yourselves treasures on earth, where moth and rust destroy, and where thieves break in and steal. But store up for yourselves treasures in heaven, where moth and rust do not destroy, and where thieves do not break in and steal. For where your treasure is, there your heart will be also. (Matthew 6:19-21)

Jesus counseled us like this because he himself will be coming to do away with the world. He ought to know! It's like a bomber sending a warning letter ahead of time to let people get out of the building by a certain time, before the bomb goes off.

Step Three

One more point about the destruction of the world. It will be a *miraculous* event, not due to the natural causes that the scientists predict about the world's end. Creation was a miracle, despite science's "evidence" to the contrary. The Flood was a miraculous event, too. The end of the world will have all the marks of one of God's miracles: it will be impossible according to natural causes (in other words, nobody will be able to see anything of cause and effect, or natural disasters, or even the hand of man, to account for how it happens). It will be sudden and catastrophic. It will draw everyone's attention to God, because they will know God's hand is in it.

> Then the kings of the earth, the princes, the generals, the rich, the mighty, and every slave and every free man hid in caves and among the rocks of the mountains. They called to the mountains and the rocks, "Fall on us and hide us from the face of him who sits on the throne and from the wrath of the Lamb! For the great day of their wrath has come, and who can stand?" (Revelation 6:15-17)

It will destroy the world completely, because his miracles do the job well – nothing will be left. Do people not believe that such a thing could happen? People didn't believe in God's earlier miracles either!

> First of all, you must understand that in the last days scoffers will come, scoffing and following their own evil desires. They will say, "Where is this 'coming' he promised? Ever since our fathers died, everything goes on as it has since the beginning of creation." But they deliberately forget that long ago by God's word the heavens existed and the earth was formed out of water and by water. By these waters also the world of that time was deluged and destroyed. By the same word the

Step Three

present heavens and earth are reserved for fire, being kept for the day of judgment and destruction of ungodly men. (2 Peter 3:3-6)

It's interesting that modern unbelievers also flatly reject the first two miracles in this passage, due to our modern scientific sophistication. Yet unbelief didn't save the wicked in those days; they *died* in their unbelief. And now, in our day, people also don't believe in the end of the world as the Bible describes it. They will be just as surprised in this miracle-working God when he comes in power as their earlier counterparts were.

Depend On God directly

There's another surprising aspect of our life in that third phase of God's plan that must be mentioned. And to understand it, we have to first look at our existence in this physical world.

We all know what it means to live in a physical world. We eat food, we breathe air, we walk on solid ground, we manipulate a physical world to achieve our ends. There is cause and effect in our world; we expect matter and energy to work a certain way, by physical laws, and we're comfortable with that when we use it to our advantage.

Even as Christians, everything we enjoy, everything that we call a blessing from God, comes by way of a physical world. Does he feed his creatures? He does it by way of parents, farmers, grocery stores – in other words, physical means of distributing physical food. We thank him for those things, because we know it all came from him; but the fact remains that we take these blessings from his hands *by way of* a physical system between him and us. We call this Providence.

Step Three

Heaven won't be like that. When we go to live with God forever, we will live directly from his hand – there will be no physical system between us to act as his distribution channel. He himself will feed us, he himself will speak to us face to face, he himself will hold us up and surround us with his power and love and righteousness.

> I did not see a temple in the city, because the Lord God Almighty and the Lamb are its temple. The city does not need the sun or the moon to shine on it, for the glory of God gives it light, and the Lamb is its lamp. (Revelation 21:22-23)

The reason this is important is that from that time on, God will be our complete world, our "all in all." In the Bible we read passages like this –

> But whenever anyone turns to the Lord, the veil is taken away. Now the Lord is the Spirit, and where the Spirit of the Lord is, there is freedom. And we, who with unveiled faces all reflect the Lord's glory, are being transformed into his likeness with ever-increasing glory, which comes from the Lord, who is the Spirit. (2 Corinthians 3:16-18)

But we don't have much time in our busy lives to do much of that! We have lots of responsibilities in this world that take away any time we'd like to devote to the Lord's business. Even the most zealous Christian has to eat, sleep, and work for a living to support his family. What none of us have ever experienced, however, is living totally in God's presence, doing everything for him, not having to divert our attention to anything else. Such a thing is impossible in this world – but in Heaven it will be the work of every saint. There we will experience what

Step Three

the word "sanctified" really means: set aside for God's use alone.

People make jokes about Heaven, as if we're going to sit around and play harps on clouds forever. They don't even have a clue about what our work for God will be like then. Jesus gave us a clue in his story about the talents:

> Then he sent for the servants to whom he had given the money, in order to find out what they had gained with it. "The first one came and said, 'Sir, your mina has earned ten more.' "'Well done, my good servant!' his master replied. 'Because you have been trustworthy in a very small matter, take charge of ten cities.' "The second came and said, 'Sir, your mina has earned five more.' "His master answered, 'You take charge of five cities.' (Luke 19:15-19)

Think about what he's saying here. If we're responsible with the little that God has given us here, he's going to give us tremendous responsibility there when we arrive in the new Kingdom. We aren't told what "ruling ten cities" means in the context of Heaven (perhaps there are hints in Genesis from the first time that God gave Adam the command to rule over his Creation), but we can imagine that we won't be lounging around and wasting our time! God will have lots to do there, and he needs skillful workers who have a heart for the work and know what they're doing already – *before* they get there.

Living in two worlds

Though we're told about the third step of God's plan, we know that those times haven't come yet. The warning is to get ready for the second coming of the King – which is still in the

Step Three

future. Right now it's time to take the warning seriously and get ready.

Wise people get ready for things ahead of time. They don't want to be caught at the last minute unprepared. If a student waits until the last minute before preparing for a test, he will probably fail the test. Whoever wants to win, spends a lot of time practicing beforehand – otherwise they are sure to lose. An actor practices his lines over and over before the play, a businessman rehearses his sales pitch before the big presentation to the client – everyone understands the value of doing one's preparation before the big event.

> Go to the ant, you sluggard; consider its ways and be wise! It has no commander, no overseer or ruler, yet it stores its provisions in summer and gathers its food at harvest. (Proverbs 6:6-8)

The same thing is true of the coming Kingdom of God. The changes that will happen are going to be so sweeping and devastating, the old will be completely gone, the new world won't work at all like the one we're used to – anybody who doesn't do some studying and getting ready for that colossal event is a fool.

> Since everything will be destroyed in this way, what kind of people ought you to be? You ought to live holy and godly lives as you look forward to the day of God and speed its coming. That day will bring about the destruction of the heavens by fire, and the elements will melt in the heat. But in keeping with his promise we are looking forward to a new heaven and a new earth, the home of righteousness. So then, dear friends, since you are looking forward to this, make every effort to be found spotless, blameless and at peace with him.

Step Three

Bear in mind that our Lord's patience means salvation. (2 Peter 3:11-15)

Who then is the faithful and wise servant, whom the master has put in charge of the servants in his household to give them their food at the proper time? It will be good for that servant whose master finds him doing so when he returns. I tell you the truth, he will put him in charge of all his possessions. (Matthew 24:45-47)

The answer, we are told, is to live with one foot in each kingdom, so to speak. We live here, but we don't have to put our whole heart into this world. We live as if we're in constant preparation for a move to a better home:

All these people were still living by faith when they died. They did not receive the things promised; they only saw them and welcomed them from a distance. And they admitted that they were aliens and strangers on earth. People who say such things show that they are looking for a country of their own. If they had been thinking of the country they had left, they would have had opportunity to return. Instead, they were longing for a better country—a heavenly one. Therefore God is not ashamed to be called their God, for he has prepared a city for them. (Hebrews 11:13-16)

There's nothing here that we love more than what's in Heaven. We don't want anything to tie itself round our hands and heart so that we don't want to move on. And when we finally do go to Heaven, we don't want to look back – there will be no longing to return, only a relief that it's all over and behind us. Abraham first experienced this when he wandered through Canaan, as we've just seen in Hebrews 11.

Step Three

Jesus himself set the pattern for all the people of God. He had no place to lay his head, he was despised wherever he went, he held no places of earthly honor that he would be reluctant to leave, and he longed for his return to Heaven. All during his stay here, he lived as if he could just as easily leave it all behind (and give away everything he owned before he left!). He counseled us to take his example:

> I tell you the truth, at the renewal of all things, when the Son of Man sits on his glorious throne, you who have followed me will also sit on twelve thrones, judging the twelve tribes of Israel. And everyone who has left houses or brothers or sisters or father or mother or children or fields for my sake will receive a hundred times as much and will inherit eternal life. But many who are first will be last, and many who are last will be first. (Matthew 19:28-30)

You can see here why he is so willing to leave behind the things of the world. He knew that the Father has a better world waiting for us, a world filled with treasures that put the baubles and beads of this world's wealth to shame. If we can see that new world, we will have no problem turning our backs on this worn-out, fallen moral disaster that the wicked love so much.

> But whatever was to my profit I now consider loss for the sake of Christ. What is more, I consider everything a loss compared to the surpassing greatness of knowing Christ Jesus my Lord, for whose sake I have lost all things. I consider them rubbish, that I may gain Christ and be found in him, not having a righteousness of my own that comes from the law, but that which is through faith in Christ —the righteousness that comes from God and is by faith. I want to know

Step Three

Christ and the power of his resurrection and the fellowship of sharing in his sufferings, becoming like him in his death, and so, somehow, to attain to the resurrection from the dead. (Philippians 3:7-11)

Therefore we do not lose heart. Though outwardly we are wasting away, yet inwardly we are being renewed day by day. For our light and momentary troubles are achieving for us an eternal glory that far outweighs them all. So we fix our eyes not on what is seen, but on what is unseen. For what is seen is temporary, but what is unseen is eternal. (2 Corinthians 4:16-18)

Life here won't be easy, however. We still have to work and live, provide for our families, get along with unbelievers somehow – and most important, win as many others as we can over to our side so that *they* don't have to be here either when destruction comes. Jesus knew how hard it would be to wait for our move. He prayed that the Father might protect us from the most deadly danger threatening us while we're still here in this dark world:

My prayer is not that you take them out of the world but that you protect them from the evil one. (John 17:15)

The devil's business is twofold: *first*, oppression and persecution; *second*, lies. He can do a tremendous amount of damage with both weapons. What Jesus was concerned about, therefore, was that while we're waiting for the Lord to take us home, we don't succumb to the lies and deceits of the devil. He's going to try to talk us out of the truth that saved us and drew us to Jesus in the first place. He wants us to give up, to lose heart, to mistake God's ways for God's displeasure and caprice and unfair practices. He wants God's people to fall back

Step Three

into the sin that they were rescued out of. He wants them to dishonor God. The assaults of the enemy on our minds and lives will be daily, vicious, and treacherous. He will work through even those who are closest to us, our friends and relatives, even through the authorities that lead us. Jesus' prayer is that we withstand the devils' schemes and hold on to the faith that we first professed to the end.

> He who stands firm to the end will be saved.
> (Matthew 24:13)

Another thing that we have to realize, while we're waiting here for the next world, is that there's a lot to do while we're waiting. We have basically two jobs to work on: *first*, to be delivered from our sins, and *second*, to get ready for Heaven. The first job is on the top of God's agenda, and it ought to be on ours. By no means did we get rid of all of our sin when we first believed! The thing that happened at our conversion was that we were introduced to our Savior, who made a solemn covenant to deliver us from our sins. But that will take us an entire lifetime! We have to learn how to follow the Spirit as he crucifies that sin in our hearts, daily, through the Word and the power of God:

> You, however, are controlled not by the sinful nature but by the Spirit, if the Spirit of God lives in you. And if anyone does not have the Spirit of Christ, he does not belong to Christ. But if Christ is in you, your body is dead because of sin, yet your spirit is alive because of righteousness. And if the Spirit of him who raised Jesus from the dead is living in you, he who raised Christ from the dead will also give life to your mortal bodies through his Spirit, who lives in you. Therefore, brothers, we have an obligation — but it is not to the sinful nature, to live according to it. For if you live

Step Three

according to the sinful nature, you will die; but if by the Spirit you put to death the misdeeds of the body, you will live, because those who are led by the Spirit of God are sons of God. (Romans 8:9-14)

We *must* crucify those sins. God doesn't want sinners in Heaven. He hates sin; he can't stand to be in its presence. And as the King and Creator of his universe, he has the right to feel that way – and the right to demand that we reform if we want to live with him! What we have to do is find out how to crucify that sin on a daily basis: to live by faith in Christ, to pray in the Spirit, to bear fruit by the Spirit, to confess and repent of what's in our hearts, to turn our backs on this world and its empty promises and lies. It's a daily struggle, it takes a lot of wisdom and dedication, and it won't be easy.

While we're working on our sins, we should also be getting ready for Heaven. Heaven is a special place that not everyone would like if they saw it. It's also a strange world, not at all like this one, and it will take some getting used to for those who do go to live there. For example, Jesus taught us that anyone who wants to be in Heaven has to be robed in righteousness:

So the servants went out into the streets and gathered all the people they could find, both good and bad, and the wedding hall was filled with guests. "But when the king came in to see the guests, he noticed a man there who was not wearing wedding clothes. 'Friend,' he asked, 'how did you get in here without wedding clothes?' The man was speechless. "Then the king told the attendants, 'Tie him hand and foot, and throw him outside, into the darkness, where there will be weeping and gnashing of teeth.' "For many are invited, but few are chosen." (Matthew 22:10-14)

Step Three

This means, of course, the righteousness of Christ – which is the only perfect righteousness that would satisfy God. We learn in Romans 8 (along with other passages) *how* to get that righteousness from God.

We also have our part to do in the building of God's Kingdom. Like Nehemiah and the Jews who returned from Exile, everyone has their part to rebuild the walls of Jerusalem. Everyone has a gift, a job to do in the Church, to build up each other in the faith:

> It was he who gave some to be apostles, some to be prophets, some to be evangelists, and some to be pastors and teachers, to prepare God's people for works of service, so that the body of Christ may be built up until we all reach unity in the faith and in the knowledge of the Son of God and become mature, attaining to the whole measure of the fullness of Christ. (Ephesians 4:11-13)

If we take a laid-back approach to our work – by either refusing to do our part, or by doing a sloppy job about it, then we can't expect to be commended for such irresponsible work. Judgment Day won't be totally wonderful for everyone, not even for those who call themselves Christians:

> If any man builds on this foundation using gold, silver, costly stones, wood, hay or straw, his work will be shown for what it is, because the Day will bring it to light. It will be revealed with fire, and the fire will test the quality of each man's work. If what he has built survives, he will receive his reward. If it is burned up, he will suffer loss; he himself will be saved, but only as one escaping through the flames. (1 Corinthians 3:12-15)

Step Three

Our goal is to become like Christ:

> And we, who with unveiled faces all reflect the Lord's glory, are being transformed into his likeness with ever-increasing glory, which comes from the Lord, who is the Spirit. (2 Corinthians 3:18)

This is because God loves his Son: Jesus is perfect, he's exactly what the Law describes as a righteous man, and he and the Father live as one in perfect love and peace. God will only be satisfied with us if we have the same looks about us that Jesus has.

One last point to notice here is that we can get a taste now of what that future life will be like. God graciously gives us the opportunity of enjoying some of those treasures now, so that we will have the hope and faith to keep struggling through this life in order to reach the fullness of God's inheritance in the next. For example, Jesus counseled us to store up treasures in Heaven:

> Do not store up for yourselves treasures on earth, where moth and rust destroy, and where thieves break in and steal. But store up for yourselves treasures in heaven, where moth and rust do not destroy, and where thieves do not break in and steal. For where your treasure is, there your heart will be also. (Matthew 6:19-21)

Those treasures will come in handy when you're facing the troubles and trials of this world and there isn't any other help at hand.

Step Three
Theories of the end times

There are several standard theories about how the world will end. Most of these theories have been around as long as the Church has existed. Following is a short summary of these theories:

- **Premillenial view:** According to this view, Jesus will suddenly appear to rapture his saints from their graves, set up a 1000 year reign on earth, and after that destroy this world to make a new heavens and a new earth. There are different opinions about how the specific events that will happen when he comes to become King over the earth.

- **Amillenial view:** According to this view, the 1000 year reign is a symbol of the current spiritual reign that Jesus already has over the earth. When Jesus comes the second time, he will destroy the earth then and set up the new heavens and earth.

- **Post-millenial view:** According to this view, the Church will enter into a 1000 year period where the influence of the Gospel will spread around the world and there will be general peace and righteousness over the kingdoms of the earth. Then after that period Jesus will come, destroy the world, and create a new heavens and earth.

Unfortunately, Christians have fought bitterly all through history about which one of these theories is correct. There have been spiritual, scholarly Christians on each side of the debate. The fierceness of the argument is embarrassing; supposedly

Step Three

Christians love each other, and are one in Christ – but this issue divides Christians all over the world. Whole denominations battle with each other about it, and too often they refuse to work with or even fellowship with brothers of a different persuasion.

The problem is that the Bible isn't 100% clear about how the world will end! There are some very clear statements in the Bible about certain events during the last days – there's no mistaking the meaning of certain passages, and it has to be a literal event that they talk about. But as far as a whole picture, a step-by-step description of the exact sequence of events, there's no such thing in the Bible. It's foolish to argue about the end times when there's no clear statement about it.

Jesus himself didn't know when the Last Day would happen.

> No one knows about that day or hour, not even the angels in Heaven, nor the Son, but only the Father. (Matthew 24:36)

One would think that the Son of God would have known the mystery of the end of time, since he was usually in on the counsels of his Father. But when he claimed that he didn't know when the Second Coming would happen, or when the old Creation would be destroyed and the new Creation put over top of the ashes, that should give us reason to pause and think. There is mystery surrounding the next phase of God's plan. That day will come like a thief, Jesus told us:

> It will be good for those servants whose master finds them ready, even if he comes in the second or third watch of the night. But understand this: If the owner of the house had known at what hour the thief was coming, he would not have let his house be broken into. You also must be ready, because

Step Three

> the Son of Man will come at an hour when you do not expect him. (Luke 12:38-40)

The knowledge that God does give us about it should tell us what to focus our attention and time on. The point isn't to figure out exactly how or when it's going to happen; the point is to *get ready for what's going to happen*. The timing of events, the exact sequence of events, doesn't matter as far as what we need to do to get ready. Trying to figure that out only stimulates curiosity, and takes away our desire to focus on what's important. I've seen unbelievers who don't even pretend to love God or Christ get fascinated with "Christian" books that supposedly describe in detail what the future will be like. That should tell you something. The sensational, the spectacular, the "Hollywood" special effects that so fascinates people – and worries them, since those stories all deal with losing physical life and property – is pretty much worthless in saving their souls from sin and death.

What will probably happen is that the end will surprise everyone. When Jesus came the first time, a student of the Bible could back-track and see how everything in the Old Testament was fulfilled in Christ's life and ministry. The match between his life and the prophecies were perfect. But the Jews missed it, didn't they? They were familiar with those prophecies too, but they read them in a certain way (a way that fit in better with their materialism and sin) and missed the point about Jesus. Christians too should get ready for a surprise. The prophecies that we think we understand so well may just turn out far different than we expect. The truth probably lies somewhere between the separate views.

What the New Testament Teaches

What the New Testament Teaches

On the surface, it seems as though the message of the New Testament is simple enough: it's the story of Jesus' life, the beginning of the Church, and final instructions from the Apostles to individual churches.

When we look beyond the New Testament, however, to the Old Testament, the picture gets more complicated. Somehow the two fit together. Jesus' ministry means little unless we see that he came to do the works of God that were first worked out in the history of the Israelites. The Old Testament is constantly quoted in the New Testament – and most of those "quotes" aren't really direct quotes, but it's obvious that the apostles had particular passages in mind.

Paul's letters, to many present-day experts, appear to describe Christ with new concepts that we can't really see in the Gospel histories. He must have seen something in Jesus that had to be brought out into the open; otherwise, if we only had the Gospels we wouldn't have fully understood Christ.

The apostles also seemed to have made the transition from the old Jewish system (with the Temple, Palestine, the Law, and so on) to the new Church system and Christianity with no difficulties. How did they do that? Even Jesus' teachings don't really lead us to believe that events would have made such a drastic leap into the Gentile Church age.

So, what seems obvious at first becomes more interesting and complex. Are there themes that hold the entire New Testament together? Is there a single point that summarizes the New Testament? Are all the separate books of the NT talking about the same themes?

The point of the New Testament

The New Testament does deal with a single overall point, which can be expressed very clearly and simply.

**The New Testament describes the New Man,
and how we become one with him.**

Let's break this down into separate ideas so that we can understand what's going on.

- **The New Man** – The Old Testament Law described what God considers to be a perfect man. God demands perfection; the least sin bothers him so much that he promises that all sinners, no matter how small their sin, will never be allowed in Heaven. Those stiff requirements might seem too strict, but that's only because we don't realize how holy God is and how pure his house must be in order to glorify him. The Jews tried at times to live up to those exacting specifications, but usually they pursued their own goals and preferred to live in immorality. The result was predictable: God punished them again and again because not only did they willfully fail him in this matter, they *couldn't* do it – the power of sin over their hearts was just too strong to break.

What was needed was a new kind of man who could really live a perfect life. Jesus did what no man before him could do: he kept the Law perfectly, all 613 commands (that's how many commands the Jews claim is in the Mosaic Law). And not only did he perfectly keep the Law, he kept the Law to its infinite spiritual depth. When we read the Sermon on the Mount in Matthew 5-7, we are amazed at what Jesus said was the true depth of the Law: it reaches the thoughts and intents of the heart, not just the outward actions. Yet the Law has absolutely no claim against Jesus, because he was absolutely sinless.

In order to make this the standard lifestyle among all of God's people, Jesus came to do three things:

First, he became a man like us. He took on flesh and blood in order to share our circumstances in a physical world.

> Since the children have flesh and blood, he too shared in their humanity so that by his death he might destroy him who holds the power of death—that is, the devil — and free those who all their lives were held in slavery by their fear of death. For surely it is not angels he helps, but Abraham's descendants. For this reason he had to be made like his brothers in every way, in order that he might become a merciful and faithful high priest in service to God, and that he might make atonement for the sins of the people. Because he himself suffered when he was tempted, he is able to help those who are being tempted. (Hebrews 2:14-18)

This thing had to be done by a man, if the benefits were to go to men in the end. He couldn't do it only as the Son of God, because naturally we would expect that God would be holy and careful to fulfill his own righteousness. But *as a man* he fulfilled the Law; now the Law has seen *a perfect man*, and the Father can justly reward *a man* with righteousness, the Heavenly inheritance, and all the covenant promises.

Second, he was filled with the Spirit of God. Notice that at the beginning of his ministry he was anointed by the Holy Spirit:

> As soon as Jesus was baptized, he went up out of the water. At that moment heaven was opened, and he saw the Spirit of God descending like a dove and lighting on him. (Matthew 3:16)

The reason for this is that he was again setting a precedent for us – a pattern that the rest of us must follow if we want what he got. In order to live the perfect life, in order to live in the presence of God, in order to fulfill God's purposes in our lives, we have to have the Spirit of God in us. The Spirit makes it possible for us to do all of this. He reveals God to us, he makes God's will known to us, he directs us in God's plan for our lives, he empowers us with the resources and power from Heaven to do the work of God and help build the Kingdom of God. But did Jesus need the Spirit in order to do what he did? As the Son of God, probably not (though that's debatable – the power behind all of God's works is the Spirit – see Zechariah 4:6); but as a man it was necessary to fulfill all righteousness. In other words, this (the filling of the Holy Spirit) is what *a man* needs to please God with a righteous life.

What the New Testament Teaches

The New Man lives by the power of the Spirit. Paul describes what life is going to be like in the Kingdom of God:

> So will it be with the resurrection of the dead. The body that is sown is perishable, it is raised imperishable; it is sown in dishonor, it is raised in glory; it is sown in weakness, it is raised in power; it is sown a natural body, it is raised a spiritual body. If there is a natural body, there is also a spiritual body. So it is written: "The first man Adam became a living being"; the last Adam, a life-giving spirit. The spiritual did not come first, but the natural, and after that the spiritual. The first man was of the dust of the earth, the second man from Heaven. As was the earthly man, so are those who are of the earth; and as is the man from Heaven, so also are those who are of Heaven. And just as we have borne the likeness of the earthly man, so shall we bear the likeness of the man from Heaven. (1 Corinthians 15:42-49)

This New Man is done with sin, he has laid down the old physical body that was prone to the temptations of sin, and he has returned to the old ideal of the first Creation: a person created in the image of God, created in righteousness, serving him alone and glorifying him in all that he does. We can see what this righteousness looks like in the life of a man by studying the life of Christ in the Gospels.

Third, he overcame sin, death, the grave – and rose to Heaven's throne. He had to suffer the consequence of sin – which is death – in order to free us from our bondage of judgment. Jesus himself was no sinner; he couldn't sin:

> For we do not have a high priest who is unable to sympathize with our weaknesses, but we have one who has been tempted in every way, just as we are —yet was without sin. (Hebrews 4:15)

But before we could hope to take advantage of what he was putting together in the New Man, he had to remove the judgment of the Law against us. This is the idea behind the Sacrifice that takes away the sin of the world. (See John 1:29) The Lamb was put to death for our sake; he died so that we wouldn't have to die. The Sinless One willingly gave us life for sinners, and the Law is satisfied – now his people have no condemnation against them and they can get on with the task of becoming righteous. Until that sacrifice took place, we had no hope of doing anything pleasing to God: we were condemned criminals who had only punishment to look forward to. But now that this critical issue is satisfactorily resolved, we can move on to the matter of preparing to live with God forever.

- **Becoming one with Christ** – Step one was creating the New Man. Jesus accomplished the goal in himself and became the "last Adam." (1 Corinthians 15:45) He is the firstborn of the new race of perfect spiritual beings:

> For those God foreknew he also predestined to be conformed to the likeness of his Son, that he might be the firstborn among many brothers. (Romans 8:29)

What the New Testament Teaches

Now Step two begins. God starts bringing some of us into the program. His intention is to make New Men out of us too – the ultimate goal is that we will look exactly like Jesus, the pattern of the New Man:

> And we, who with unveiled faces all reflect the Lord's glory, are being transformed into his likeness with ever-increasing glory, which comes from the Lord, who is the Spirit. (2 Corinthians 3:18)

But the way he will do this is so clever! Instead of using Jesus as an example, and demanding that we live up to that example, he resorts to a fail-safe method. He knows that we can't reach Jesus' high ideal of perfection on our own. He also doesn't want us to fail. So to insure success, *he makes us one with Jesus* – like melting two bars of metal together to form one. Actually there isn't a really good analogy of what happens, because neither Christ nor we lose our individual natures, yet it's a fact that we take on Christ's nature to replace our old sinful nature. There is a real spiritual union that happens, but the union isn't like the Oriental religions that preach the obliteration of the soul.

These are the steps he uses to make us one with the life of Christ:

> **First**, God puts the Spirit of Christ in us. That immediately establishes a line of communication between us and Christ. Now we can live in the presence of God; now we can hear his voice (John xx), and follow him as he leads us. We can see things now, through the new ability called "faith" – it's a spiritual

insight that our souls have now to be able to see the world of God.

Second, God crucifies the sin in our physical nature. Since we still have bodies, and the old nature is still strong in us, we have to get free of sin's destructive power in our lives. So the power of Christ's indestructible life, and the power of his perfect righteousness, is brought to bear on our sinful nature. The old flesh is starved out, and our spirits are set free to walk in holiness before God. It's the hand of God doing the impossible – we could never do it on our own.

Third, the Spirit of God prepares us for our eternal home in Heaven. God still has strict standards for those who want to live with him; he demands perfection, humility, service, and glory. A great deal of work remains to be done to shape our natures into something that will please him. Again, the New Man that Jesus became is the pattern: that's the goal that the Holy Spirit aims at. But since we are *one with Christ*, it's just a matter of transforming our nature – molding us to fit the pattern that we are now a part of – so that we look like Jesus. The molding will happen, it can't fail to happen, since Jesus is that perfect New Man – and we are in him already. It's like pouring a cake mix in a pan: it's just a matter of time till we eventually really do look like Jesus, since God has "poured us into him already.

What the New Testament Teaches
Fulfillment of the Old Testament

The Old Testament fits in hand-in-glove with the New Testament. They both talk about the same ideas, though one does it on a physical level and the other on a spiritual level. It's the same God doing the same kinds of things for the same goals.

What the New Testament does for us is explain the mystery behind that. At first glance it would appear that the two books are describing a different God who does things in completely different ways. But we dare not think that! If that was true, we would lose precious truths of the Old Testament and be cast adrift into a sea of doctrinal problems. Christians have often despised the Old Testament due to ignorance and willfulness, and suffered because of it. We can avoid the errors of cults, heresies, imbalances, and unnecessary denominational biases if we listen more carefully to what the New Testament has to say about its Old Testament foundations.

Let's take the most important example in the Old Testament and examine how valuable is the New Testament witness to it. The Lord gave the covenant to Abraham and his heirs in Genesis 12-17. That covenant made an eternal promise of four things: the land, the son, the nation, and the blessing to all nations on earth. Those four things were worked out in physical terms throughout the rest of Israelite history; the sharp student will realize that every good thing given to the Israelites came from nowhere else but the covenant they inherited from their father Abraham.

But the New Testament makes an extraordinary claim: that covenant wasn't meant just for the physical descendants of Abraham but to his *spiritual* descendants. The Jews were wrong to think that they were the sole heirs to the covenant. In fact, any student who reads the story about God giving Abraham the covenant and thinks it was ultimately about physical blessings is wrong about it. Abraham himself knew that the promises were spiritual and eternal. We have proof of that from the New Testament.

For example, Abraham knew that the son that God promised him wasn't just Isaac but Christ:

> Your father Abraham rejoiced at the thought of seeing my day; he saw it and was glad. (John 8:56)

Abraham knew that the land that God promised him wasn't just the physical property of Canaan, but a Heavenly city where *all* of his spiritual heirs – Jews and Gentiles – would live with God forever:

> For he was looking forward to the city with foundations, whose architect and builder is God. (Hebrews 11:10)

Abraham knew that the blessing that God promised to the nations of the world through him was nothing less than resurrection from the dead – the very gift that we have in Christ's resurrection:

> Abraham reasoned that God could raise the dead, and figuratively speaking, he did receive Isaac back from death. (Hebrews 11:19)

And if Abraham didn't know in his lifetime, he does know *now* that the promise of the nation includes not just Jewish descendants but Gentile believers as well:

> The time came when the beggar died and the angels carried him to Abraham's side. (Luke 16:22)

What the New Testament Teaches

> I say to you that many will come from the east and the west, and will take their places at the feast with Abraham, Isaac and Jacob in the kingdom of Heaven. (Matthew 8:11)

Unless we had read all this in the New Testament, we would certainly have missed the fact by just reading the Old Testament story of Abraham. There aren't any hints there that Abraham knew these things. But that's the value of the New Testament for our faith: not only does it tell us what was really going on in the Old Testament, but it shows us how fundamental, how critical, how absolutely necessary is the faith that the Old Testament taught. What would we Christians have if you take away the covenant made to Abraham and his heirs? What else would we want from God except these four covenant promises? So quite literally our Christian faith is made up of Old Testament principles: take the Old Testament away from us, and we have nothing to believe in or hope for.

Hope for people of God

The New Testament lifts our faith up from the physical realities that the Jews were hoping for to a new spiritual realm. In the Old Testament, God spelled out the covenant blessings in physical terms: the land Canaan, the physical Temple in an earthly Jerusalem, an earthly kingdom of David, the physical blessings and miracles that he did for his people, and so on. Naturally they expected Jesus to continue the tradition if he was what he claimed to be – the Son of their God.

But we learn in the New Testament that those old physical events and blessings were pictures of the reality, no more. They were schoolbook lessons for God's children. With the advent of Christ, he brought his people into their maturity:

What the New Testament Teaches

> Before this faith came, we were held prisoners by the law, locked up until faith should be revealed. So the law was put in charge to lead us to Christ that we might be justified by faith. Now that faith has come, we are no longer under the supervision of the law. (Galatians 3:23-25)

Now we're going to deal with the spiritual world that God had intended all along. Abraham, as we've just seen, knew that the spiritual Kingdom was God's real aim from the beginning. But now in the New Testament it's not going to be hints and symbols and types any more. Christians are going to deal with the actual currency of Heaven: faith, Heavenly treasures, the indwelling of the Spirit, the sacrifice of Christ, fighting Satan and his "principalities and powers," and so on. This is a real world that the Jews knew next to nothing about and had almost no experience in. The Church of God has come of age in the New Testament.

Paul tells us to set our eyes and minds on things in Heaven now:

> Since, then, you have been raised with Christ, set your hearts on things above, where Christ is seated at the right hand of God. Set your minds on things above, not on earthly things. For you died, and your life is now hidden with Christ in God. (Colossians 3:1-3)

The reason is that this world, we know now, isn't what's valuable for our souls. God's world is our eternal rest; we must struggle to enter into *that* rest now, not the rest and pleasures of this world:

What the New Testament Teaches

> Let us, therefore, make every effort to enter that rest, so that no one will fall by following their example of disobedience. (Hebrews 4:11)

We have an altar in Heaven now, not in an earthly Temple in Jerusalem, before which we are required to present ourselves before God:

> Let us then approach the throne of grace with confidence, so that we may receive mercy and find grace to help us in our time of need. (Hebrews 4:16)

Christ told us to forget about amassing treasures on earth – they will do us no good spiritually; but rather store up a new kind of treasure:

> Do not store up for yourselves treasures on earth, where moth and rust destroy, and where thieves break in and steal. But store up for yourselves treasures in Heaven, where moth and rust do not destroy, and where thieves do not break in and steal. For where your treasure is, there your heart will be also. (Matthew 6:19-21)

In order to take advantage of this new spiritual world, we have to live by the Spirit. The Spirit is the key to both knowing what God's new Kingdom is like, and taking advantage of it. Without the Spirit we can't even see what's there, let alone reach out and take hold of it. But with the Spirit forming the link between us and Heaven, we can now walk in God's presence, see the spiritual treasures there for our benefit, and take hold of those things so that we can be saved and prepared for our spiritual life.

> We have not received the spirit of the world but the Spirit who is from God, that we may understand what God has freely given us. (1 Corinthians 2:12)

Being able to live a spiritual existence like this of course means that life here will change considerably. If you despise worldly wealth and instead look forward to the riches in Christ, you're going to have different priorities than other people do! While they struggle to gain material wealth, you're pursuing the Kingdom of God instead:

> So do not worry, saying, 'What shall we eat?' or 'What shall we drink?' or 'What shall we wear?' For the pagans run after all these things, and your Heavenly Father knows that you need them. But seek first his kingdom and his righteousness, and all these things will be given to you as well. (Matthew 6:31-33)

You're going to look strange to them since you're not interested in wealth, pleasure, and reputation: to you the important things of life are the building of the Kingdom, the glory of God, loving the members of Christ's church, and fighting the spiritual forces of a dark world. You're going to look like an outsider to them with your different value system and lifestyle:

> All these people were still living by faith when they died. They did not receive the things promised; they only saw them and welcomed them from a distance. And they admitted that they were aliens and strangers on earth. People who say such things show that they are looking for a country of their own. (Hebrews 11:13)

What the New Testament Teaches

> They think it strange that you do not plunge with them into the same flood of dissipation, and they heap abuse on you. (1 Peter 4:4)

Hope is whatever we value, what we set our hearts on, what prompts us to live the way we do. And Christian hope isn't about a "maybe" world where we "hope" that Heaven will be good. Christian hope is based on faith: in other words, we have already seen what God has for his children. We hope in what we know is true, what we know already exists there in Heaven. Our "hope" is a longing for *that*, and the willingness to turn away from what this world offers us because we prefer Heaven's treasures.

The reason this is important is because we can't serve two masters. The world, and Satan, wields the treasures of earth like a bribe: put your heart and soul into getting ahead in this world, and you will *have* to serve the enemy as he steers you away from Heaven. All your time and energy will go into material happiness instead of the saving of your soul. The needs of the Church will go begging while you build your own house; you literally won't have time for the things of God. At the end of life you will discover that you will be poverty stricken before God, spiritually poor, with nothing in Heaven waiting for you. You will also find yourself treacherously left on your own as Satan leaves you at God's Judgment Seat empty-handed after serving him your entire life.

In order to serve God, we have to turn our back on the idea of making this world our hope and home. This is only a stopping place, a wayside inn where we can get the minimum to live – food, drink, clothing, a house over our heads (more than Jesus himself had!) while we put our remaining energies into the important job of getting ready for the next world. There is so much to do that we simply have to rearrange our schedules to make the Kingdom of God a priority, while setting other things behind in second place.

The world of course doesn't understand that kind of life, but then they don't share our hope of Heaven.

The nature of the Church

It's also in the New Testament that we get a final, clear understanding of who makes up the Church of Christ. In the Old Testament we may be confused over who are the people of God: there was great sin among the Israelites, great spiritual confusion, the Spirit of God seemed to be limited to the prophets and a select few individuals, and the promises appeared to include the Jewish race alone – leaving the Gentile "outsiders" out in the cold.

But starting with the ministry of Christ, we discover the true boundaries of the people of God – and the true requirements for membership. Jesus came to sinners, the despised of society, the "untouchables," and offered them the Gospel:

> It is not the healthy who need a doctor, but the sick. But go and learn what this means: 'I desire mercy, not sacrifice.' For I have not come to call the righteous, but sinners. (Matthew 9:12-13)

He seemingly couldn't get along with the religious leaders, the Pharisees who supposedly were experts in the Law and were therefore counted as the most righteous people in Jewish society. But we discover that the Pharisees weren't as holy as they claimed to be:

> Woe to you, teachers of the law and Pharisees, you hypocrites! You are like whitewashed tombs,

which look beautiful on the outside but on the inside are full of dead men's bones and everything unclean. In the same way, on the outside you appear to people as righteous but on the inside you are full of hypocrisy and wickedness. (Matthew 23:27-28)

Now we see that God demands perfection from the heart, not just from outward actions. The Law has an inward force, it plumbs to the depths of the heart and demands that the "thoughts and intents of the heart" are pure and holy.

"Are you still so dull?" Jesus asked them. "Don't you see that whatever enters the mouth goes into the stomach and then out of the body? But the things that come out of the mouth come from the heart, and these make a man 'unclean.' For out of the heart come evil thoughts, murder, adultery, sexual immorality, theft, false testimony, slander. These are what make a man 'unclean'; but eating with unwashed hands does not make him 'unclean.'" (Matthew 15:16-20)

Jesus also showed us the importance of the heart in matters where people are most likely to get mistaken. For instance, we love those who can contribute the most money to the cause. But to Jesus the intention of the heart – not the size of the purse – is what impresses God:

Jesus sat down opposite the place where the offerings were put and watched the crowd putting their money into the temple treasury. Many rich people threw in large amounts. But a poor widow came and put in two very small copper coins, worth only a fraction of a penny. Calling his disciples to him, Jesus said, "I tell you the truth, this poor widow has put more into the treasury than all the others. They all gave out of their wealth; but she, out of her poverty, put in everything — all she had to live on." (Matthew 12:41-44)

To Jesus, the Laws of his Kingdom are spiritual and matters of the heart. The Sermon on the Mount – Jesus' statement on how he intends to run his Kingdom, and who will be allowed in – is a remarkable "constitution" of the Kingdom of God. No government on earth, no matter how tyrannical, would expect obedience to that extent, to the very thoughts of our minds. But Jesus does, because he knows two things: **first**, God can't abide the least sin, not even of the heart and mind; **second**, he knows what the Spirit can do to transform a sinner to a saint. The goal of our salvation is to make us *perfect* with his personal righteousness, nothing less.

> Be perfect, therefore, as your Heavenly Father is perfect. (Matthew 5:48)

The apostles all taught about the Church in some form, from many angles. Paul describes the Church as the body of Christ:

> The body is a unit, though it is made up of many parts; and though all its parts are many, they form one body. So it is with Christ. For we were all baptized by one Spirit into one body — whether Jews or Greeks, slave or free — and we were all given the one Spirit to drink ... Now you are the body of Christ, and each one of you is a part of it. (1 Corinthians 12:12-13,27)

This is so critical for our survival. If we are so inseparably united with Christ, we can count on at least three things happening:

What the New Testament Teaches

First, everything that happens to Christ will happen to us also. If he lives, we will live. If he enjoys the treasures of Heaven as an heir, so will we. If he rules over God's Kingdom, so will we, since the whole body sits on the throne. If God considers Christ to be his Son, then we are all children of God (we by adoption, Christ by nature) and enjoy the fellowship of the family of God.

Second, he *will* lead us – the head always makes the decisions for the body. This point is often overlooked in the Church, as if Jesus only saved us in the beginning and then left us on our own to make our own decisions. Jesus is not an irresponsible Lord: he intends to lead us, he demands to lead us, and he wants us to learn how to listen to and obey him as he leads us. This takes some wisdom on our part, being able to discern the Lord's leading – since he's not here in person, and works through the Spirit of God working among us, it requires a spiritual discernment to know the presence of Christ among us. But unless we develop this spiritual sensitivity we will often find ourselves working against him instead of working with him! Things don't work when we lead; things always work when we follow his leading.

Third, we are part of a unit – one body – so that we all share in what happens to the body. We already saw that Paul makes a point about this very thing.

We are one with each other, because of the fact that we are one in Christ. What one person suffers, we all suffer. When one person doesn't do his part, we are all in need. Most churches don't operate as if this is true – they like to limit their church activities to one or two hours a week, because otherwise they would fight and not get along – but that's the reason that those churches are so sick spiritually. *We need each other*: the Spirit gives each one of us some gifts for the benefit of the whole group.

Kingdom of God

In the Old Testament we learn about the Kingdom of God mainly through the kingdom of David and his descendants. There we learn how God wants his kingdom to be set up and how it operates. David was a man after God's own heart (1 Samuel 13:14), and he was therefore careful to rule over God's people in the way that God wanted.

In the New Testament, we see the same thing come together – only in the Kingdom of Christ, the son of David. Christ of course did the same things his father David did, in the same way – otherwise he would have been guilty of setting up a kingdom contrary to God's specifications. The Son of God would never do that!

But the kingdom he set up was different in one important respect: it was a spiritual kingdom, not an earthly one. That totally confused his followers. They fully expected Jesus to march on Jerusalem, set up David's old throne, and assume control over Judah. He never showed the slightest interest in doing that. Not only did he refuse to do anything along the lines of setting up a physical kingdom, he wouldn't even save himself when challenged by Pilate to prove his royal claim:

"Do you refuse to speak to me?" Pilate said. "Don't you realize I have power either to free you or to crucify you?" Jesus answered, "You would have no power over me if it were not given to you from above." (John 19:10-11)

The kind of kingdom that Jesus was interested in was one in which the typical features of earth would be strangely but significantly absent. Gone would be the usual things that we depend on in our earthly kingdoms: money, glory to man, morals that allow us to sin, materialism, a religion without God, and so on. Even the materials that we use to build our nations and communities are worthless. It's like the Tower of Babel: the workers used brick and tar instead of stone and mortar; in God's eyes, earth's wealth and resources aren't good enough for what he wants to do.

Jesus actually started building his kingdom when he called his disciples together. True to form, he was following the precedent of his father David. He was laying the foundation for the Heavenly city of Jerusalem. This foundation – spiritual, not physical – would soon support the structure of the entire Church of God:

> Consequently, you are no longer foreigners and aliens, but fellow citizens with God's people and members of God's household, built on the foundation of the apostles and prophets, with Christ Jesus himself as the chief cornerstone. (Ephesians 2:19-20)

The reason that the apostles are the foundation of the Church is that their eyewitness testimony of Christ and his ministry ended up as our New Testament! Without that testimony we wouldn't have a Christian faith. It's been the one standard that has stood firm through war, heresy, division, false religions, and all the other threats that our great enemy has thrown at us. The New Testament is an unchanged account of the truth as it is in Jesus.

I warn everyone who hears the words of the prophecy of this book: If anyone adds anything to them, God will add to him the plagues described in this book. And if anyone takes words away from this book of prophecy, God will take away from him his share in the tree of life and in the holy city, which are described in this book. (Revelation 22:18-19)

Jesus taught us what the kingdom would be like in his Kingdom parables. He described its growth, its characteristics, its goals, the problems involved and how those problems would be solved. Here are a few examples of his description of the Kingdom:

> He told them another parable: "The kingdom of Heaven is like a mustard seed, which a man took and planted in his field. Though it is the smallest of all your seeds, yet when it grows, it is the largest of garden plants and becomes a tree, so that the birds of the air come and perch in its branches."

> He told them still another parable: "The kingdom of Heaven is like yeast that a woman took and mixed into a large amount of flour until it worked all through the dough." (Matthew 13:31-33)

> The kingdom of Heaven is like treasure hidden in a field. When a man found it, he hid it again, and then in his joy went and sold all he had and bought that field.

> Again, the kingdom of Heaven is like a merchant looking for fine pearls. When he found one of great value, he went away and sold

What the New Testament Teaches

everything he had and bought it. (Matthew 13:44-46)

The Kingdom of Christ grows according to spiritual principles, by the power of the Spirit, and will eventually become an entirely new Heavens and earth where God's people will live. We shouldn't be surprised that the way it works differs greatly with the way this world works. For example, Jesus said some surprising things about Heavenly financing that no doubt disturbed his listeners who were used to "common sense" when dealing with money:

> I tell you, use worldly wealth to gain friends for yourselves, so that when it is gone, you will be welcomed into eternal dwellings. (Luke 16:9)

But to God, this way of dealing with money makes perfect sense – when you can see the spiritual Kingdom that it's benefiting. There were many other examples of Jesus' spiritual viewpoint leading him to a different lifestyle and value system than those who couldn't see that kingdom he was in.

The ultimate victory will be when the spiritual kingdom of Christ will eventually be unveiled so that everyone can see it. It will be finished then; the world that Christ went away to prepare for us will be complete. Then this world that we live in now will be done away with; there will be no more need for the physical, because the new world will support us completely.

> I declare to you, brothers, that flesh and blood cannot inherit the kingdom of God, nor does the perishable inherit the imperishable. Listen, I tell you a mystery: We will not all sleep, but we will all be changed — in a flash, in the twinkling of an eye, at the last trumpet. For the trumpet will sound, the

dead will be raised imperishable, and we will be changed. For the perishable must clothe itself with the imperishable, and the mortal with immortality. When the perishable has been clothed with the imperishable, and the mortal with immortality, then the saying that is written will come true: "Death has been swallowed up in victory." (1 Corinthians 15:50-54)

We don't know much about what Heaven will be like. But we do know some facts about it that will help us in our preparation for it:

First, God will be there. That should be good news for those who love God, and terrible news for the wicked. God will be the center of Heaven, and all of our "time" there (if such a thing as time can be imagined in eternity) will be taken up completely with him. God is, after all, the source of all that we enjoy, and the goal of our hearts. If we don't know much of him now, that will be remedied in Heaven when we will spend eternity studying and appreciating his limitless richness and glory. It will be pure bliss to behold him.

Second, Heaven will be holy and righteousness. God insists on his surroundings being without spot or blemish. He has a right to feel that way, since it *is* his house! This means that we have to be changed: we will no longer sin, nor will we want to sin, nor will we be able to sin ever again. And that should be a relief to his people; sin is our dread sickness, the reason we suffer and die. It will be worth being in Heaven if only to finally escape the poison of the sin in our hearts!

What the New Testament Teaches

Third, Christ rules there. That new world is a Kingdom, and his Law will hold over everyone there. We will be his servants. His will reigns; we will not be doing our own thing there, and we won't even want to. His will, our service to him, will be our delight. Paul even hints that we will participate in his reign:

> Do you not know that we will judge angels? (1 Corinthians 6:3)

Fourth, it will be spiritual. So our bodies must be changed, as we've already seen. And though the New Testament talks about "streets of gold" and gates of precious gems, we have to understand that these are, again, pictures of the realities. Heaven can't be described in earthly terms, because it won't consist of anything of earth. We will depend on God directly, instead of receiving his blessings through created things as we do now. When Paul got a chance to visit Heaven, he came back speechless – in fact, he was forbidden to even try to describe what he saw there. Any attempt to describe it (beyond what the Bible already gives us) would do it injustice and no doubt confuse us about what it's really like there.

> And I know that this man — whether in the body or apart from the body I do not know, but God knows — was caught up to paradise. He heard inexpressible things, things that man is not permitted to tell. (2 Corinthians 12:3)

What the New Testament Teaches
Fulfilling the Law through the Spirit

The Old Testament is often equated with the Law of Moses, though that's an unfair comparison. What really rules the content and historical sweep of the Old Testament is the covenant made with Abraham and his children. The Law was only one aspect of the Kingdom of God, though an important one.

But to the Jews, the Law was everything. The Pharisees virtually worshipped the Law. They even extended the application of the Law (with their own commentaries that they considered just as authoritative as the Bible itself) to thousands of pages of legal decisions that ruled every aspect of life.

The problem about the Law is that we can't follow it. The Jews were mistaken in thinking that they could keep the Law in a way that would be pleasing to God. They didn't realize that the Law is infinitely deep: it requires a pure heart, not just pure actions. The Jew who mastered the external matters of righteousness could still be, and actually was, a Law-breaker in his heart.

In several places in the Old Testament we get hints that this was God's view on the matter:

> The LORD your God will circumcise your hearts and the hearts of your descendants, so that you may love him with all your heart and with all your soul, and live. (Deuteronomy 30:6)

> These people come near to me with their mouth and honor me with their lips, but their hearts are far from me. Their worship of me is made up only of rules taught by men. (Isaiah 29:13)

What the New Testament Teaches

The heart is deceitful above all things and beyond cure. Who can understand it? (Jeremiah 17:9)

But in the New Testament the Lord takes the veil away and we see the real problem. Nobody can keep the Law. Everyone has broken it in some way. The Law is spiritual, and anybody who relies on keeping the Law to please the thrice-holy God is a fool:

There is no one righteous, not even one; there is no one who understands, no one who seeks God. All have turned away, they have together become worthless; there is no one who does good, not even one." (Romans 3:10-12)

The trouble is that God's requirements haven't therefore been set aside, just because we can't attain those requirements! The Law is still the description of the perfect man, as God sees it. It still describes sin, as God sees it. Just because people can't keep the Law doesn't mean that God is going to relax his standards.

The New Testament shows us the true extent of the problem about sinful man trying to please God on his own efforts – it's impossible. But God isn't playing games with us. He doesn't set a standard for us only to condemn us all. *He has provided a way of escape.* There is a solution for those who wish to live with God. There is a way to reach that high level of righteousness that the Law describes – but it's not at all what we thought it would be!

The Jews were required to keep the Law on their own strength and will. They of course failed, because no man (except Jesus) can keep the Law perfectly, nor do we want to. But for his people, God sends the Spirit to live in our hearts.

What that means is that we now have the means to achieve perfect righteousness! We can have, as a matter of fact, the perfect righteousness of Christ – if we live by the Spirit. The Spirit of holiness is the key to our salvation.

Romans 8 and Galatians 5 deal with this extensively. The process is simple, yet amazing. The Spirit leads us away from our sin and prepares us for living in Heaven. He crucifies the sin in our heart – he takes the desire for it away (starves it, in other words) and puts the desire for holiness in its place. He trains us to set our eyes on Heavenly treasures, which means that the desire for the world will die away. He leads us in obedience to Christ's commands, which, as we do that, will end up fulfilling the demands of the Law. Without actually dealing with the Law itself, we end up fulfilling the Law in our walk of faith in Jesus.

> And so he condemned sin in sinful man, in order that the righteous requirements of the law might be fully met in us, who do not live according to the sinful nature but according to the Spirit. (Romans 8:3-4)

See the appendix "Led by the Spirit" for more information about how this works.

How to study the New Testament

How to study the New Testament

Reading the New Testament through, like reading any other book, is a good idea. It helps you get familiar with its teachings in general: its history and doctrines, with the characters involved, with the works of God, and with Christian morals and faith.

But *just* reading it through isn't good enough if you want to get the most out of it. It's the Word of God, which means that it has a depth that one can't appreciate with only a quick reading. The Bible is the product of an infinite mind. The more you study it, the more you realize that it has layers of meaning and insight that only come to light with some effort – and in many cases, with a great deal of effort. It's like a diamond mine: the treasures aren't usually lying on the surface. You have to dig to get rich.

Many students of the Bible have found proven methods for studying the New Testament. These methods most easily uncover the truth in the Bible; they've found what works, in other words, and it would be wise of us to use those effective means of study. Where many people go wrong, when they study the Bible, is by not using proven methods of study. It's possible to get the wrong meaning from the Scriptures! That's where many of the cults and strange religious groups today have gotten their supposedly "Biblical" teachings – from mangling the Bible into saying what it most definitely doesn't say.

What we want to do here, then, is to look over the "tools" we have for opening up and understanding the New Testament in the way that God wants us to see it.

Start with prayer

The entire Bible is God's book. He made certain that the human authors would write what he wanted in it; nothing is in it that God didn't say and wants us to believe. The Bible is the product of the Spirit of truth, who was literally the inspiration behind the prophets and apostles who first penned the original manuscripts.

Therefore, this is the mind of God – this is his viewpoint on the world, his own revelation of himself, the "inside" look of the Creator at his creation. And we can't hope to understand the mind of God unless we ask him for help.

> We have not received the spirit of the world but the Spirit who is from God, that we may understand what God has freely given us. This is what we speak, not in words taught us by human wisdom but in words taught by the Spirit, expressing spiritual truths in spiritual words. The man without the Spirit does not accept the things that come from the Spirit of God, for they are foolishness to him, and he cannot understand them, because they are spiritually discerned. The spiritual man makes judgments about all things, but he himself is not subject to any man's judgment: "For who has known the mind of the Lord that he may instruct him?" But we have the mind of Christ. (1 Corinthians 2:12-16)

How To Study the New Testament

> If any of you lacks wisdom, he should ask God, who gives generously to all without finding fault, and it will be given to him. (James 1:5)

Even though it seems that we *can* learn the Bible, and even memorize its verses, without God's help, we won't see the real point of it until God opens the eyes of our hearts to see it. The best examples of people who thought they could understand the Bible without God's help were the Pharisees – they considered themselves experts in the Word of God. The sad truth is that, even though they knew the words, they missed the meaning behind those words entirely. Jesus actually charged these experts of God's Word with ignorance:

> You diligently study the Scriptures because you think that by them you possess eternal life. These are the Scriptures that testify about me, yet you refuse to come to me to have life. (John 5:39-40)

> You are in error because you do not know the Scriptures or the power of God. (Matthew 22:29)

On the other hand, whenever someone saw the real meaning behind the words, the Bible makes it clear that they saw it only because God opened their eyes to see it. We can't *know* about his spiritual world unless God reveals it to us.

> I tell you the truth, no one can see the Kingdom of God unless he is born again ... I tell you the truth, no one can enter the Kingdom of God unless he is born of water and the Spirit. (John 3:3,5)

Therefore, if we hope to understand the mystery of Christ, the hidden mystery of the Gospel that Paul revealed to the Churches, and the mystery that the Jews entirely missed (even though their own Scriptures taught them about it) we have to turn to God who teaches us. He has to take away the veil of sin from our minds and hearts so that we can willingly hear the truth. He has to clean out the spiritual cobwebs in our souls and free us from the ignorance and lies that we've been trained in all of our lives.

We can't make the mistake of believing that a little bit of study will make us knowledgeable about Jesus. The wisdom that God wants to give us is complex and extensive; it's a university training in Heavenly treasures. There are some things that we won't see for a long time – at least until we get some of the basics down first. Usually a Christian will learn the fundamentals first, move on to more difficult subjects, and years later will learn even more that will show him how to pull all the pieces together that he's been learning in years past. Our understanding grows gradually, not overnight.

When we become Christians, we find ourselves sitting at the feet of Jesus like Mary did. (Luke 10:38-42) Our education in God's world starts in earnest then. As did the disciples, when they realized that they'd been taught wrong in the past and they needed instruction, we need to come to Jesus and ask him to teach us. He's pleased with us when we realize that *he* has to lead us by the hand. He'll honor a request like that. Then when he does, everyone will know that we've been taught by the Master himself and we didn't come up with our "knowledge" on our own. Those kind of credentials will get us far in the work of the Kingdom.

The Old Testament lays the foundation

We really must go back to the Old Testament to understand most of what happens in the New Testament. We've already looked at how the two sections relate to each other, so we won't repeat any of that here. But we can make a few general observations.

First, the Lord first worked out the entire plan of salvation through the history of the Israelites. He worked it all out on a physical level so that it would be easy to understand. Everyone can understand a rich land where pilgrims can rest. Everyone can understand the blood of a sacrifice. The miracles showed a real God at work solving impossible situations. But when you back up and look at the grand sweep of things, you can see that Old Testament events describe what our God was doing – saving his people, and living among them – in graphic form. What happened in the Old Testament is the same theory, the same principle, that we see in the New Testament. The New Testament actually didn't teach a single thing new to us that hadn't already been touched on in some way in the Old. The Jews should have recognized the same God at work in Christ.

Second, the reason that there's so much material in the Old Testament is that Jesus Christ is an amazingly complex person, and his work can't be described simply or shortly. In the Old Testament the Lord takes the opportunity (through historical events, using physical realities), to examine in detail every single thing about our salvation so that we can fully understand it. The New Testament doesn't repeat much of what the Old Testament teaches because that would be redundant. It assumes you've already done your homework, and it moves on to other issues.

So the point is that you must first learn the fundamentals of the Old Testament. Also, you should assume that a particular passage that you're studying in the New Testament isn't as simple or plain as you might suppose – it probably rests on a particular truth that the *Old* Testament spent a lot of time explaining for you.

A Spiritual level

The Jews learned about their God on a physical level. God promised Abraham certain things, and although his ultimate intentions were a spiritual fulfillment of that covenant, he first worked it out through physical realities.

But the New Testament lifts us up out of the physical level into God's spiritual Kingdom. We learn now that God isn't interested in the physical Temple but in the Body of Christ, which is the eternal Temple of God. We learn that Canaan isn't his intended resting place for his people, but the Heavenly Jerusalem. Every promise that God made the Israelites becomes a spiritual reality for Christians.

There's a reason for this: what God has planned for his people is a spiritual, eternal world. The things of this earth can't build a new world like God has in mind for us. He plans to destroy the first Creation; it has no more purpose than to simply provide a "stage" for his spiritual purposes to work themselves out for now. When the new world is ready, he will sweep away all physical things and replace it all with the new Kingdom of perfection, peace, justice, holiness, love, and joy.

Interpreted History

We've already looked at this point, but it bears repeating. The New Testament records those things that have to do with our faith. It isn't interested in satisfying our idle curiosity about people or history.

The story of the life of Christ in the Gospels obviously leaves a lot of details out. But what *is* given to us is for our spiritual growth. These are the things we need to know about Christ. Every single detail is a powerful treasure out of Heaven that we can learn, store away, and use to solve problems and draw closer to God. These truths are food for our soul.

This is the way God wants you to look at things. We are tempted to hold our own opinions on things, so much so that we even listen to the truths of the Bible with skepticism. But that's a fatal attitude to take toward God's truth. These things save the soul, just as a life raft will save a drowning man. If we make the mistake of doubting the truth of the Bible, we are throwing away the very thing that will save us from sin and death. The rich man who despised Lazarus at his front gate found out too late that the truth which Lazarus believed can save the soul. (Luke 16:19-31) We may live in a country that prides itself on giving freedom of thought and action to its citizens, but none of us are free to doubt God, let alone sin against him. We have to give up this idea of being free to doubt the truth. Such thinking poisons the soul and shuts the gate to Heaven; there's no hope for the person who refuses to bend his knee in submission to the Lord of the New Testament.

> I told you that you would die in your sins; if you do not believe that I am the one I claim to be, you will indeed die in your sins. (John 8:24)

God-centered

Always read the Bible to look for God. That's the primary purpose of the Bible – to reveal God to us. Students most often miss the point of the Scriptures when they forget why this book was written. We *are* in the book, but we aren't its primary subject.

The reason we have to look for God in the New Testament is because there is only salvation *in God*, never in our own actions. We have to find out what it is about God that we need so badly. We know what our problems are already; what we need to know now is whether God can help us.

I've seen well-meaning teachers encourage their students to "have faith in Christ," "believe in Christ," "obey Christ," "worship Christ," "follow Christ" – as if *our* actions were the whole point! Although it sounds good, their teaching is man-centered: do this, do this, do this. Can they answer this question, however: which Christ are you referring to? What does Jesus do? What is he like? Without a good understanding of Jesus, they can make up any religion and call it Christianity, and there's nothing there to save our souls.

For example, there are two ways to teach the Sermon on the Mount. It's obviously filled with instructions and commands. And it's easy to run off with this list of instructions and get busy trying to do them. But if we aren't satisfied with a superficial religion, it won't be long before we find out that we don't have the spiritual understanding, courage, or strength to carry out these amazingly severe requirements! That's because we failed to look at the One who taught them.

The King spoke those words to us. Stop and look at the circumstances, and what he's saying. He taught them to his followers from a hillside, with them sitting at his feet – the Jews wouldn't have missed the fact that he was claiming royal authority over his subjects, since kings and mountains went together in those days. And he was laying the Law down — which again a King would be interested in doing. The King has a responsibility to set up a government of just laws among his subjects. These are the laws of Christ's Kingdom among his people; if we want to live with him forever, we may as well accept the fact that he expects us to measure up to these requirements if we want his favor.

Furthermore, these laws are obviously severe! Even the thoughts and intents of the heart are within the reach of the King's law. Can any of us hope to achieve this kind of perfection? Does this tell you what has to happen to you before you can be accepted into his perfect Kingdom? Does this tell you how perfect that Kingdom is going to be? This is obviously a Kingdom that this world has never seen before! The requirements are beyond what an ordinary sinner can hope to achieve on his own; they must be referring to a Kingdom somewhere else – such a place can't exist here. Do you see where this is leading us? This is, ultimately, his eternal Kingdom that will be the "new Heavens and the new earth" that was promised in the prophets.

Reading a passage to learn about God – and, of course, Christ – puts an entirely different light on things. It steers us into the right direction to think, instead of what we would have assumed after a superficial reading. One's conclusions are entirely different if God is the point instead of ourselves.

Testimony

One of the most important aspects of the New Testament is that it's a collection of affidavits from eyewitnesses. *These people saw God at work.* We mustn't forget how powerful a tool that is for bringing people face to face with the Word of God.

A testimony is a legal device in a court of law that goes a long way to solving a case. Since the court doesn't know whether the defendant is guilty or innocent, and since the consequences can be life changing, we really need a fail-safe way of finding out the truth. Not knowing the truth will mean confusion, injustice, frustration, hurt, and even death. In the case of knowing whether Jesus is really the Son of God, whether we can trust him with our souls, whether we really are in the danger he said we are and he can get us out of that danger – we simply have to have reliable facts about him. Philosophy, and even religion, isn't good enough.

The witness provides us with that proof. He was there; he saw Jesus do certain things, and say certain things. We can rely on his testimony because he's as reliable as any one of us would have been if we had had the chance to be there ourselves. And we can't reject his testimony unless we can come up with a more reliable witness of our own who can prove that the Bible's witnesses were liars.

Since there are no other witnesses, this means that the testimony of the apostles makes the New Testament a reliable and *legally binding* document. It has authority that no other religion or philosophy has. We are obligated to believe the eyewitnesses, as we would be in a court of law. God used this device to give us absolute confidence in the Gospel of Christ. This is the only truth, and the only way to look at Jesus and his ministry.

This also means that we can use this truth in the same way that the Biblical witnesses used them. If Jesus has all power (as their testimony tells us), we can go to him too for answers to our problems. If he has all wisdom (as their testimony tells us) then we can turn to him to teach us the truth too. If he really is the King, the Master, the Creator (as their testimony tells us) then we too had better bow before him and serve him, or he will treat us as he did rebels in his day.

Symbol, type, allegory

The Old Testament is full of symbols and types. These are literary devices to teach us more truth about certain principles than a doctrinal treatise could ever teach us. Pictures convey a tremendous amount of meaning that simple words can't do for us.

But in the New Testament the need for symbols and types isn't so great. The reality that the Old Testament pointed to had now come – Christ was what all those old stories and types were referring to. He is the living fulfillment of all the principles of God's kingdom.

> The blood of goats and bulls and the ashes of a heifer sprinkled on those who are ceremonially unclean sanctify them so that they are outwardly clean. How much more, then, will the blood of Christ, who through the eternal Spirit offered himself unblemished to God, cleanse our consciences from acts that lead to death, so that we may serve the living God! (Hebrews 9:13-14)

The challenge is to connect Jesus up with the pictures of the Old Testament! Sometimes we're told what Old Testament principle illustrates some aspect of Jesus' life and ministry, but often we aren't told. We have to be sharp students to see the connection. But it's necessary to do that study. Jesus didn't do anything apart from his Father's will – and his Father's will was to "fulfill all righteousness." That means that all the hard work that went into the plan of salvation before he came (in Old Testament times) must be brought to a finish.

For example, we've already seen how important the link is between Jesus and David. David shows us what a king *must* do in order to build and secure God's Kingdom. Since the Scriptures compare every son of David with the model, we have to assume that Jesus himself would be careful to "do as his father David had done" – since God's requirements haven't changed.

But there are still some symbols and allegory that remain in the New Testament. For example, our practice of Communion is a symbol of the body and blood of Christ, sacrificed for us as a Passover Lamb. Baptism is a symbol of our union with Christ in his death and resurrection, and the pouring out of the Spirit on us. There are rich studies to be done in this area.

Read in faith

The switch from the old physical system to the new spiritual system means that a lot of people are going to be left out in the cold. It was hard enough to see God's eternal purposes in the Old Testament, but it was easy to appreciate the fact that there *was* a God in those days – he did real miracles, he led them to a real Promised Land, and he punished them with real enemies. It was very easy to see.

But in the New Testament the physical props are taken away from us. The first problem is Jesus himself: he was born in a poor family, was never accepted by the leaders of Israel, and was crucified as a common criminal. People found it impossible to believe that he was really what he said he was.

Plus, the kingdom that he preached was, he himself admitted, impossible to see with one's physical eyes. His followers could never expect to have any more than their Master – persecution, homelessness, poverty, hunger. The Church itself was made up of the "despised" of the community:

> Brothers, think of what you were when you were called. Not many of you were wise by human standards; not many were influential; not many were of noble birth. But God chose the foolish things of the world to shame the wise; God chose the weak things of the world to shame the strong.

He chose the lowly things of this world and the despised things — and the things that are not — to nullify the things that are, so that no one may boast before him. (1 Corinthians 1:26-29)

Our hope is an invisible world. Jesus is gone who knows where, because nobody can see him now. The Church is universal around the world, but there's nothing visible that ties us together. Our entire religion deals with things we can't see our touch.

This is the meaning of living by faith. It's a New Testament concept that makes our religion possible. Whereas other religions rely on stone or gold gods that its devotees can see to worship, we worship a God we can't see with our eyes – only with our souls.

We live by faith, not by sight. (2 Corinthians 5:7)

Faith, as we've seen before, is living in the light of God's world. The world of God becomes real to us because of the way the Spirit of God opens up our souls to its reality. We don't live by hopes and guesses and opinions, but by what we *know* – what the Spirit has shown us to be real.

But we may as well figure that we'll never be able to prove our faith to anybody. We have nothing we can point to! If someone is going to see what we see, and know that such things are real, the Spirit will have to open their hearts and minds to those things that we see.

How To Study the New Testament

Appendices

Led by the Spirit

The most precious gift that Christ has given his people is the Holy Spirit. Yet we know so little about him, probably because he is just *that* – Spirit – and we can't see him or sense his presence nearly so easily as the disciples did Jesus. And what we can't see, we don't concern ourselves with very much. So most of us think almost nothing about the Spirit, much to our spiritual hurt.

But the Bible tells us that the purpose of the Spirit's coming – the reason that Jesus gave him to us – is so that we might be *led by the Spirit*. Christ promised us that he isn't going to leave us alone in this world; and the Spirit is the fulfillment of that promise. There's too much that can go wrong in our lives if we don't listen to, and act on, some spiritual guidance from someone who knows the way.

Some people have formed their own opinion on what being "led" by the Spirit means. For instance, they long for the ability to have visions, or ecstatic utterances, or some sort of spiritual high during worship. Others on the other end of the spectrum want the Spirit to lead them into material wealth – they are "men of corrupt mind, who have been robbed of the truth and who think that godliness is a means to financial gain." (1 Timothy 6:5) But neither of these is what the Scripture means by being "led by the Spirit." In the first instance, *every* Christian must be led of the Spirit – but not every Christian will experience spiritual highs like the Old Testament Prophets sometimes did. In the second instance, the Spirit is leading God's people *away* from the world's riches, toward a reward that is far better than silver and gold.

The special work of the Spirit

Usually we think of the Spirit in terms of sanctification — that is, making us free from sin, or holy. "But you were washed, you were sanctified, you were justified in the name of the Lord Jesus Christ and by the Spirit of our God." (1 Corinthians 6:11) "To God's elect ... who have been chosen according to the foreknowledge of God the Father, by the sanctifying work of the Spirit, for obedience to Jesus Christ and sprinkling by his blood." (1 Peter 1:1-2)

But that's not the *primary* work of the Spirit according to the Bible. In a total of over 80 different passages that talk about what the Spirit does, I found only five places where it refers to his work of cleansing from sin, and some of those are marginal. Over half of the passages teach that the Spirit *reveals* the things of God, and the other half talk about the Spirit's *empowering* work.

- *The Spirit reveals the world of God.* " 'No eye has seen, no ear has heard, no mind has conceived what God has prepared for those who love him' — but God has revealed it to us by his Spirit." (1 Corinthians 2:9-10)

If we want to know more about Heaven, the first hurdle that we have to get over is the fact that we are so earthbound. Since the day we were born, we have known only what we can see, smell, touch, taste, and hear. This world that we live in has been, to us, the *only* real world, as far as we can tell. The things that we put value on and the things that we own are in *this* world; the issues that we consider important are in *this* world; the people we respect are in *this* world; the forces that we fear are in *this* world. Most people live and die knowing nothing more than what is in this physical world, and they really don't care if there is another world — it seems like unrealistic stories anyway, myths and fairy tales.

But there is another world that's different from this one, even if we don't know anything about it: it's the world that God lives in. God is not of this world. That's a fundamental doctrine of Christianity. We have to believe that God's world is a completely different place than this world that we live in, that he can and does exist without any dependence on the physical world. He is the Creator: he made the universe, and he doesn't depend on it in the least — it depends on him. We could all snap completely out of existence and he wouldn't change in the least. He is what he is, and he will always be what he is, without our help or interference.

God's spiritual world is completely different from ours. Whereas ours is always changing, always falling apart and needing to be built up again, his is unchanging. Ours is completely physical, which means that the One who made it can unmake it just as easily (which he intends to do someday, by the way); but God's world is spiritual and therefore eternal. Our world looks good on the outside, and promises to satisfy us — but those are hollow promises, because it can't deliver on those promises (God intentionally made it unable to satisfy us); God's world doesn't look so appealing to our senses but it does satisfy the soul's deepest needs. Our world struggles under the curse of sin and death, and God has already passed judgment on it — its time will come; God's world remains untouched by that stain and therefore remains God's only choice for where spiritual life can thrive.

What about this completely "other" world that we don't know anything about? We can, and do, live our entire lives in complete ignorance that it even exists. The two worlds actually run parallel to each other, like two cities on either side of a railroad track; and if it weren't for certain historical events that forced a link between the two we would still not know how the people lived "on the other side of the tracks."

One of the most important historical events that forged a bridge between the two worlds was the giving of the Holy Spirit. The Spirit reveals, makes plain, uncovers, makes "see-able" this other world that God lives in. It's like taking the veil away from a statue so that the public can see it for the first time. It's like opening a window into Heaven so that we can see inside.

The first occasion in the Bible where we find the Spirit doing this type of work is in connection with the Tabernacle. God was concerned that Moses and the Israelites build their central place of worship in the right way; not just anything would do. So instead of running the risk that the makers of the Tabernacle would misunderstand his instructions, no matter how plain he made them, the Lord poured out his

Led by the Spirit

Spirit on the two men in charge of the building project:

> See, the LORD has chosen Bezalel son of Uri, the son of Hur, of the tribe of Judah, and *he has filled him with the Spirit of God*, with skill, ability and knowledge in all kinds of crafts ... And he has given both him and Oholiab son of Ahisamach, of the tribe of Dan, the ability to teach others ... so Bezalel, Oholiab and every skilled person to whom the LORD has given skill and ability to know how to carry out all the work of constructing the sanctuary are to do the work just as the LORD has commanded. (Exodus 35:30,34-35; 36:1)

And what did the Spirit show them?

> They serve at a sanctuary that is a copy and shadow of what is in Heaven. This is why Moses was warned when he was about to build the tabernacle: "See to it that you make everything according to the pattern shown you on the mountain." (Hebrews 8:5)

The Spirit showed these men what the Heavenly Tabernacle, in God's world, looked like. To what extent we don't know, but at least we know that they saw the essentials so that they could pattern the earthly tabernacle after it in a way that would satisfy God.

Led by the Spirit

In Isaiah there is a prophecy of the Messiah, and it tells us that he will be filled by the Spirit:

> The Spirit of the LORD will rest upon him — the Spirit of wisdom and of understanding, the Spirit of counsel and of power, the Spirit of knowledge and of the fear of the LORD ... He will not judge by what he sees with his eyes, or decide by what he hears with his ears ... (Isaiah 11:2,3)

In other words, he won't rely on his senses to judge how to work in this world, but by what the Spirit tells him — knowledge from another world than this one.

Jesus said that when we face authorities who persecute us for our faith, the Spirit of God will give us the right words to say — words that we wouldn't ordinarily think of on our own. (Mark 13:11) He also promised to send the Spirit to us, who would "guide you into all truth." (John 16:13) The Spirit of God opened Stephen's eyes to see Christ standing at God's right hand when the Jews were stoning him. (Acts 7:55-56) The Spirit tells us what to pray for and how to pray when we don't know what to say. (Romans 8:26) The mystery of Christ "has now been revealed by the Spirit" to the Church." (Ephesians 3:5) Paul said that whoever rejects the teaching of Scripture isn't rejecting man but the Spirit, who is actually doing the teaching. (1 Thessalonians 4:8) The Spirit gives us a taste of the Heavenly gift, and enlightens us about the world of God. (Hebrews

6:4) The Prophets, Peter tells us, always spoke as they were "carried along by the Holy Spirit" — the Spirit told them what to say. (1 Peter 1:21) The Spirit testifies to the cleansing power of Christ's blood. (1 John 5:6) John the Apostle was praying in the Spirit when he had his revelation of Christ. (Revelation 1:10) The Spirit says things to the churches of Christ that they need to hear. (Revelation 2:11)

This is just a sampling from the Bible about the work of the Spirit as he reveals the world of God to our minds and souls.

- ***The Spirit gives power.*** "But you will receive power when the Holy Spirit comes on you; and you will be my witnesses in Jerusalem and in all Judea and Samaria, and to the ends of the earth." (Acts 1:8)

The kind of power that this verse is talking about isn't any power that we are familiar with. Simon made that mistake when he saw the Apostles working miracles and tried to buy the power of the Spirit from them. (Acts 8:9-24) The power that the Spirit gives is a new thing, something that this world doesn't know anything about.

The first time that we find the empowering work of the Spirit in the Bible is in Genesis.

> In the beginning God created the Heavens and the earth. Now the earth was formless and empty, darkness was over the surface of the deep, and the Spirit of God

was hovering over the waters. (Genesis 1:1-2)

What exactly was there at the beginning, the building blocks that God used to make the world, we don't know; we do know that it was "without form" and "without substance" (as the Hebrew words mean), which are the two necessary characteristics of matter as we know it. In other words, the Spirit brought non-existence into existence; he gave life and substance to what used to be nothing. The earth and plants and animals and man all exist because the Spirit gave us the ability to exist. Without him we would return to nothingness.

That's what happened to the world when the Spirit moved in the beginning. What happens in men's souls now? Here is where we need the Spirit most of all, because we are all dead to the world of God from our birth. (Ephesians 2:1-3) Even if we see God (the first job of the Spirit), and even if we *know* the truth about God and his world, we still can't do anything about it. God requires obedience from us — but we can't obey him because we are so bound up in our sin, and without power to obey his commands. He requires faith from us — but we can't believe in him because we are so confused, wandering in this dark world. He calls us to live in *his* world, but we can't get out of our world. At the very least we are to "love the Lord your God with all our heart and with all your soul and with all your mind" (Matthew 22:37), but unfortunately we aren't interested — there are other things that we love more.

Led by the Spirit

When the Spirit works on the heart, however, that person wakes up to God's world, like opening one's eyes on a bright morning. "Wake up, O sleeper, rise from the dead, and Christ will shine on you." (Ephesians 5:14) He can see things now that he hasn't seen before. Even this dark world that we live in gets a new light: the Spirit shines on our lives, on circumstances, on other people, like a spotlight and shows us things that we couldn't see before.

The Spirit not only wakes us up to the world of God, he makes us *able* to live in God's world. "Flesh and blood cannot inherit the Kingdom of God" (1 Corinthians 15:50), simply because the conditions there would kill us. The air is different, the food is different, the light is different (I'm using symbols of the realities, you understand; "air" and "food" and "light" in Heaven are spiritual things, whereas we think of our physical world when we hear those words.) Paul said that before we can hope to rise into Heaven, some things about us have to change:

> So it will be with the resurrection of the dead. The body that is sown is perishable, it is raised imperishable; it is sown in dishonor, it is raised in glory; it is sown in weakness, it is raised in power; it is sown a natural body, it is raised a spiritual body. (1 Corinthians 15:42-44)

In order to live before God and not die, we have to change completely. Our natures as they are now can neither survive before God's glory, nor can we understand or appreciate what we would see there. Our physical senses weren't made to be aware of the things of God. Unless, of course, the Spirit gives life to our souls — our souls *were* made to be aware of God. That's why the Bible talks about having "eyes to see" and "ears to hear." The Spirit makes us alive spiritually (which Jesus called, appropriately, being "born again" — John 3:3) so that our spiritual senses can start picking up on the things of God. In order to pick up the signals from a radio station, you have to first turn the radio on. In the same way, before anybody can hope to know God, their souls must be made alive first.

The Spirit makes it possible for us to obey God's commands; without him we could never do it. (Ezekiel 36:26-27) The Law is spiritual, Paul says (Romans 7:14), and the Spirit shows us what God means by his Law and how he will make us conform to its requirements. The Spirit of God blew over the bones in Israel and made them alive again. (Ezekiel 37:1-14) The Lord will build his Kingdom "not by might nor by power, but by my Spirit" (Zechariah 4:6); because of this, his Kingdom will be eternal and it will consist of things that will satisfy both him and us. Jesus drove out demons by the Spirit of God. (Matthew 12:28) Jesus said that, when someone has the Spirit in him, it will be a spring of water welling up inside to eternal life. (John 4:14) "The Spirit gives life, the flesh counts for nothing" (John 6:63) — and Jesus' words were Spirit because they give us spiritual life, the awareness of God and ability to live for God. Peter, the disciple whom the Jews had last seen denying the Lord, stood up at Pentecost full of the Spirit and preached the eternal Gospel to the Jews — with thousands of conversions as a result. (Acts 2) The Holy Spirit gives joy to God's people. (Romans 14:17) It's because of the Spirit's work that we have faith in Christ — a faith that comprehends the breadth and depth of Christ's person and work. (Ephesians 2:8; 3:16) The Spirit washes and renews us so that we become heirs of God's promises. (Titus 3:5)

Our journey to Heaven

You may have noticed something important in the previous discussion. The Spirit reveals – what? The world of God! He shows us the spiritual Kingdom that God lives in, the one that we've been called to live in ourselves. And the Spirit empowers us – to do what? To live in that Kingdom of Heaven! God's world is of such a nature that the Spirit has to make us *able* to come into God's presence, *able* to take advantage of the treasures that God put in Christ for us. In other words, the primary focus of the Spirit in our lives is *to make us fit to live in the Kingdom of God.*

When a person becomes a Christian, his heart changes. Jesus described it to Nicodemus (who, by the way, should have known about this already, because he was an expert in the Old Testament!).

> I tell you the truth, no one can see the Kingdom of God unless he is born again … I tell you the truth, no one can enter the Kingdom of God unless he is born of water and the Spirit. Flesh gives birth to flesh, but the Spirit gives birth to spirit. You should not be surprised at my saying, 'You must be born again.' The wind blows wherever it pleases. You hear its sound, but you cannot tell where it

comes from or where it is going. So it is with everyone born of the Spirit. (John 3:3,5-8)

Our souls, dead to God at birth and completely unable to sense his presence or feel any inclination to be interested in him, suddenly become alive to God. The Spirit blows from Heaven in a way that none of us can describe or predict and, for some reason, we are suddenly interested in the things of Heaven. We can tell now that there really is a God; we know he's there. More specifically, we find that we fear this God (which means we want to be careful how we act around him), and we hope in this God (which means that we know that he has what we need).

When this happens, we discover that we have a practical problem on our hands. It's such a precious gift to become a child of God, an heir to the eternal Kingdom, with the right to enjoy our Heavenly inheritance. But we find ourselves still on earth, with physical bodies and physical needs! We would like to leave for Heaven immediately and be done with this world! But it can't be, not yet at any rate. Even Jesus prayed about our problem:

> I have given them your Word and the world has hated them, for they are not of the world any more than I am of the world. My prayer is not that you take them out of the world but that you protect them from the evil one. They are not of the world, even as I am not of it. (John 17:14-16)

What we have here is a dual-identity problem. In Hebrews we find a description that fits all of God's children, as long as they remain here in this world:

> All these people were still living by faith when they died. They did not receive the things promised; they only saw them and welcomed them from a

distance. And they admitted that they were *aliens and strangers* on earth. People who say such things show that they are looking for a country of their own. If they had been thinking of the country they had left, they would have had opportunity to return. Instead, they were longing for a better country — a Heavenly one. Therefore God is not ashamed to be called their God, for he has prepared a city for them. (Hebrews 11:13-16)

As long as we remain here, we actually have one foot on earth and one foot in Heaven. Our hearts are in another world, and our eyes are focused on the Throne of God. We know that we don't belong here anymore. We aren't supposed to love the things in this world anymore; as Jesus told us –

Do not store up for yourselves treasures on earth, where moth and rust destroy, and where thieves break in and steal. But store up for yourselves treasures in Heaven, where moth and rust do not destroy, and where thieves do not break in and steal. For where your treasure is, there your heart will be also. (Matthew 6:19-21)

We could go on and on, listing the passages from the Bible about our new life in Christ, our new spiritual inheritance, and God's command to turn our backs on this world. It really is a new life that we've begun because of what Christ did in our hearts.

Here, now, is where the Spirit comes in. Becoming a Christian isn't just a matter of changing from the old way of life to a new way, or holding to a different set of beliefs about God. As Paul says, "If only for *this* life we have hope in Christ, we are to be pitied more than all men." (1 Corinthians 15:19) Our goal now is *Heaven*. We have begun a journey: from the moment that we woke up spiritually and saw our Savior, the rest of our lives will be a steady progress *from* earth *to* Heaven. And the Spirit is doing two things for us: leading us in the right way to Heaven, and slowly making us fit to arrive there in perfect condition and pleasing to our Master. We are making plans for *leaving* this world – and that fact should become more apparent to others as time goes on.

In the Old Testament Temple, there were certain vessels and articles that the priests used for purposes of worship only. The Law strictly forbade anybody from using these articles for common use; the priests sprinkled each article with blood and "set it aside" for this sacred use in the Temple. That's exactly what the word "sanctify" means in Hebrew – to "set aside for sacred use." Once a pot, for example, was sanctified, it couldn't be used for ordinary cooking anymore. Even if it was broken by accident, it had to be destroyed – the people were forbidden to use it for any common purpose once it had been sanctified.

That's exactly what the Spirit is doing to us. God is so holy, and the Temple in Heaven is so overwhelmingly holy, that it's forbidden that any common, ordinary, wicked sinner should ever be allowed there. Earth is full of sinners; but Heaven has, and shall have, *none*. There won't even be the hint of sin in the presence of the holy God. But you can probably see the problem here: if God calls us to come up before him, and especially to share the inheritance with Christ as God's children, what are we going to do about our sin? And even if we *were* allowed inside his Temple, what in the world would we say or do there? We know nothing about the place! So the Spirit is going to prepare us for life in Heaven. And here is how he will do it:

- ***Crucify the flesh:*** "Flesh and blood cannot inherit the Kingdom of God, nor does the perishable inherit the imperishable." (1 Corinthians 15:50) We like to pamper our flesh, to line our nests in this world. We want comfortable jobs, respectability in the community, plenty of friends and good times. We also like to indulge in our lusts from time to time.

But there is nothing in Heaven for the flesh to lust for! There are no earthly pleasures, no wealth that we are familiar with, no lusts allowed – or even possible! Remember that Jesus told us that "at the resurrection people will neither marry nor be given in marriage; they will be like the angels in Heaven." (Matthew 22:30) Not too promising for anybody looking forward to pampering their flesh! The pleasures there are purely spiritual. The physical as we know it will be gone, remade, unrecognizable. The physical has to die, like a seed, so that the spiritual can be born and live in a spiritual Heaven.

Now before we can be ready for such a strange place, and before we can even *want* to go to such a place, the Spirit has to work on us and make us into spiritual creatures who love God's spiritual Kingdom. The flesh must die.

- ***Renew the mind:*** "Do not conform any longer to the pattern of this world, but be transformed by the renewing of your mind." (Romans 12:2) Our minds are remarkable tools for enabling us to get along in this world. In fact, we pride ourselves at being "savvy" or intelligent, and we hate to play the fool and show our ignorance.

But when it comes to the world of God, we know almost nothing about it. We don't know what it looks like, we don't know much about God himself, we don't know the immense riches in

Christ or how to get at them, we don't know how to act in front of God and Heaven's hosts when we pray – there is so much we don't know about God's world, that the first sight of it will surely humble us!

That's what the Spirit is going to do. He's going to renew our minds, make them able to see and understand spiritual truths and realities, and make us skilled at knowing and using Heavenly treasures.

> We have not received the spirit of the world but the Spirit who is from God, that we may *understand* what God has freely given us. This is what we speak, not in words taught us by human wisdom but in words taught by the Spirit, expressing spiritual truths in spiritual words. (1 Corinthians 2:12-13)

- ***Fruits of righteousness:*** "But the fruit of the Spirit is love, joy, peace, patience, kindness, goodness, faithfulness, gentleness and self-control. Against such things there is no law." (Galatians 5:22-23)

What naturally comes out of a human being's heart? Read the newspapers! Earth is full of wickedness; it's been that way since the fall of Adam and Eve. None of us can claim moral perfection; even the best of us have failed God at some point in our lives.

But God can't tolerate the least trace of sin! He is so holy – Isaiah said that he is "holy, holy, holy!"

Led by the Spirit

(Isaiah 6:3) – that he would sooner have us all put to death than pollute his pure environment with our wickedness. Notice that he didn't have any qualms about destroying sinners in the past! Read the stories of Noah, and Korah, and the Exile, and Sodom and Gomorrah, for proof of his hatred of sinners.

But the Spirit is going to take care of this spiritual cancer in our hearts. Knowing that we can't appear before God in our own wretched rags of "morality" which haven't made us any more righteous in God's eyes, he's going to replace them with the robe of righteousness that Jesus bought for us with his obedience. Slowly, he's going to *make* us do what pleases God in our lives, day by day. Slowly but surely he's going to remake our hearts in holiness instead of leaving them in wickedness.

- *True worship:* "Yet a time is coming and has now come when the true worshipers will worship the Father in Spirit and truth, for they are the kind of worshipers the Father seeks." (John 4:23)

The ways that we invent to worship God in our churches and denominations can be pretty pitiful. We believe firmly that the way *we* worship God is the only right way; but, if you think about it, we can't *all* be right! We all have different versions of how to do worship. But so much of what we do is simply because of our preferences, traditions and culture.

Almost none of it, unfortunately, fits in with the way the servants of God worship him in Heaven. In fact, we probably would feel completely out of place there – we wouldn't know the first thing to do if we were presented to God in person! What would we say? What would we do? Even if we could think of what to do for the first five minutes, what would we do for the rest of the day? For a year? For eternity? Remember that the worship of God is going to be our work in Heaven *forever*. Do we have any idea of how to go about such work?

The Spirit, then, has to train us in spiritual worship. He has to show us what God likes, and what he expects from us. He has to make us skilled at saying and doing things for God that please him. He has to show us the real work going on in Heaven and what our part in it will be.

- **Walk by faith:** "For in the gospel a righteousness from God is revealed, a righteousness that is by faith from first to last, just as it is written: 'The righteous will live by faith.'" (Romans 1:17)

What most people mean by "faith" is a poor substitute for the tremendous spiritual gift that God has given us in true faith. Most people think it means believing in some doctrine or Biblical truth. So they think that they have faith when they, for example, believe that there is a God. James ridicules such "faith!" "You believe that there is one God. Good! Even the demons believe that – and shudder." (James 2:19)

What would happen if God would suddenly lift you up from earth and set you in Heaven? Would you recognize anything? Would everything be totally new to you? Would you be like a foreigner, lost and wandering, friendless, homeless, without a clue as to what is going on around you? If God would invite you to share in the spiritual treasures in Christ, which is your inheritance, would you even know what those treasures are? Or where to find them?

Faith is walking in the light of God's world. It's the result of the light of Christ coming down from Heaven, that the Spirit shines down on us as he reveals to us the things of God. We *know* God, we *see* God, through our faith. We see the riches in Christ; that's why we reach out to *him* when we need help. We see a world that others can't see. That "seeing" is what true faith is all about. With true faith, this physical world means little to us, and the world of God becomes our only hope. Living by faith means we conform our daily lives to spiritual realities – things that other people can't see and don't know. The Spirit, as he reveals these things to us, makes such a faith possible.

- *Hope in Heaven:* "For in this hope we were saved." (Romans 8:24) The last point leads to this one, naturally. We hope in whatever we set the greatest value on. If we love this world with all of its "riches" and "glory," and we long to fill our physical lusts with earthly pleasures, then we won't have much interest in a spiritual world where there is none of that sort of thing.

When we are brought before God's judgment seat on the Last Day, it will be plain for everyone to see what we have been putting our hope in. If our hearts have been set on things on earth, we will look with great disappointment and fear at this God that we haven't been paying any attention to. We will cringe before a Heaven without worldly pleasures. We will look back, like Lot's wife, at the earth burning behind us, destroyed by God's punishing hand, wishing that we were there instead of in this spiritual world with God and his people. What will we do if Heaven turns out to be so foreign and offensive to us?

So the Spirit is going to wean us from the world now, and set our hearts on Heavenly things. He works in us to will and do God's perfect will. He helps us pray – for spiritual treasures. He sets our eyes on Christ, seated at God's right hand, above all earthly powers and pleasures. When he gets done with us, there will be nothing on earth that we desire but God, and nothing in Heaven that so wins our hearts but God. (Psalm 73:25) The longer we live with the Spirit, the more we will *long* for Heaven.

The Spirit blows where he wills

The Israelites were bound to obey the Law that God gave them at Mt. Sinai. The Law was, simply put, a list of rules and regulations that described the government of God over his people. He expected obedience – strict obedience, upon pain of death. There was no leeway in this, either; one single broken Law and they were in trouble. The Law often required death as a punishment.

The key to understanding the Law is that *the Israelites themselves had to keep the Law*. "And if we are careful to obey all this Law before the LORD our God, as he has commanded us, *that* will be our righteousness." (Deuteronomy 6:25) They had to *do* what the Law said. When they did, God considered them righteous; if they didn't, God punished them.

Led by the Spirit

The history of the Israelites is a lesson on what happens when God turns us loose with the Law: we fail miserably. None of us can keep the Law as God requires it. The Israelites couldn't. Their sin and ignorance, the temptations of the world, the deceits of the enemy, all of that conspired to trip them up in their attempted obedience to the Law. The only man who ever kept the Law completely, to God's satisfaction, was Jesus – the Son of God.

Jesus did more than keep the Law, however. He bought a righteousness for us that none of us could achieve on our own. Now he is busy applying that righteousness of his to our souls – we're getting righteous the easy way! We are reaching a spiritual level that no Israelite could do on his own. But in order to pull this off, we have to be careful and let the Spirit guide us into that righteousness.

This is a subtle point that many people often miss. Though we claim to be Christians, and we understand that nothing that we do can save us or make us righteous in God's eyes, we still try our best to follow the Law! As if we could do what the Jews couldn't do! It's so tempting to follow the Law that the Galatians fell for the mistake, and Paul had to write rough rebukes to them for attempting to do what they couldn't do and they weren't allowed, as followers of Christ, to do.

> Are you so foolish? After beginning with the Spirit, are you now trying to attain your goal by human effort? Have you suffered so much for nothing — if it really was for nothing? Does God give you his Spirit and work miracles among you because you observe the Law, or because you believe what you heard? (Galatians 3:3-5)

A Christian isn't obligated to keep the Law; he can't anyway, so it's no use trying. He has a much better approach for becoming righteous: the Spirit of God is going to do it for him. Paul describes it this way:

> For what the Law was powerless to do in that it was weakened by the sinful nature, God did by sending his own Son in the likeness of sinful man to be a sin offering. And so he condemned sin in sinful man, in order that *the righteous requirements of the Law might be fully met in us*, who do not live according to the sinful nature but according to the Spirit. (Romans 8:3-4)

In other words, follow the Spirit, wherever he leads, and you will walk right into righteousness. He will change your heart for you, in a way that you couldn't dream of doing. His whole purpose is to take the righteousness of Christ – which is perfection, something the Law can never find fault with – and shape your soul with it. You will have the heart of a righteous man, and now you will automatically do the works of a righteous man without even thinking about it – as Jesus lives in you. When the Spirit is done with you, you will shine in the image of Christ. (2 Corinthians 3:18)

So the result is the same – a righteous man – but the methods are completely different. The Law just stands coolly off to one side, arms crossed, demanding that we obey or be punished. No help, no encouragement, no hope. But the Spirit goes about it in a different way: he gives us three spiritual skills: faith, hope and love. We find these three skills listed in several places in the New Testament.

> And now these three remain: **faith**, **hope**, and **love**.
> But the greatest of these is love. (1 Corinthians 13:13)

> ... we have heard of your **faith** in Christ Jesus and of the **love** you have for all the saints – the faith and love that spring from the **hope** that is stored up for you in Heaven ... (Colossians 1:4-5)
>
> ... your work produced by **faith**, your labor prompted by **love**, and your endurance inspired by **hope** in our Lord Jesus Christ. (1 Thessalonians 1:3)
>
> ... he has given us new birth into a living **hope** ... who through **faith** are shielded by God's power ... though you have not seen him, you **love** him ... (1 Peter 1:3, 5, 8)

Why are these skills so crucial for making us ready for Heaven?

> - *He gives us faith.* Faith, as we have seen, is walking in the light of Heaven. By faith we are enabled to see the reality of God, the reality of the treasures of Heaven, the true nature of Christ, the true state of our souls, the true nature of the world that we live in and why we don't want to stay here. Faith opens our spiritual eyes so that we can see the truth, just as the Bible describes it. Without faith we can see nothing.
>
> The Spirit has to open our eyes like this. And when he does, the sin, ignorance and misery that we used to live in falls away. It's the first step toward life. A person who can't see where his salvation is, will remain in darkness and die in his sins, though he might work as hard as he can at being pleasing to God. But the person who sees

how to reach salvation, and where it is, can start moving in that direction.

- *He gives us hope.* Hope isn't just wishing that something *might* come true; it's the assurance that it *will* be true. It's what we are waiting for, not wishing for; it's been promised to us, and it's only a matter of time until we receive it. Hope, as the Spirit gives it, keeps us going even when we have no other encouragement in this world, because we know what is waiting for us at the end.

Only the Spirit can give us this kind of hope. People without hope from the Spirit have no idea how God will receive them at Judgment Day; they "hope" that he will be merciful to them, but they have no reason for their "hope." But a Christian has already heard encouraging words from his Savior. He knows that Jesus went "to prepare a place" for him in Heaven, and the Father is waiting to receive them into an eternal family. Remember, the Spirit reveals the things of God: he shows us the heart of God, the love of God, the certainty of the promises of God. He shows us Christ, who came to save sinners and restore them to a relationship with their Father. When the Spirit shows us how certain these things are, we put our sights on Heaven now instead of earth. The temptations, the sins, the darkness of this world take on their true colors and we willingly turn our backs on all of that. It's not difficult to hate what is ugly and deadly; it becomes easy to love life.

- *He gives us love.* There are different kinds of love, but the kind of love that the Spirit puts in

Led by the Spirit

our heart is a self-sacrificing love. The New Testament word is **agape** (pronounced, ah-GAWP-ay). John tells us what this kind of love means:

> This is how we know what love is: Jesus Christ laid down his life for us. And we ought to lay down our lives for our brothers. (1 John 3:16)

Jesus said that our duty is to –

> 'Love the Lord your God with all your heart and with all your soul and with all your mind.' This is the first and greatest commandment. And the second is like it: 'Love your neighbor as yourself.' (Matthew 22:37-40)

A sinner isn't going to do this on his own; he sees no reason to love God whom he hates, nor love anybody else other than himself. But when the Spirit reveals the Father to us, especially the love of the Father in Christ Jesus, a love for God is born in our hearts. We love this God who first loved us. Why does this love suddenly show up in a hard heart, in a sinner who formerly didn't want anything to do with God? We can only account for such a thing by the Spirit re-making the heart and giving it the ability to love God. And because of our love for God, we won't settle for anything in this world – what we want is to be with *him*.

Someone who loves God will also love God's children, because they bear the image of their

Led by the Spirit

Father. Jesus is the oldest brother of a family, and we know that we are among our spiritual brothers and sisters. Again, this love comes because the Spirit works it into our hearts, revealing our family to us and showing us their spiritual needs that we can fulfill. And we want to fulfill those needs for them, because we want them in Heaven with us – just as Jesus wants all of us with him there. (John 17:24)

When the Spirit gives us these three skills – faith, hope, and love – we are now in the position to start walking with the Spirit and having our hearts conformed to the righteousness of Christ. Whereas someone under the Law had to try to obey the commandments, without the benefit of any outside help, a Spirit-led Christian finds himself lifted up into a spiritual world – through what he sees, hopes in, and loves. These abilities and feelings aren't natural to him – the Spirit works them into his heart – but they enable him to walk in a world of love, of wanting and living for the treasures of Heaven, of "hating even the clothing stained by corrupted flesh." (Jude 22) When we walk with God, with the help of the Spirit, the righteousness of Christ comes naturally to us. His life is the *only* life possible in Heaven! Anybody who lives completely in the world of sin and death will live as the world lives: Paul lists those sins in Galatians 5:19-21. But whoever lives in God's Kingdom will experience the life of Christ in their hearts:

> Love, joy, peace, patience, kindness, goodness, gentleness, faithfulness, and self-control. Against such things there is no Law. (Galatians 5:22-23)

Problems along the way

We need to pause for a minute and take a reality check. It's nice to talk about being led by the Spirit, and we Christians claim that we *want* God to lead us, but I'm afraid that there are going to be problems along the way. Though we say that we want to go to Heaven, and be made ready to serve God forever, we find the actual process too painful to bear. Like Lot's wife, we look back longingly at the world which the Spirit is leading us away from.

- *The treasures on earth* – We love our riches, our comforts, our reputations, our good life. We panic when any of that is threatened. We think that life isn't worth living if we have to go without the good things of the world. And while we argue with God about what we get to keep and what we have to get rid of, the Spirit shows us treasures in Heaven that are overwhelmingly more valuable than the entire universe. As if gold and silver come anywhere close to the value of the spiritual riches we have in Christ! For example, the Spirit counsels us that –

> Blessed is the man who finds wisdom,
>   the man who gains understanding,
> for she is more profitable than silver
>   and yields better returns than gold.
> She is more precious than rubies;
>   nothing you desire can compare with her.
> Long life is in her right hand;
>   in her left hand are riches and honor.
> Her ways are pleasant ways,
>   and all her paths are peace.
> She is a tree of life to those who embrace her;
>   those who lay hold of her will be blessed.
>   (Proverbs 3:13-18)

Of course this makes no sense to an unspiritual person. Gold we understand, but wisdom – and that means the wisdom from God's Word – we just don't see the importance of. We tend to love what we see, not what we don't see, and we work for what we love, not for what we don't love. So we usually fight against the Spirit as he tries to lead us toward Heavenly treasures and away from earthly ones.

- ***Our glory*** – Glory is when we take the credit for something. Just about everything we do is for our own glory. We like to be in the limelight; we like to think that we're in control of our lives, that our successes are due to our own decisions and good judgment. When we fail, we blame others – not ourselves. Anything that puts a good light on our character, our image, our social standing, our reputation – we're in favor of that. What we don't like is to appear helpless and in need of anything or anybody.

And this is precisely what the Spirit is trying to do to our proud hearts! He wants to show us that we are spiritually helpless unless God has mercy on us. He wants to prove that, without God, we are nothing and will be nothing. "But you do not realize that you are wretched, pitiful, poor, blind and naked." (Revelation 3:17) We have no hope unless God saves us, cleans us, remakes our hearts, renews our minds, sets us in the right direction, gives us a path to walk on, gives us the strength to walk, gives us the light to see by, gives us the wisdom we need to know the truth, and guides us every step of the way. To appear so helpless in this world, in front of our friends and especially our enemies, is one of the greatest fears we have.

- *Feed the flesh* – Our well-being and contentedness comes first in life. We look out for Number One first; everyone else, including God, has to wait their turn. We listen to and feed our lusts, because pleasure is our primary reason for living. We cry when we don't get what we want, and we ignore others in their need when we are well-fed and satisfied. And we like our pleasures so much that we work to make sure that we can repeat them whenever we want; we surround ourselves with opportunities to feed our flesh with the temptations of the world.

But the Spirit knows that this is death, not life. Living for this world means that we have no concern for the next world, where the real treasures are. He knows that the only way to open our eyes to the treasures of Heaven is to cut away the flesh, to crucify the flesh, to put the flesh to death – so that when what we love is *gone*, we will then look at what Christ has for us instead. This won't be easy. The flesh and the Spirit are at war with each other. (Galatians 5:17) The Spirit is out to kill the flesh with its lusts and rebellion, because nothing short of that will prepare us for Heaven. And the flesh resists the Spirit's sanctifying work at every turn because it knows that its death is at hand.

- *Our own kingdom* – Man was born to be a ruler – God made him a ruler over the earth – but now, in his sin and death, he does things to destroy himself and the world, not to build them up. Look at the mess we've created! We are best at hatred, killing, misery and persecution, ignorance, pollution, slaughter, greed, stealing and robbery, adultery and fornication, destruction of the family – the ugly list goes on.

We have clearly demonstrated what happens when we are in control of things. Now it's time for God to rule over us, and straighten out the mess. But as the Spirit works to build God's Kingdom among us, we aren't going to want to turn control over to him. We are going to question his authority, resist his influence, ignore his commands, doubt his good intentions, speak ill of his holy character, and generally do whatever will undermine his work among us.

He knows this will happen. Bring in a new King, set up new laws and regulations, start working toward a new society, and all the rebels will rise up in protest. It's bound to happen. We are going to fight and disagree and disobey at almost every turn. We might *say* that we bow to the Lord as our King, but in our hearts we despise his rule over us.

This is ugly, but unfortunately it's too often true of us. And when we fight the very one who came to help us, it positively grieves him. He has our well-being at heart! He wants to save us. And then we respond to his love by biting him, like a dog biting the one who tries to help him get loose from a trap that's killing him. It doesn't make sense.

"And do not grieve the Holy Spirit of God, with whom you were sealed for the day of redemption." (Ephesians 4:30) The Holy Spirit sealed us to be *saved* on the Last Day; why do we fight him and run away from our salvation? As he leads us to Heaven, using methods that are designed to make us holy, why do we resist his work in us?

"Do not put out the Spirit's fire." (1 Thessalonians 5:19) The Spirit fires our hearts, burning off the chaff of sin and worldliness, purifying the gold of God's grace and righteousness in our hearts. Why do we do things that fight against that purifying process? Why do we keep dumping things back into our hearts that quench the fires, that drown our hearts in the sludge and muck of the world's pigsty? He's getting us ready for Heaven; why do we insist on letting go of our salvation and drowning in an ocean of wickedness?

Only those who persevere to the end will be saved. (Matthew 10:22) Our theology should glorify God who can save anybody, but we can't hide behind our theology and lay back unconcerned in our sin. If we resist the Spirit, what hope do we have? When he leads us in God's ways, how can we expect to be saved when we go off in our own directions? When he applies the knife to our hearts to cut out the sin and lust, why do we think we will be saved when we run away and feed those lusts again – all the while claiming to be Christians?

> It is impossible for those who have once been enlightened, who have tasted the Heavenly gift, *who have shared in the Holy Spirit*, who have tasted the goodness of the word of God and the powers of the coming age, if they fall away, to be brought back to repentance, because to their loss they are crucifying the Son of God all over again and subjecting him to public disgrace. (Hebrews 6:4-6)

It's not time for theological arrogance, but for a genuine fear of God whom we are offending with our hypocrisy! Although many Biblical scholars have debated the meaning of

Hebrews 6:4-6, those who resist the Spirit's leading to life and holiness will learn its meaning all too well in the end.

How does he lead us?

Since our goal is Heaven, we have an immediate problem on our hands: how will we get there? Since Heaven is a spiritual place, there isn't anything on earth that can help us get there. In fact, most religions don't even pretend to deal with Heaven now, since we can't see it or feel it or know for sure that it even exists. Some of them promise Heaven in the end, but nobody knows for certain that such a place is real. Least of all do they offer us a way to get there *now*, before we die.

That's where the Spirit of God comes in for Christians. He does two things for us: ***first***, he shows us that Heaven is very real; he lets us taste the fruits of that Promised Land before we arrive there. ***Second***, he leads the way along certain prescribed paths; he shows us the way to Heaven.

Those paths to Heaven are well known to most people. Of course, many people make up their own roads to Heaven, claiming that they can reach God in any way that they please. They're wrong, and they will find out how wrong they were on Judgment Day when they stand face to face with a God they never knew! Their paths led them to their own gods, not to the God of the Bible. But many other people have heard about the true roads to Heaven, and have been taking those roads for a long time.

But it's entirely possible – in fact, it usually happens – that most people try to travel on these roads to Heaven *without* the Spirit leading them. One may as well try to drive on a road in pitch-black darkness! It's possible to try that, but it's impossible to arrive safely at your destination if you do. The Spirit has to show us the way as we travel that road; he sheds just enough light to show us the road at our feet, so that we know where to go next. Without him we will head off in the wrong direction, run into things that stop us, get into trouble, and get hopelessly lost.

These five roads lead to Heaven. Just remember two things: we have to take the right road, and the Spirit has to lead us on that road. We must at least get on these roads if we hope to see God, because no other roads will lead to him. But keep in mind that as we travel these roads, we have to keep tuned to the Spirit and let *him* do the driving!

- ***The Word of God*** – Man is a rational creature, the only one on the planet. And when God created Adam and Eve, he gave them a unique job: to rule over the creatures on earth in his place, in his Name. In order to do this, they had to have a mind capable of understanding God, the world, and what God wanted done in his new world. As they ruled the earth, they were to get their instructions and goals from the King of kings and see to it that God's wishes were carried out on earth.

  Adam and Eve fell into sin and created a gigantic mess as far as their original responsibilities were concerned. But now Christians have a second chance. They too are called by God to a special job: this time, they are lifted up higher than Adam and Eve and made kings and priests in God's spiritual Kingdom. (Revelation 20:6) Their calling is to help expand and rule over God's spiritual Kingdom (which is done this time by serving others, as Jesus pointed out – see Matthew 20:25-28).

  Again, in order to do this job, we need *information*. We need to know the mind of God,

Led by the Spirit

his instructions and will, his purposes, his likes and dislikes. We need to know what the seat of the Kingdom is like (Heaven), and we need to know the ways we can carry out his will on earth. There is a tremendous amount of information that we need if we are to do our jobs well.

This information comes from the Bible, the Word of God. That's the reason that God gave us this book: so that we will know what his will is, what his Kingdom is like, what our place is in his plans, what our resources are, what we are called to do, and what only God can do.

> "No eye has seen, no ear has heard, no mind has conceived what God has prepared for those who love him"— but God has revealed it to us by his Spirit. The Spirit searches all things, even the deep things of God. For who among men knows the thoughts of a man except the man's spirit within him? In the same way no one knows the thoughts of God except the Spirit of God. We have not received the spirit of the world but the Spirit who is from God, *that we may understand what God has freely given us*. This is what we speak, not in words taught us by human wisdom but in words taught by the Spirit, expressing spiritual truths in spiritual words. (1 Corinthians 2:9-13)

The Spirit shows us the truth, which men have searched for throughout history and never found. Here, though, in the Bible, we find out what is really going on – God reveals the truth about

Led by the Spirit

ourselves, our world, about himself. We also see that other religions and philosophies have been deceiving us! This may sound narrow-minded, but it was Jesus himself who put us on to this idea: "*Your Word* is truth." (John 17:17)

So, if you want to see God, study the Bible. Spend time in it; learn it; meditate on it; master it; use it. Here is the information you need to fulfill your destiny as king and priest in God's Kingdom. You can't do your job to God's satisfaction without it. For example, here are a few passages that show how important it is to get God's wisdom: "I have hidden your Word in my heart that I might not sin against you." (Psalm 119:11) "Give me wisdom and knowledge, that I may lead this people, for who is able to govern this great people of yours?" (2 Chronicles 1:10) "My people are destroyed from lack of knowledge. Because you have rejected knowledge, I also reject you as my priests." (Hosea 4:6) "If you remain in me and *my words* remain in you, ask whatever you wish, and it will be given you." (John 15:17)

If you "meditate" on the Word of God, "by day and night" (Psalm 1:2), then expect to find the Spirit of God there. This is his testimony to you about the spiritual world of God. He is behind all the Bible, behind everything that every writer wrote and what every person saw and heard about God. The Spirit of God is the primary "eyewitness" to the reality of God, and he helps all of us to see and know God – from the Apostle Paul to the least saint in Christ's Church. He lives in this Book. He is ready to help you see God in it, if you come to him in the right way.

But remember that we *could* take matters in our own hands and try to drive this road without the help of the Spirit. Most people, sad to say, do this very thing. They know the Scriptures by heart; they know doctrine and theology; they can quote chapter and verse. Many of them are masters of the Bible. The trouble is, they have no spiritual understanding of any of it – and you can tell, because they aren't any closer to Heaven or more skillful in spiritual duties for all their knowledge. They aren't being made to look like Christ.

The Jews in Jesus' day were famous for this. Jesus uncovered their problem in a revealing condemnation:

> You have never heard his voice nor seen his form, nor does his word dwell in you, for you do not believe the one he sent. You diligently study the Scriptures because you think that by them you possess eternal life. These are the Scriptures that testify about me, yet you refuse to come to me to have life. (John 5:37-40)

They knew the Old Testament far better than we know our New Testaments today! But they were driving down the road of Scripture by themselves; turning their backs on the Spirit, they could only see what they wanted to see – not what God wanted to show them in the Bible. So for all their Biblical knowledge, they actually got farther away from Heaven!

Led by the Spirit

We do this all the time, each in our own way. We are blind to certain subjects in the Bible, because we don't want to think about them or we were deceived about them by others. We form our own opinions that take the place of what the Bible teaches – so that instead of getting our knowledge about God from the Bible, we simply make up what we want our God to be instead. Or we will get off-balance, emphasizing one idea in the Bible so much that we ignore other important ideas that we also ought to be studying. And we often find ourselves reading the Bible for the wrong reasons: instead of coming to listen to God and receive whatever he says to us there, we search through it for support for our own special purposes, things that the Bible was *not* written for.

But in order to be led of the Spirit when we read the Bible, we must come humbly, ready to listen and learn, ready to throw out what we thought we knew and replace it all with new information – *his* information. When we come like this, the Spirit will do something for us that we could have never done on our own: he will make the world of God real, so much so that we will know the *certainty* of what we read about. He will let us taste the fruit of Heaven, and see the treasures waiting for us that Jesus talked about. We will see who Jesus really is – not a dead, historical figure that only exists in a dusty Bible, but a living Savior that is ready to do for us everything that we read about in the Biblical account of him. The Spirit makes this world of God come alive for us. When we read the Bible in the Spirit, we *know* (we can't prove it to anybody, but that doesn't make it any less real!) that there is a God and that it pays to live for him. (Hebrews 11:6)

And when we study the Bible in the Spirit, ready to be led and taught by him, he will show us what God thinks is important for us to know, not what many people *think* is important to know. For example, many people think that it's important to know one's system of doctrine, according to the denomination or local church or traditions handed down to them from the past. But the Bible tells us plainly that there are certain things that we *must* know in order to please God and be able to serve him faithfully – and usually these things aren't often taught in the local church! For a start, look at Psalm 105:1-11. This says that we must know about his Name, his works, his covenant with Abraham, his judgments, his miracles, and true worship. You will find that these are *not* topics in a standard theology textbook! And for that reason, very few people know much about these topics. But in order to please God, according to this passage, we must know a great deal about *these* subjects. Do you?

- ***Prayer and Worship*** – Obviously, if we want to get in touch with God, one of the primary ways of doing that is through prayer and worship. Now there are two ways to pray: you could either stay here on earth and try sending a message Heavenward, hoping that it gets there somehow; or you could deliver the message in person – right into the presence of God.

Ordinarily, people don't understand the second approach. Prayer to them means saying a formula, or even pouring out their heart with deep meaning and feeling – by *long distance*. They hope that their prayer reaches Heaven; but they don't know for certain that it does. But it really doesn't matter, because they are so used to praying in this way that they don't know that there is another way.

This is what I meant by driving by yourself. Many people pray, because they instinctively know that prayer is one of the roads to Heaven. What they don't know, however, is that in order to get there they have to turn control over to the Spirit and let him take them there.

This is so important that Paul counsels us –

Pray *in the Spirit* on all occasions with all kinds of prayers and requests. (Ephesians 6:18)

He knew that we can't hope to reach God in prayer without the Spirit leading us there.

"Praying in the Spirit" is a highly charged subject today due to the charismatic movement. We are not defining it here, though, as many do – visions, ecstatic utterances, prayer languages, etc. The answer is very straightforward and simple – we do it exactly as the Bible says. When you pray in the Spirit, this is what will happen: you will come into the presence of God. You won't be stuck on earth anymore; spiritually you will be lifted up and brought before God. You will see the Temple in Heaven, and the saints gathered there. You will hear continuous worship from the multitudes which surround God's throne.

Led by the Spirit

> But you have come to Mount Zion, to the Heavenly Jerusalem, the city of the living God. You have come to thousands upon thousands of angels in joyful assembly, to the church of the firstborn, whose names are written in Heaven. You have come to God, the judge of all men, to the spirits of righteous men made perfect, to Jesus the mediator of a new covenant, and to the sprinkled blood that speaks a better word than the blood of Abel. (Hebrews 12:22-24)

Isaiah saw this. When the Spirit enabled him to enter Heaven, this is what he saw:

> In the year that King Uzziah died, I saw the LORD seated on a throne, high and exalted, and the train of his robe filled the temple. Above him were seraphs, each with six wings: With two wings they covered their faces, with two they covered their feet, and with two they were flying. And they were calling to one another: "Holy, holy, holy is the LORD Almighty; the whole earth is full of his glory." At the sound of their voices the doorposts and thresholds shook and the temple was filled with smoke. "Woe to me!" I cried. "I am ruined! For I am a man of unclean lips, and I live among a people of unclean lips, and my eyes have seen the King, the LORD Almighty." (Isaiah 6:1-5)

Led by the Spirit

The Apostle John was in the Spirit, we are told, when he saw Jesus in his glory:

> On the Lord's Day I was in the Spirit ... I turned around to see the voice that was speaking to me. And when I turned I saw seven golden lampstands, and among the lampstands was someone "like a son of man." (Revelation 1:10, 12-13)

I hope you realize that you will experience the reality of Heaven only as you read his Word. The two go hand in hand. You can't see the true Heaven apart from the only revelation of Heaven; you can only hear God speak to you when you open the book in which he spoke to you. And it's not as if we must get a full-scale vision like the old prophets did; the Spirit stands ready to take *any* believer to Heaven, through the Word, and enlighten their minds and understanding with its reality. We *all* must worship this way. Jesus put it in a nutshell:

> Yet a time is coming and has now come when the true worshipers will worship the Father *in Spirit and truth*, for they are the kind of worshipers the Father seeks. God is Spirit, and his worshipers must worship *in Spirit* and *in truth*. (John 4:23-24)

We aren't prone to do things this way; we would rather pray and worship under our own power. What we usually do, therefore, since we can't see God or any part of his spiritual Kingdom, is focus on ourselves in prayer. (This is inevitable when we won't use the Bible as our prayer book.)

Led by the Spirit

We want God to come down to *us*. This comes out most clearly in our "Christmas lists" that we haul out during prayer. We naturally have our own interests at heart, and we want God to get started working on certain things in order to please us. In other words, we tell him what *we* want! We come up with the answers and expect him to get busy filling our list. This is always wrong. God is the Lord, we are his servants. If the Spirit were really leading us in prayer, we would come in humility before the King who is waiting for us to listen to *him* and be ready to do what he wants. Solomon taught us how to worship like this:

> Guard your steps when you go to the house of God. Go near to listen rather than to offer the sacrifice of fools, who do not know that they do wrong. Do not be quick with your mouth, do not be hasty in your heart to utter anything before God. God is in Heaven and you are on earth, so let your words be few. As a dream comes when there are many cares, so the speech of a fool when there are many words. (Ecclesiastes 5:1-3)

Another way we end up driving prayer and worship on our own is by insisting on certain rules and traditions made by men, as if "true worship" has to be done according to methods that *we* approve. This is obviously ridiculous. If there are a million churches in the world, and if we think that just *our* church is worshipping God in the only correct way, then 999,999 churches are doing false worship! That's not true. The rules of worship are made in Heaven, not on earth, and only the Spirit can show us what those rules are and enable us to follow them in a spiritual way. It's closer to the truth to say that a little of true worship happens in many churches around the world – usually in spite of man's traditions and efforts! We will discover that the outward practices that we've invented in our forms of worship do us little good in the spiritual court of Heaven, where flesh and blood can't go, and where all creatures must worship God *in Spirit*.

And we also show that we are doing the driving when we worship false gods. None of us in our Christian circles would claim to do such a thing, of course; we all take the name of Christ upon us and claim to be worshipping the one God. But think of this: if we say that our God is like such and such, but the Bible's description of him is different than what we say he is, how can we claim to be worshipping the Bible's God? Many people worship a "God" who allows sin, who doesn't do miracles for his people, who "helps those who helps themselves," who doesn't require a sacrifice for sin. This is *not* the Bible's God – therefore we can assume that the Spirit is *not* leading them in their prayers.

When the Spirit leads us in prayer and worship, we *see* what we hope in – the one true God. We can also expect to get answers. Those treasures in Heaven that we see through the Spirit are for us. Those are the answers for our prayers, waiting to be given out. Praying in the Spirit means that we get close enough to God to take what he has given us in Jesus. In other words, prayer done in the

Led by the Spirit

Spirit *will* get answers from Heaven, because that's what true prayer is all about.

In case you're worried about whether you *can* pray in the Spirit, God has that problem covered too. Of course we can't simply press a button that instantly turns our prayer into a spiritual success. Often when we pray, we feel anything but successful – we wonder if we're getting through to God at all. But if you come to him prepared to let him lead, prepared for what he has in store for you, then rest assured that he *will* make it work. Even if we don't know what to do, he will get us to Heaven and train us in how to act in God's presence:

> The Spirit helps us in our weakness. We do not know what we ought to pray for, but the Spirit himself intercedes for us with groans that words cannot express. And he who searches our hearts knows the mind of the Spirit, because the Spirit intercedes for the saints in accordance with God's will. (Romans 8:26-27)

- *Walking in Faith* – Christians are people of faith. One of the best known passages concerning this life of faith is found in Romans:

> For in the Gospel a righteousness from God is revealed, a righteousness that is by faith from first to last, just as it is written: "The righteous will *live by faith*." (Romans 1:17)

Led by the Spirit

What isn't so obvious is what this means. Faith isn't just believing in a set of doctrines, or holding onto your religious beliefs with all your heart. If this is faith, then just about everyone would have faith – and be headed to Heaven! But we know that's not true.

Faith is living in the light of God's world. Until we have faith, we have no idea of the true nature of this world, or of our hearts, or even who God really is. We are blind and spiritually in the dark. But when God makes us alive in Christ, he makes our formerly-dead souls alive spiritually so that we can see now. We can see him, we can hear him, we know when he touches us. Spiritual things aren't hearsay for us anymore, but realities. We can't prove them to others who are still blind, but we know, nevertheless, that they are real.

> Faith is *being sure* of what we hope for, and *certain* of what we do not see. (Hebrews 11:1)

That is, we don't see them with our physical eyes, but with our new spiritual eyes. We see these things because the Spirit shines his light down from Heaven all around us. We are living in light, and we can see what is around us now. Now when we walk around, we know what dangers to avoid – we can see that they *are* dangerous and what they will do to us. We can see our spiritual brothers and sisters and pick them out from among the people we know. We know what they need, and we know that we can and ought to help them. We can see Jesus for what he is, and we know why we need him for all of our spiritual needs. We can see that God filled Jesus with treasures of Heaven. We can hear God speak to us in his Word – "The sheep ... know his voice." (John 10:4)

Walking by faith, in other words, is living according to certain spiritual realities that *you* can see, but others can't see. They are going to think you're crazy for being a Christian! It's because they don't have that faith, that ability to see God and his Kingdom, so naturally they will live in a different way. They are on the road to death and they don't know it. You are on the road to life and, by the mercy of God, you know that you are.

Again, I hope you realize that this can't happen unless you study God's Word (where that spiritual world is laid out before you) and are led by the Spirit (who reveals all spiritual realities to God's people). We keep coming back to this, don't we?

But there is a way of having "faith" without the Spirit's help; most people have this kind of "faith." They hold to a set of "beliefs" that they feel describe what they need to know to get along in life. They might have gotten it from their ancestors – a set of traditions, in other words – or they got it from their culture, or they came up with it on their own. Wherever they got it, they hold to it as Gospel truth. They think that if they faithfully stick to these beliefs then everything will turn out all right for them in the end.

That's not what the Bible describes as true faith, however. We know this because these people keep saying things that directly contradict what the Bible teaches! For instance, these misguided people feel very comfortable in this world, and have found ways to rely on the world in many ways and look to the world to fulfill their needs. But the Bible warns us with a revelation about the world:

> Do not love the world or anything in the world. If anyone loves the world, the love of the Father is not in him. For everything in the world — the cravings of sinful man, the lust of his eyes and the boasting of what he has and does — comes not from the Father but from the world. The world and its desires pass away, but the man who does the will of God lives forever. (1 John 2:15-17)

God has plans to destroy the world. There is nothing in the world that can help our souls, or even fulfill the great spiritual needs in our hearts. The world is full of darkness, deceit, wickedness, violence, death, destruction, failure and hopelessness. The world is enemy territory – God's people don't belong here! We are actually "aliens and strangers" as long as we are still in this world! (Hebrews 11:13; 1 Peter 2:11) Our home is Heaven, where Jesus has gone to prepare a place for us. (John 14:1-4) Only someone who lives by faith will see this.

Another way we turn our backs on the Spirit is when we try to control our own destiny, when we dream up what *we* want to do and then demand that God go along with our plans. We piously call this "living by faith" – meaning that we are going to believe, with all our hearts, that God will do what *we* want. But that isn't living by faith. "In his heart a man plans his course, but the LORD determines his steps." (Proverbs 16:9) The Spirit must lead us through life, putting us through trials and troubles that God has determined is for our good. He teaches us in his Word the things we are responsible to do, and gives us strength from Heaven to perform those duties faithfully. Only as we go where *he* tells us to go in life will he bless us with success.

The key to living by faith is to take advantage of what the Spirit has put at our disposal. Through the Word, and because of his promise to take us there, we are to –

> … set your hearts on things above, where Christ is seated at the right hand of God. Set your minds on things above, not on earthly things. For you died, and your life is now hidden with Christ in God. (Colossians 3:1-3)

When we have our eyes set on the things in Heaven, naturally our hearts will follow after. We will be working toward that, instead of things on earth. And that's what we want: there is life there with God, and only death here on earth.

You prove that your faith is genuine when you follow Christ's advice:

> Do not store up for yourselves treasures on earth, where moth and rust destroy, and where thieves break in and steal. But store up for yourselves treasures in Heaven, where moth and rust do not destroy, and

Led by the Spirit

where thieves do not break in and steal. For where your treasure is, there your heart will be also. (Matthew 6:19-21)

This makes no sense to someone who can't see those treasures. And for those who like the sound of it, but still can't see it, they won't have any *certainty* that they are really doing the right thing and they might think longingly on the pleasures that they could have had from the world. But those who live by the Spirit can easily see what is in store for them in Heaven, and their walk through life (which often means doing without the pleasures of earth) is much easier in that light.

Walking by the faith that the Spirit gives means that we don't go by outward appearances. This world looks too good to pass up; its temptations are tempting, its treasures look valuable, its dangers appear frightening. But when we get true faith, we see that the world's treasures and temptations are empty promises that don't fulfill us. We see that dangers are toothless monsters that can do nothing to those protected by God. Paul describes it this way: "We live by faith, not by sight." (2 Corinthians 5:7) We don't go by what our physical senses tell us, but by what our spiritual senses tell us – since we are now spiritually aware of God's world.

- ***The Church*** – Amazingly, through good times and bad, there has always been a true Church. Tyrants have been unable to destroy it, and power and prosperity have been unable to permanently corrupt it. Not that the Church has always been in good spiritual health – it usually isn't – but its persistence is impressive proof of its divine birth.

Let's define our terms at the beginning, however, before we get confused. By the "Church" I mean the body of Christ, the true believers who have found eternal life in him. They are adopted children of God, marked out to be "kings and priests" in his Kingdom, and appointed to receive the inheritance of Heaven waiting for them. They were once like all wicked people, living in darkness and sin and death; but Christ saved them from that moral and spiritual disaster and, through the Spirit, is making them fit for eternal life in the presence of the holy God.

This isn't the same as the "churches" that we go to on Sundays. Members of the true Church attend these services, and sit next to people who aren't part of the true Church. What people mistakenly call "church" is usually a social event, or religious meeting, at which little if anything spiritual actually goes on.

This may sound harsh, but history bears out the picture. It's awful what has happened in the name of Christ's Church throughout history. True believers would never claim the ridiculous and painful episodes of churches doing what God never told them to do.

When a person becomes a Christian, he automatically becomes part of the Church of Christ – no matter where or when he lives in the world, no matter what his culture or race or sex or political stripe. And with that "membership" comes certain spiritual privileges: he is heir to God's promises, he is part of the family of God (with Jesus as our elder brother), he is marked to escape the destruction coming on the world, his sins are put away "as far as the east is from the west," and many more privileges.

But though these things are automatic, *living* in the Church isn't. It really takes a spiritual maturity to live with others who are in that same fellowship, which is one of the ironies of Christianity. Though we are new creatures, brothers and sisters under one Father, possessed of one Spirit and one faith, we can't seem to get along with each other! Where there ought to be peace, there is usually war and division. Often one has more enemies *in* the Church than outside of it!

The Bible says that God intends us to be *one body*. In Christ he united both Jew and Gentile to make one man. (Ephesians 2:14-18) As you would expect, then, Jesus told us to live as if we were one family: "My command is this: love each other as I have loved you." (John 15:12) And since God is love, "whoever does not love does not know God, for God is love." (1 John 4:8)

The trouble is that we can't possibly do this without the Spirit of God. So, to make the impossible happen, God sent his Spirit to dwell among us. It's *in the Church* that the Spirit lives and works among us. In one of the most beautiful images of the Old Testament, we see how God works on us:

Led by the Spirit

> How good and pleasant it is
>   when brothers live together in unity!
> It is like precious oil poured on the head,
>   running down on the beard,
> running down on Aaron's beard,
>   down upon the collar of his robes.
> It is as if the dew of Hermon
>   were falling on Mount Zion.
> For *there* the LORD bestows his blessing,
> even life forevermore. (Psalm 133:1-3)

Oil was a symbol of the Spirit, and Aaron represents the high priest – who is, for us, Jesus. The Spirit comes down on us from the Head, who is Christ. But look at what he says about eternal life – it will be found *in the body of Christ*, as the Spirit works among us. In other words, we can't continue to be loners, not if we want to get to Heaven. The road to eternal life is by way of the Church of Christ.

One of the most powerful ways that the Spirit works on us in the Church is through the spiritual gifts. They are listed for us in several places; here is one list:

> But to each one of us grace has been given as Christ apportioned it. This is why it says: "When he ascended on high, he led captives in his train and gave gifts to men." ... It was he who gave some to be Apostles, some to be prophets, some to be evangelists, and some to be pastors and teachers, to prepare God's people for works of service, so that the body of Christ may be built up until we all reach unity in the faith

and in the knowledge of the Son of God and become mature, attaining to the whole measure of the fullness of Christ. (Ephesians 4:7-13)

This passage also shows us *why* the Spirit gives gifts in the Church: to "prepare God's people for works of service." Do you remember that we were given a job to do in God's Kingdom? Here is how you will be trained to do that job! As others do their job for your spiritual benefit, you will grow enough to start doing your job for the benefit of others. It was for good reason that the Bible likens it to a living body: each part does its job for the benefit of the whole.

But the reason that this doesn't often happen in a local church is that people don't want to follow the Spirit when they "do church." They immediately take control away from the Spirit and do things their own way. Instead of listening to the Head of the Body – that is, Christ – and letting him run things, they assume that things won't get done unless *they* do it. So they volunteer for jobs that they have no spiritual skill for. They decide what the worship service will be like, even though little of it focuses on God or directs people toward him. They draw attention to themselves. They get followings, and they criticize everyone who won't join willingly in *their* program. They try to do the church's work in the ways that the world would go about things, instead of the ways that God likes to work.

They obviously don't have any trust at all that the Spirit knows how to run the Church! If they would do things God's way, and wait on God to provide what they need in a local church, much of the sin, ignorance and failure in our churches today wouldn't be happening. When God does things, they work; when *we* are running the show, however, nothing works – at least in a spiritual sense. For a while it may appear that we are achieving our purposes in our church programs, but it's only a superficial success and time will show how empty and powerless they were.

One of the surest ways to grieve the Spirit in the life of the Church is to say almost nothing about God and Christ in the service. For some reason, this spiritual shortsightedness seems to be rampant in today's churches. Take notes during a service and you will see what I mean. God's name is used a lot, but almost nothing is said *about* him. The emphasis is almost always, "*We* must do this, *we* must be this way, *we* must avoid sin, *we* must have faith, *we* must carry the cross, *we* must pray, *we* must persevere, *we* must trust in God." As you can see, the content of the message is *man*, not God. There is no salvation in that! When we worship, supposedly we are come together to meet *him* and to see *him*. The teaching, the preaching, the hymns, the testimony, the encouragement – all of it is supposed to uncover and reveal our God so that we can all see him more clearly. When that happens, then we see him well enough to know him and put our trust in him. That's what the Spirit does: he reveals God, and Christ our Savior. Without this revelation in church, we have no God and therefore no hope for our lives.

Led by the Spirit

Jesus said that to *know God* is eternal life. (John 17:3) So tell me about him! What is he like? What does he do? What are his ways? What is his Kingdom like? When I learn something about God, *then* I know where I fit into his world. For example, if Paul would have written Ephesians 4-6 (our spiritual responsibilities) without first writing Ephesians 1-3 (knowledge about God in Christ) it would have made no sense, and we would have no hope of ever achieving such an impossible lifestyle.

One other way that people "do church" without the Spirit is to turn the whole thing into a social affair. They know down inside that they need "religion" in some form, and "religion" happens at church, so they go to church to get some "religion." But since true religion doesn't get into us this way, what results is just a time for gossip and play and politicking and conversations about everything under the sun except spiritual matters! This doesn't help us to grow spiritually, obviously, so we can assume that the Spirit has nothing to do with church meetings like this.

When Christians rely on the Spirit to make the Church work for them, spiritual impossibilities happen. People learn about God there; they see him at work there. They get trained in spiritual skills and go out into the world ready to work. They share God's concern for a lost and dying world. They hear about Heaven and see others living for the treasures of Heaven, and so are encouraged to do the same. They learn to love each other, they see precious children of God in each other, and they gladly do things for each other that may even cost them something. They get strong there – there is strength in unity – and successfully frustrate the work of the enemy, both in the Church and in the world where they live and work. And they become shining lights in the darkness, living witnesses to the power of God in a holy life.

A church led by the Spirit *works*. There isn't spiritual failure there, but success. It looks like this:

> As a prisoner for the Lord, then, I urge you to live a life worthy of the calling you have received. Be completely humble and gentle; be patient, bearing with one another in love. Make every effort to keep the unity of the Spirit through the bond of peace. There is one body and one Spirit — just as you were called to one hope when you were called — one Lord, one faith, one baptism; one God and Father of all, who is over all and through all and in all. (Ephesians 4:1-6)

If a church doesn't look like this, and *stay* like this, then the Spirit isn't leading them.

- ***The Cross*** – Now for the fatal flaw of our human nature. When we think that we have Heaven wrapped up, that we can have anything there that we want, that God will just let us cruise painlessly into his Kingdom without giving up anything along the way, along comes Paul with some bad news:

Led by the Spirit

I declare to you, brothers, that flesh and blood cannot inherit the Kingdom of God, nor does the perishable inherit the imperishable. (1 Corinthians 15:50)

God is Spirit, and whoever worships him must do it in Spirit and in Truth. (John 4:24) Heaven is spiritual, and all the inhabitants there are spiritual. Physical things can't exist in such a rarefied atmosphere; we would die from the lack of a physical framework to support us.

There's an additional problem. We were born into sin, so much so that we naturally follow the lusts of our flesh for everything we want. We are slaves to the temptations of the world, which deceive us and lead us into finding ways of fulfilling those lusts. But we were not originally designed to live like this! God made us to control the inclinations of our bodies and follow his instructions only, enjoying the physical world only within the limitations of his Law. But ever since Adam made the fateful decision to be ruled by his own feelings, desires and opinions, we turned our backs, collectively as a human race, on God and his will. Living according to what we want and feel has resulted in the misery and wickedness and death that constantly surrounds us.

Paul tells us plainly what our flesh leads us into:

> For the sinful nature desires what is contrary to the Spirit, and the Spirit what is contrary to the sinful nature. They are in conflict with each other, so that you do not

Led by the Spirit

do what you want ... The acts of the sinful nature are obvious: sexual immorality, impurity and debauchery; idolatry and witchcraft; hatred, discord, jealousy, fits of rage, selfish ambition, dissensions, factions and envy; drunkenness, orgies, and the like. I warn you, as I did before, that those who live like this will not inherit the Kingdom of God. (Galatians 5:17,19-21)

The solution is to crucify the flesh. This isn't good news; it means pain, suffering, trials, discipline, hard times. It means doing without what our flesh desperately wants. It means traveling a lonely road when others do exactly what they please, and putting up with their mocking. It means walking with Jesus, who suffered for his faith, and parting company with those who refuse to go to God for life.

Someone once described the flesh as being like a vicious dog. Feed it, and it will get stronger and meaner. But starve it, and it will grow weaker and eventually die – and cease to be a problem! That's what Paul meant when he said, "So I say, live by the Spirit, and you will not gratify the desires of the sinful nature." (Galatians 5:16) Quit feeding the flesh with the temptations that it wants, and it will lose the strength and power that it once had. Then the soul, fed by the Spirit from the Master's table in Heaven, will daily grow in strength to the point that we will be able and willing to live by God's will instead.

Many people know about the "cross" in life, but they are mistaken as to what it really means.

Led by the Spirit

They think that they have to take care of this matter of crucifying the flesh themselves – without God's help. You probably have heard about those who invent crosses to carry: they beat themselves, they give up something for Lent, they deny themselves legitimate blessings in life, they become hermits, they create new rules and conform to outward customs and traditions to set themselves apart from the world, and so on. But none of this works – it doesn't really please God, because it's all on the outside and does nothing to change our souls into the righteous person that he requires.

> Since you died with Christ to the basic principles of this world, why, as though you still belonged to it, do you submit to its rules: "Do not handle! Do not taste! Do not touch!"? These are all destined to perish with use, because they are based on human commands and teachings. Such regulations indeed have an appearance of wisdom, with their self-imposed worship, their false humility and their harsh treatment of the body, but they lack any value in restraining sensual indulgence. (Colossians 2:20-23)

But when the Spirit is free to determine what our cross will be, it changes our souls. I like the image in Isaiah that talks about this:

> My loved one had a vineyard on a fertile hillside. He dug it up and cleared it of stones and planted it with the choicest vines. He built a watchtower in it and cut out a winepress as well. Then he looked for

a crop of good grapes, but it yielded only bad fruit. (Isaiah 5:1-2)

God plants us as vines, in the soil of this world, and tends us as a gardener. He clears our hearts of the stones of sin and hardness to him. He builds a winepress – trials and troubles designed to squeeze our hearts – so that he can get good juice out of us (the fruit of the Spirit). Those troubles, in other words, are crosses that are specially designed to determine what we really are inside, spiritually. If we fail our test, we fail him. And unfortunately this is precisely where we often fail God – in how we handle the hardships of life that he takes us through.

We don't like to think that our problems are due to God's testing us, but it's true. We are his children! And in order to make us fit to live in his house, he has to trim the old nature from us, and clothe us in the righteousness of Christ. The writer of Hebrews puts the thing into perspective for us.

> Endure hardship as discipline; God is treating you as sons. For what son is not disciplined by his father? If you are not disciplined (and everyone undergoes discipline), then you are illegitimate children and not true sons. Moreover, we have all had human fathers who disciplined us and we respected them for it. How much more should we submit to the Father of our spirits and live! Our fathers disciplined us for a little while as they thought best; but God disciplines us for our good, that we may share in his holiness. No discipline

seems pleasant at the time, but painful. Later on, however, it produces a harvest of righteousness and peace for those who have been trained by it. (Hebrews 12:7-11)

Paul tells us that "we know that in all things God works for the good of those who love him, who have been called according to his purpose." (Romans 8:28) It's a beautiful sight to see a Christian accepting the Spirit's leading and shouldering the cross that God provides. Someone who willingly and cheerfully accepts hardships as opportunities for spiritual growth is a wise Christian. They resemble Paul, who said –

> To keep me from becoming conceited because of these surpassingly great revelations, there was given me a thorn in my flesh, a messenger of Satan, to torment me. Three times I pleaded with the Lord to take it away from me. But he said to me, "My grace is sufficient for you, for my power is made perfect in weakness." Therefore I will boast all the more gladly about my weaknesses, so that Christ's power may rest on me. That is why, for Christ's sake, I delight in weaknesses, in insults, in hardships, in persecutions, in difficulties. For when I am weak, then I am strong. (2 Corinthians 12:7-10)

However, you will often find that those who rely the most on their own outward signs of their religion will fall the hardest when God puts *his* crosses on them. Putting your trust in your own crosses will turn you into a spiritual wimp;

naturally you will go easy on yourself, especially in those areas where you want the least interference. But that's the target that the Spirit aims for, and when he hits you with a cross that crucifies your favorite area you are really going to hurt! That's what separates the sheep from the goats.

You don't always have to get hit so hard, however – if you are used to following the Spirit, that is. If you already know that he wants you to put away a certain sin, then you can work *with* him in this instead of against him. If you fight him, he's going to come back with discipline and *make* you conform to God's righteous standards. But if you walk *with* him, then you'll know not to stray into areas that he doesn't approve.

> Dear friends, I urge you, as aliens and strangers in the world, to abstain from sinful desires, which war against your soul. Live such good lives among the pagans that, though they accuse you of doing wrong, they may see your good deeds and glorify God on the day he visits us. (1 Peter 2:11-12)

Just say no! You can avoid a lot of trouble from sin that way, and you'll avoid getting into trouble with God too. That's what Paul meant by "keeping in step with the Spirit." (Galatians 5:25)

Led by the Spirit?

To sum up, it's entirely possible *to try* to get to Heaven on your own. Many people try it, and fail. The reason they fail is because they reject the means of getting there, which God has graciously provided for us in the Spirit.

The Spirit knows how to get us to Heaven, and he is capable of getting us there safely and ready to enjoy the new world of God. He also knows that you must *change*: and there is a lot of work to be done on your soul before you are ready for Heaven. You aren't going to particularly like the ways he prepares you, but you have to submit yourself to his leading, wherever that takes you, knowing that God has your good at heart.

But for those who give up trying to get there on their own goodness and works, and give up trying to keep the Law on their own, living in the power and revelation of the Spirit is a refreshing change. Things work when he leads us.

The Names of Christ

Jesus' names mean something. Our names don't necessarily mean anything special, but God's names do. They are either special Hebrew or Greek words that have particular meanings, or they are descriptions of his character or work. Every name of Jesus has a meaning that we must study and meditate on. There is a reason for his name: either there is a problem in our lives that the name will solve, or it is a weapon that we can use against our enemies, or it is a source of strength and nourishment that we aren't getting from the world. We can't afford to miss *any* of his names, any more than we can do without a well-balanced diet. We might not know how to use a particular name yet, but rest assured that it has a use and we will need it someday. Jacob, for example, needed the "God of Abraham and the God of Isaac" for the kinds of trials he was about to face and the lessons he needed to learn. (Genesis 28:13)

What are the names of Jesus? The Bible is full of them — the problem is deciding which names to take time out to study! Here are some of the more important names and what they mean.

The Names of Christ

Advocate	*Job 16:19*
All & in all	*Colossians 3:11*
Alpha & Omega	*Revelation 21:6*
Altar	*Hebrews 13:10*
Ark	*Hebrews 11:7*
Atoning sacrifice	*1 John 4:10*
Author of our faith	*Hebrews 12:2*
Banner	*Isaiah 11:10*
Bright morning star	*Revelation 22:16*
Brother	*Hebrews 2:11*
Clothing	*Romans 13:14*
Cornerstone	*1 Peter 2:6*
Creator	*Colossians 1:16*
Dew	*Hosea 14:5*
Door	*John 10:9*
Everlasting Father	*Isaiah 9:6*
Example	*John 13:15*
Faithful witness	*Revelation 19:11*
Firstborn	*Colossians 1:15*
Food	*John 6:51*
Foundation	*1 Corinthians 3:11*
Fountain	*Zechariah 13:1*
Freedom	*John 8:36*
Friend	*Matthew 11:19*
Good Shepherd	*John 10:11,14*
Head	*Colossians 1:18*
High Priest	*Hebrews 4:14*
Holiness	*1 Corinthians 1:30*
Holy One of God	*Mark 1:24*
Hope	*1 Timothy 1:1*
Horn	*Luke 1:68,69*
Husband	*Ephesians 5:25*
I am	*Exodus 3:14*
Immanuel	*Matthew 1:23*
Jesus	*Matthew 1:21*
King of kings	*Revelation 19:16*

The Names of Christ

Ladder	*Genesis 28:12*
Lamb of God	*John 1:29*
Life	*Colossians 3:4*
Light	*John 12:46*
Lion of Judah	*Revelation 5:5*
Master	*Matthew 23:8*
Messiah	*John 1:41*
Mighty God	*Isaiah 9:6*
Overseer of souls	*1 Peter 2:25*
Passover	*1 Corinthians 5:7,8*
Peace	*Ephesians 2:14*
Physician	*Luke 4:23*
Portion	*Lamentations 3:24*
Prince of Peace	*Isaiah 9:6*
Prophet	*Deuteronomy 18:15*
Redemption	*1 Corinthians 1:30*
Refuge	*Hebrews 6:18*
Resurrection	*John 11:25-26*
Reward	*Genesis 15:1*
Righteousness	*Jeremiah 23:6*
Root of Jesse	*Isaiah 11:10*
Salvation	*Psalm 118:14*
Sanctification	*1 Corinthians 1:30*
Savior of the world	*John 4:42*
Shield	*Genesis 15:1*
Son of David	*Matthew 12:23*
Son of God	*Matthew 16:16*
Son of Man	*Matthew 16:13*
Song	*Psalm 118:14*
Strength	*Philippians 4:13*
Sun of righteousness	*Malachi 4:2*
Supply	*Philippians 4:19*
Teacher	*Matthew 23:10*
Temple	*Revelation 21:22*
Treasure	*Matthew 13:44*
Truth	*John 1:17*

The Names of Christ

<u>Vine</u>	*John 15:5*
<u>Way</u>	*John 14:6*
<u>Wisdom</u>	*1 Corinthians 1:30*
<u>Wonderful Counselor</u>	*Isaiah 9:6*
<u>Word</u>	*John 1:1*

The Prophecies Concerning Christ

The Old Testament is filled with prophecies of Christ. We know many of them because the New Testament was careful to point them out to us. There are many prophecies about him, though, that we would miss if we aren't careful. It requires a careful reading of the Old Testament and some digging in the New to pull some of them out and make the connections.

The following Scriptures are the standard prophecies concerning Christ's person and life. In the left column is the Old Testament prophecy, and in the right is either the New Testament passage that is the direct fulfillment of it, or it is an illustration of how the prophecy was fulfilled (you can find several more of your own if you wish).

These prophecies, hopefully, will help you find a deeper value in the story of Christ, which ought to spill over into your teaching about him. Sometimes you may wish to use one of them for a lesson; usually, however, they will provide background knowledge about him that you will keep in mind when you work through the Gospel stories.

GENESIS 3:15 And I will put enmity between you and the woman, and between your offspring and hers; he will crush your head, and you will strike his heel.

GENESIS 17:19 Then God said, "Yes, but your wife Sarah will bear you a son, and you will call him Isaac. I will establish my covenant with him as an everlasting covenant for his descendants after him."

GENESIS 18:18 Abraham will surely become a great and powerful nation, and all nations on earth will be blessed through him.

GENESIS 22:18 Through your offspring all nations on earth will be blessed, because you have obeyed me.

GENESIS 49:10 The scepter will not depart from Judah, nor the ruler's staff from between his feet, until he comes to whom it belongs and the obedience of the nations is his.

NUMBERS 24:17 I see him, but not now; I behold him, but not near. A star will come out of Jacob; a scepter will rise out of Israel. He will crush the foreheads of Moab, the skulls of all the sons of Sheth.

DEUTERONOMY 18:15 The LORD your God will raise up for you a prophet like me from among your own brothers. You must listen to him.

GALATIANS 4:4 But when the time had fully come, God sent his Son, born under Law.

MATTHEW 1:2,16 Abraham was the father of Isaac, Isaac the father of Jacob, and Jacob the father of Judah and all his brothers ... and Jacob the father of Joseph, the husband of Mary of whom was born Jesus, who is called Christ.

ACTS 3:25 And you are heirs of the prophets and of the covenant God made with your fathers. He said to Abraham, "Through your offspring all peoples on earth will be blessed."

EPHESIANS 2:13 But now in Christ Jesus you who once were far away have been brought near through the blood of Christ.

LUKE 3:33 The son of Amminadab, the son of Ram, the son of Hezron, the son of Perez, the son of Judah.

LUKE 3:34 The son of Jacob, the son of Isaac, the son of Abraham, the son of Terah, the son of Nahor.

JOHN 6:14 After the people saw the miraculous sign that Jesus did, they began to say, "Surely this is the Prophet who is to come into the world."

The Prophecies Concerning Christ

PSALMS 2:6-9 "I have installed my King on Zion, my holy hill." I will proclaim the decree of the LORD: He said to me, "You are my Son; today I have become your Father. Ask of me, and I will make the nations your inheritance, the ends of the earth your possession. You will rule them with an iron scepter; you will dash them to pieces like pottery."

PSALMS 2:12 Kiss the Son, lest he be angry and you be destroyed in your way, for his wrath can flare up in a moment. Blessed are all who take refuge in him.

PSALMS 16:10 Because you will not abandon me to the grave, nor will you let your Holy One see decay.

PSALMS 22:6-8 But I am a worm and not a man, scorned by men and despised by the people. All who see me mock me; they hurl insults, shaking their heads: "He trusts in the LORD; let the LORD rescue him. Let him deliver him, since he delights in him."

PSALMS 22:16 Dogs have surrounded me; a band of evil men has encircled me, they have pierced my hands and my feet.

PSALMS 22:18 They divide my garments among them and cast lots for my clothing.

EPHESIANS 1:20-22 Which he exerted in Christ when he rasied him from the dead and seated him at his right hand in the Heavenly realms, far above all rule and authority, power and dominion, and every title that can be given, not only in the present age but also in the one to come. And God placed all things under his feet, and appointed him to be head of the Church.

PHILIPPIANS 2:10 At the Name of Jesus every knee should bow, in Heaven and on earth and under the earth.

LUKE 24:6 He is not here; he has risen!

MATTHEW 27:43 He trusts in God. Let God rescue him now if he wants him, for he said, "I am the Son of God."

JOHN 19:18 Here they crucified him, and with him two others -- one on each side and Jesus in the middle.

MARK 15:24 And they crucified him. Dividing up his clothes, they cast lots to see what each would get.

The Prophecies Concerning Christ

PSALMS 27:12 Do not turn me over to the desire of my foes, for false witnesses rise up against me, breathing out violence.

MATTHEW 26:60-61 But they did not find any, though many false witnesses came forward. Finally two came forward and declared, "This fellow said, 'I am able to destroy the temple of God and rebuild it in three days.'"

PSALMS 34:20 He protects all his bones, not one of them will be broken.

JOHN 19:33 But when they came to Jesus and found that he was already dead, they did not break his legs.

PSALMS 41:9 Even my close friend, whom I trusted, he who shared my bread, has lifted up his heel against me.

MARK 14:10 Then Judas Iscariot, one of the Twelve, went to the chief priests to betray Jesus to them.

PSALMS 45:2 You are the most excellent of men and your lips have been anointed with grace, since God has blessed you forever.

JOHN 1:14 We have seen his glory, the glory of the one and only Son, who came from the Father, full of grace and truth.

PSALMS 68:18 When you ascended on high, you led captives in your train; you received gifts from men, even from the rebellious -- that you, O LORD God, might dwell there.

LUKE 24:50-51 When he had led them out to the vicinity of Bethany, he lifted up his hands and blessed them. While he was blessing them, he left them and was taken up into Heaven.

PSALMS 69:4 Those who hate me without reason outnumber the hairs of my head; many are my enemies without cause, those who seek to destroy me. I am forced to restore what I did not steal.

JOHN 15:23-25 He who hates me hates my Father as well. If I had not done among them what no one else did, they would not be guilty of sin. But now they have seen these miracles, and yet they have hated both me and my Father. But this is to fulfill what is written in their Law, "They hated me without reason."

PSALMS 69:21 They put gall in my food and gave me vinegar for my thirst.

JOHN 19:29 A jar of wine vinegar was there, so they soaked a sponge in it, put the sponge on a stalk of the hyssop plant, and lifted it to Jesus' lips.

The Prophecies Concerning Christ

PSALMS 109:4 In return for my friendship they accuse me, but I am a man of prayer.

PSALMS 109:7-8 When he is tried, let him be found guilty, and may his prayers condemn him. May his days be few; may another take his place of leadership.

PSALMS 110:1 The LORD says to my Lord: "Sit at my right hand until I make your enemies a footstool for your feet."

PSALMS 110:4 The LORD has sworn and will not change his mind: "You are a priest forever, in the order of Melchizedek."

PSALMS 118:22 The stone the builders rejected has become the capstone.

PSALMS 132:11 The LORD swore an oath to David, a sure oath that he will not revoke: "One of your own descendants I will place on your throne."

ISAIAH 2:4 He will judge between the nations and will settle disputes for many peoples. They will beat their swords into plowshares and their spears into pruning hooks. Nation will not take up sword against nation, nor will they train for war anymore.

LUKE 23:34 Jesus said, "Father, forgive them, for they do not know what they are doing."

ACTS 1:21 Therefore it is necessary to choose one of the men who have been with us the whole time the Lord Jesus went in and out among us.

1 CORINTHIANS 15:25 For he must reign until he has put all his enemies under his feet.

HEBREWS 6:20 Where Jesus, who went before us, has entered on our behalf. He has become a high priest forever, in the order of Melchizedek.

1 PETER 2:4 As you come to him, the living Stone -- rejected by men but chosen by God and precious to him ...

EPHESIANS 1:20 Which he exerted in Christ when he raised him from the dead and seated him at his right hand in the Heavenly realms.

EPHESIANS 2:15 His purpose was to create in himself one new man out of the two, thus making peace, and in this one body to reconcile both of them to God through the cross, by which he put to death their hostility.

The Prophecies Concerning Christ

ISAIAH 7:14 Therefore the Lord himself will give you a sign: The virgin will be with child and will give birth to a son, and will call him Immanuel.

MATTHEW 1:18 This is how the birth of Jesus Christ came about. His mother Mary was pledged to be married to Joseph, but before they came together, she was found to be with child through the Holy Spirit.

ISAIAH 9:1-2 Nevertheless, there will be no more gloom for those who were in distress. In the past he humbled the land of Zebulun and the land of Naphtali, but in the future he will honor Galilee of the Gentiles, by the way of the sea, along the Jordan -- The people walking in darkness have seen a great light; on those living in the land of the shadow of death a light has dawned.

MATTHEW 4:12 When Jesus heard that John had been put in prison, he returned to Galilee. Leaving Nazareth, he went and lived in Capernaum, which was by the lake in the area of Zebulun and Naphtali -- to fulfill what was said through the prophet Isaiah.

ISAIAH 9:6-7 For to us a child is born, to us a son is given, and the government will be on his shoulders. And he will be called Wonderful Counselor, Mighty God, Everlasting Father, Prince of Peace. Of the increase of his government and peace there will be no end. He will reign on David's throne and over his kingdom, establishing and upholding it with justice and righteousness from that time on and forever. The zeal of the LORD Almighty will accomplish this.

JOHN 18:37 You are right in saying I am a king. In fact, for this reason I was born, and for this I came into the world, to testify to the truth.

ISAIAH 11:1-2 A shoot will come up from the stump of Jesse; from his roots a Branch will bear fruit. The Spirit of the LORD will rest on him-- the Spirit of wisdom and of understanding, the Spirit of counsel and of power, the Spirit of knowledge and of the fear of the LORD .

JOHN 1:32 I saw the Spirit come down from Heaven as a dove and remain on him.

The Prophecies Concerning Christ

ISAIAH 28:16 So this is what the Sovereign LORD says: "See, I lay a stone in Zion, a tested stone, a precious cornerstone for a sure foundation; the one who trusts will never be dismayed."

EPHESIANS 2:20 Built on the foundation of the apostles and prophets, with Christ Jesus himself as the chief cornerstone.

ISAIAH 42:1 Here is my servant, whom I uphold, my chosen one in whom I delight; I will put my Spirit on him and he will bring justice to the nations.

MATTHEW 3:16 As soon as Jesus was baptized, he went up out of the water. At that moment Heaven was opened, and he saw the Spirit of God descending like a dove and lighting on him.

ISAIAH 50:6 I offered my back to those who beat me, my cheeks to those who pulled out my beard; I did not hide my face from mocking and spitting.

MARK 14:65 Then some began to spit at him; they blindfolded him, struck him with their fists, and said, "Prophesy!" And the guards took him and beat him.

ISAIAH 53:3-5 He was despised and rejected by men, a man of sorrows, and familiar with suffering. Like one from whom men hide their faces he was despised, and we esteemed him not. Surely he took up our infirmities and carried our sorrows, yet we considered him stricken by God, smitten by him, and afflicted. But he was pierced for our transgressions, he was crushed for our iniquities; the punishment that brought us peace was upon him, and by his wounds we are healed.

MATTHEW 8:16-17 When evening came, many who were demon-possessed were brought to him, and he drove out the spirits with a word and healed all the sick. This was to fulfill what was spoken through the prophet Isaiah: "He took up our infirmities and carried our diseases."

ISAIAH 53:7 He was oppressed and afflicted, yet he did not open his mouth; he was led like a lamb to the slaughter, and as a sheep before her shearers is silent, so he did not open his mouth.

MATTHEW 26:62-63 Then the high priest stood up and said to Jesus, "Are you not going to answer? What is this testimony that these men are bringing against you?" But Jesus remained silent.

The Prophecies Concerning Christ

ISAIAH 53:9 He was assigned a grave with the wicked, and with the rich in his death, though he had done no violence, nor was any deceit in his mouth.

MATTHEW 27:57-60 As evening approached, there came a rich man from Arimathea, named Joseph, who had himself become a disciple of Jesus. Going to Pilate, he asked for Jesus' body, and Pilate ordered that it be given to him. Joseph took the body, wrapped it in a clean linen cloth, and placed it in his own new tomb that he had cut out of the rock. He rolled a big stone in front of the entrance to the tomb and went away.

ISAIAH 53:12 Therefore I will give him a portion among the great, and he will divide the spoils with the strong, because he poured out his life unto death, and was numbered with the transgressors. For he bore the sin of many, and made intercession for the transgressors

MATTHEW 27:38 Two robbers were crucified with him, one on his right and one on his left.

ISAIAH 59:16 He saw that there was no one, he was appalled that there was no one to intervene; so his own arm worked salvation for him, and his own righteousness sustained him.

ROMANS 5:18 Consequently, just as the result of one tresspass was condemnation for all men, so also the result of one act of righteousness was justification that brings life for all men.

ISAIAH 61:1 The Spirit of the Sovereign LORD is on me, because the LORD has anointed me to preach good news to the poor. He has sent me to bind up the brokenhearted, to proclaim freedom for the captives and release from darkness for the prisoners.

MATTHEW 11:4 Jesus replied, "Go back and report to John what you hear and see: the blind receive sight, the lame walk, those who have leprosy are cured, the deaf hear, the dead are raised, and the good news is preached to the poor.

ISAIAH 63:1 Who is this coming from Edom, from Bozrah, with his garments stained crimson? Who is this, robed in splendor, striding forward in the greatness of his strength? "It is I, speaking in righteousness, mighty to save."

HEBREWS 9:14 How much more, then, will the blood of Christ, who through the eternal Spirit offered himself unblemished to God, cleanse our consciences from acts that lead to death, so that we may serve the living God!

The Prophecies Concerning Christ

JEREMIAH 23:5 "The days are coming," declares the LORD, "when I will raise up to David a righteous Branch, a King who will reign wisely and do what is just and right in the land."

JEREMIAH 31:15 This is what the LORD says: "A voice is heard in Ramah, mourning and great weeping, Rachel weeping for her children and refusing to be comforted, because her children are no more."

DANIEL 9:25 Know and understand this: From the issuing of the decree to restore and rebuild Jerusalem until the Anointed One, the ruler, comes, there will be seven 'sevens,' and sixty-two 'sevens.' It will be rebuilt with streets and a trench, but in times of trouble.

HOSEA 11:1 When Israel was a child, I loved him, and out of Egypt I called my son.

MICAH 5:2 But you, Bethlehem Ephrathah, though you are small among the clans of Judah, out of you will come for me one who will be ruler over Israel, whose origins are from of old, from ancient times.

HAGGAI 2:7 "I will shake all nations, and the desired of all nations will come, and I will fill this house with glory," says the LORD Almighty.

REVELATION 11:15 The kingdom of the world has become the kingdom of our Lord and of his Christ, and he will reign for ever and ever.

MATTHEW 2:16 When Herod realized that he had been outwitted by the Magi, he was furious, and he gave orders to kill all the boys in Bethlehem and its vicinity who were two years old and under, in accordance with the time he had learned from the Magi.

LUKE 2:1-2 In those days Caesar Augustus issued a decree that a census should be taken of the entire Roman world. (This was the first census that took place while Quirinius was governor of Syria.)

MATTHEW 2:14 So he got up, took the child and his mother during the night and left for Egypt.

MATTHEW 2:1 After Jesus was born in Bethlehem in Judea, during the time of King Herod, Magi from the east came to Jerusalem.

MATTHEW 12:6 I tell you that one greater than the Temple is here.

The Prophecies Concerning Christ

ZECHARIAH 3:8 Listen, O high priest Joshua and your associates seated before you, who are men symbolic of things to come: I am going to bring my servant, the Branch.

ZECHARIAH 9:9 Rejoice greatly, O Daughter of Zion! Shout, Daughter of Jerusalem! See, your king comes to you, righteous and having salvation, gentle and riding on a donkey, on a colt, the foal of a donkey.

ZECHARIAH 11:12-13 I told them, "If you think it best, give me my pay; but if not, keep it." So they paid me thirty pieces of silver. And the LORD said to me, "Throw it to the potter"-- the handsome price at which they priced me! So I took the thirty pieces of silver and threw them into the house of the LORD to the potter.

ZECHARIAH 12:10 And I will pour out on the house of David and the inhabitants of Jerusalem a spirit of grace and supplication. They will look on me, the one they have pierced, and they will mourn for him as one mourns for an only child, and grieve bitterly for him as one grieves for a firstborn son.

ZECHARIAH 13:7 "Awake, O sword, against my shepherd, against the man who is close to me!" declares the LORD Almighty. "Strike the shepherd, and the sheep will be scattered, and I will turn my hand against the little ones."

HEBREWS 5:5 So Christ also did not take upon himself the glory of becoming a high priest. But God said to him, "You are my Son; today I have become your Father."

JOHN 12:13-14 They took palm branches and went out to meet him, shouting, "Hosanna!" "Blessed is he who comes in the Name of the Lord!" "Blessed is the King of Israel!" Jesus found a young donkey and sat upon it, as it is written.

MATTHEW 26:15 And [he] asked, "What are you willing to give me if I hand him over to you?" So they counted out for him thirty silver coins. **MATTHEW 27:6-7** The chief priests picked up the coins and said, "It is against the Law to put this into the treasury, since it is blood money." So they decided to use the money to buy the potter's field as a burial place for foreigners.

JOHN 19:18 Here they crucified him, and with him two others -- one on each side and Jesus in the middle.

MARK 14:50 Then everyone deserted him and fled.

The Prophecies Concerning Christ

MALACHI 3:1 "See, I will send my messenger, who will prepare the way before me. Then suddenly the Lord you are seeking will come to his temple; the messenger of the covenant, whom you desire, will come," says the LORD Almighty.

JOHN 1:29 The next day John saw Jesus coming toward him and said, "Look, the Lamb of God, who takes away the sin of the world!"

The miracles of Christ

The miracles that Christ did prove who he was – he was the Son of the God of the Old Testament, doing the same kind of work that Yahweh did for the Israelites. These are the miracles that Christ did as recorded in the Gospels:

Two blind men healed	*Matthew 9:27-31*
Mute man healed	*Matthew 9:32-34*
Temple tax provided	*Matthew 17:24-27*
Deaf and muteman healed	*Mark 7:31-37*
Blind man's sight restored	*Mark 8:22-26*
Jesus passes unseen	*Luke 4:28-30*
Catch of fish	*Luke 5:1-11*
Widow's son raised	*Luke 7:11-17*
Crippled woman healed	*Luke 13:10-17*
Man's dropsy healed	*Luke 14:1-6*
Ten lepers healed	*Luke 17:11-19*
Malchus' ear healed	*Luke 22:50-51*
Water made wine	*John 2:1-11*
Official's son healed	*John 4:46-54*
Healing at the pool	*John 5:1-9*
Man born blind healed	*John 9:1-7*
Lazarus raised from dead	*John 11:38-44*
Miraculous catch of fish	*John 21:1-14*
Canaanite woman's daughter healed	*Matthew 15:21-28; Mark 7:24-30*
Feeding of 4000	*Matthew 15:32-39; Mark 8:1-10*
Fig tree withers	*Matthew 21:18-22*
Centurion's servant healed	*Matthew 8:5-13; Luke 7:1-10*
Blind and mute demoniac healed	*Matthew 12:22-32; Luke 11:14-23*
Man with evil spirit healed	*Mark 1:21-28; Luke 4:31-37*
Peter's mother-in-law healed	*Matthew 8:14-15; Mark 1:29-31; Luke 4:38-39*
Jesus calms the storm	*Matthew 8:23-27; Mark 4:35-41; Luke 8:22-25*

The Miracles of Christ

Demoniac men healed	*Matthew 8:28-34; Mark 5:1-20; Luke 8:26-33*
A leper healed	*Matthew 8:1-4; Mark 1:40-45; Luke 5:12-16*
Jairus' daughter raised	*Matthew 9:18-26; Mark 5:22-43; Luke 8:41-56*
Woman's hemorrhage healed	*Matthew 9:20-22; Mark 5:25-34; Luke 8:43-48*
A paralytic healed	*Matthew 9:1-8; Mark 2:1-12; Luke 5:17-26*
Man's withered hand healed	*Matthew 12:9-14; Mark 3:1-6; Luke 6:6-11*
Demonic boy delivered	*Matthew 17:14-20; Mark 9:14-29; Luke 9:37-43*
Two blind men healed	*Matthew 20:29-34; Mark 10:46-52; Luke 18:35-43*
Jesus walks on water	*Matthew 14:22-27; Mark 6:45-52; John 6:15-21*
Feeding of 5000	*Matthew 14:13-31; Mark 6:30-44; Luke 9:10-17; John 6:1-14*

The Parables of Christ

The parables of Christ are amazingly illuminative insights into the Kingdom of God. Through these simple stories Jesus tells us more about how the Kingdom works than we could have gotten through any other means.

The thing to remember about a parable is that it's talking about general principles, and it does it in a symbolic manner. Since the Kingdom of God is such a huge and complex subject, Jesus uses parables to show us single snap-shots, so to speak, of truths that we need to know about. Once we understand the principle he's teaching us, then we can keep it in mind when we need to rely on God's work in our lives – in other words, we know that this is the way things work when God is around. That way we can work with him, not against him; we can work for the same goals that he's working for and not on our own mistaken goals.

These are all the parables that Jesus taught which are recorded in the Gospels:

Weeds	*Matthew 13:24-43*
Hidden treasure	*Matthew 13:44*
Pearl of great price	*Matthew 13:45-46*
Parable of the net	*Matthew 13:47-50*
Unmerciful servant	*Matthew 18:21-35*
Workers in the vineyard	*Matthew 20:1-16*
Two sons	*Matthew 21:28-32*
Wedding banquet	*Matthew 22:1-14*
Ten virgins	*Matthew 25:1-13*
Talents	*Matthew 25:14-30*
Sheep and goats	*Matthew 25:31-46*
Growing seed	*Mark 4:26-29*
Household watching	*Mark 13:32-37*
Two debtors	*Luke 7:36-50*

The Parables of Christ

Good samaritan	*Luke 10:25-37*
Teaching on prayer	*Luke 11:5-13*
Rich fool	*Luke 12:16-21*
Watchful servants	*Luke 12:35-40*
Faithful steward	*Luke 12:42-48*
Barren fig tree	*Luke 13:6-9*
Great banquet	*Luke 14:15-24*
Cost of being disciple	*Luke 14:25-33*
Lost coin	*Luke 15:8-10*
Lost son	*Luke 15:11-32*
Shrewd manager	*Luke 16:1-13*
Rich man and Lazarus	*Luke 16:19-31*
Master and servant	*Luke 17:7-10*
Persistent widow	*Luke 18:1-8*
Pharisee and tax collector	*Luke 18:9-14*
Ten minas	*Luke 19:11-27*
House built on rock	*Matthew 7:24-27; Luke 6:46-49*
Yeast	*Matthew 13:33; Luke 13:20-21*
Lost sheep	*Matthew 18:10-14; Luke 15:3-7*
Light under bowl	*Matthew 5:14-16; Mark 4:21-25; Luke 8:16-18; Luke 11:33-36*
New cloth, old garment	*Matthew 9:16; Mark 2:21; Luke 5:36*
New wine, old wineskins	*Matthew 9:17; Mark 2:22; Luke 5:37-39*
Sower	*Matthew 13:1-23; Mark 4:3-20; Luke 8:4-15*
Mustard seed	*Matthew 13:31-32; Mark 4:30-32; Luke 13:18-19*
Vineyard and tenants	*Matthew 21:33-46; Mark 12:1-12; Luke 20:9-19*
Fig tree	*Matthew 24:32-35; Mark 13:28-31; Luke 21:29-33*

The Old In The New

The Old Testament is critical to the New Testament's message. Aside from the outright prophecies of Christ, there are many ideas and principles from the Old that the New uses in its stories and teachings.

The apostles were astute students of their Bibles - which, by the way, was the Old Testament! They read and thought about and prayed about the Scriptures so much that they had a deep pool of knowledge to draw from when they wrote their letters. They did the same thing that modern writers do: they quoted Old Testament passages to support and illustrate their own point (though they didn't often give the reference and only gave the name of the prophet even then!).

The following is a listing of all the Old Testament Scriptures that are quoted in the New Testament, both Gospels and Epistles. The left column is the Old Testament passage, and the right column is the place in the New Testament where that passage is quoted. Notice that some OT passages are quoted several places in the New; the OT reference isn't printed more than once in these cases.

Also notice that some of the OT references are underlined. This means that the NT writer was using the Septuagint - a Greek translation of the OT - instead of the Hebrew Bible. As is true with all translations from the original, it often didn't read the same. This accounts for the fact that the quote that the NT writer gives us is different than the passage we find when we go back to the OT and look it up; our Old Testament comes from the Hebrew Bible, not the Septuagint.

The Old in the New

Don't worry about the differences, however; it is a bit technical, but what it boils down to is that the Hebrew Bible we have now isn't the original that the prophets wrote - there were older Hebrew Bibles then that we don't have. But the Septuagint translators had those older Bibles - which is why the Spirit wants that difference in the New Testament quote instead of the present version of the Hebrew. If that doesn't make sense, just trust the Lord that the version he wanted is what the apostles used!

Finally, you will notice that I italicized the Gospel references for easy location.

(This list is taken from The Greek New Testament, © 1983 by the United Bible Societies; edited by Aland, Black, Martini, Metzger and Wikgren; pp.897-8.)

OT Passage:	Quoted in:	OT Passage:	Quoted in:
Genesis 1:27	*Matthew 19:4*	Exodus 3:15	*Matthew 22:23*
	Mark 10:6		*Mark 12:26*
Genesis 2:2	Hebrews 4:4		Acts 3:13
Genesis 2:7	1 Cor.15:45	<u>Exodus 9:16</u>	Romans 9:17
Genesis 2:24	*Matthew 19:5*	Exodus 12:46	*John 19:36*
	Mark 10:7-8	Exodus 13:2	*Luke 2:23*
	1 Cor. 6:16	Exodus 13:12	*Luke 2:23*
	Ephesians 5:31	Exodus 13:15	*Luke 2:32*
Genesis 5:2	*Matthew 19:4*	Exodus 16:18	2 Cor. 8:15
	Mark 10:6	<u>Exodus 19:6</u>	1 Peter 2:9
<u>Genesis 5:24</u>	Hebrews 11:5	Ex. 19:12-13	Hebrews 12:20
Genesis 12:1	Acts 7:3	Ex. 20:12	*Matthew 15:4*
Genesis 12:3	Galatians 3:8		*Mark 7:10*
Genesis 12:7	Galatians 3:16		Ephesians 6:2-3
Gen.14:17-20	Hebrews 7:1-2	Ex. 20:12-16	*Matt. 19:18-19*
Genesis 15:5	Romans 4:18		*Mark 10:19*
Genesis 15:6	Rom.4:3,9,22		*Luke 18:20*
	Galatians 3:6	Exodus 20:13	*Matthew 5:21*
	James 2:23		James 2:11
Gen.15:13-14	Acts 7:6-7	Ex. 20:13-15,17	Romans 13:9
Genesis 17:5	Rom.4:17,18	Exodus 20:14	*Matthew 5:27*
Genesis 17:8	Acts 7:5		James 2:11
Genesis 18:10	Romans 9:9	Exodus 20:17	Romans 7:7
Genesis 18:14	Romans 9:9	Exodus 21:17	*Matthew 15:4*
Genesis 18:18	Galatians 3:8		*Mark 7:10*
Genesis 21:10	Galatians 4:30	Exodus 21:24	*Matthew 5:38*
Genesis 21:12	Romans 9:7	Exodus 22:28	Acts 23:5
	Hebrews 11:18	Exodus 24:8	Hebrews 9:20
Gen.22:16-17	Hebr.6:13-14	Exodus 25:40	Hebrews 8:5
Genesis 22:18	Acts 3:25	Exodus 32:1	Acts 7:40
Genesis 25:23	Romans 9:12	Exodus 32:6	1 Cor. 10:7
Genesis 26:4	Acts 3:25	Exodus 32:23	Acts 7:40
<u>Genesis 47:31</u>	Hebrews 11:21	Exodus 33:19	Romans 9:15
Genesis 48:4	Acts 7:5	Leviticus 12:8	*Luke 2:24*
		Leviticus 18:5	Romans 10:5
Exodus 1:8	Acts 7:18		Galatians 3:12
Exodus 2:14	Acts 7:27-28	Leviticus 19:2	1 Peter 1:16
	Acts 7:35	Leviticus 19:12	*Matthew 5:33*
Exodus 3:2	Acts 7:30	Leviticus 19:18	*Matthew 5:43*
Exodus 3:5-10	Acts 7:33-34		*Matthew 19:19*
Exodus 3:6	*Matthew 22:32*		*Matthew 22:39*
	Mark 12:26		*Mark 12:31*
	Luke 20:37		*Mark 12:33*
	Acts 3:13		*Luke 10:27*
	Acts 7:32		Romans 13:9
Exodus 3:12	Acts 7:7		Galatians 5:14

345

OT Passage:	Quoted in:	OT Passage:	Quoted in:
Leviticus 19:18	James 2:8		1 Timothy 5:18
Leviticus 23:29	Acts 3:23	Deut. 25:5	Matthew 22:24
Leviticus 24:20	Matthew 5:38		Mark 12:19
Leviticus 26:12	2 Cor. 6:16		Luke 20:28
		Deut. 27:26	Galatians 3:10
Numbers 9:12	John 19:36	Deut. 29:4	Romans 11:8
Numbers 16:5	2 Timothy 2:19	Deut. 30:12-14	Romans 10:6-8
Numbers 30:2	Matthew 5:33	Deut. 31:6,8	Hebrews 13:5
		Deut. 32:21	Romans 10:19
Deut. 4:35	Mark 12:32	Deut. 32:35	Romans 12:19
Deut. 5:16	Matthew 15:4	Deut. 32:35-36	Hebrews 10:30
	Mark 7:10	Deut. 32:43	Romans 15:10
	Ephesians 6:2-3	Deut. 32:43	Hebrews 1:6
Deut. 5:16-20	Matt. 19:18-19		
	Mark 10:19	1 Samuel 13:14	Acts 13:22
	Luke 18:20		
Deut. 5:17	Matthew 5:21	2 Samuel 7:8	2 Cor. 6:18
	James 2:11	2 Samuel 7:14	2 Cor. 6:18
Dt. 5:17-19, 21	Romans 13:9		Hebrews 1:5
Deut. 5:18	Matthew 5:27	2 Samuel 22:50	Romans 15:9
Deut. 5:21	Romans 7:7		
Deut. 6:4	Mark 12:32	1 Kgs 19:10,14	Romans 11:3
Deut. 6:4-5	Mark 12:29-30	1 Kings 19:18	Romans 11:4
Deut. 6:5	Matthew 22:37	Job 5:13	1 Cor. 3:19
	Mark 12:33	Job 41:11	Romans 11:35
	Luke 10:27		
Deut. 6:13	Matthew 4:10	Psalm 2:1-2	Acts 4:25-26
	Luke 4:8	Psalm 2:7	Acts 13:33
Deut. 6:16	Matthew 4:7		Hebrews 1:5
	Luke 4:12		Hebrews 5:5
Deut. 8:3	Matthew 4:4	Psalm 4:4	Ephesians 4:26
	Luke 4:4	Psalm 5:9	Romans 3:13
Deut. 9:4	Romans 10:6	Psalm 8:3	Matthew 21:16
Deut. 9:19	Hebrews 12:21	Psalm 8:4-6	Hebrews 2:6-8
Deut. 17:7	1 Cor. 5:13	Psalm 8:6	1 Cor. 15:27
Deut. 18:15	Acts 7:37	Psalm 10:7	Romans 3:14
Deut. 18:15-16	Acts 3:22	Psalm 14:1-3	Rom. 3:10-12
Deut. 18:19	Acts 3:23	Psalm 16:8-11	Acts 2:25-28
Deut. 19:15	Matthew 18:16	Psalm 16:10	Acts 2:31
	2 Cor. 13:1	Psalm 16:10	Acts 13:35
Deut. 19:21	Matthew 5:38	Psalm 18:49	Romans 15:9
Deut. 21:23	Galatians 3:13	Psalm 19:4	Romans 10:18
Deut. 24:1	Matthew 5:31	Psalm 22:1	Matthew 27:46
	Matthew 19:7		Mark 15:34
Deut. 24:1,3	Mark 10:4	Psalm 22:18	John 19:24
Deut. 25:4	1 Cor. 9:9	Psalm 22:22	Hebrews 2:12

OT Passage:	Quoted in:	OT Passage:	Quoted in:
Psalm 24:1	1 Cor. 10:26	Psalm 118:22	Luke 20:17
Psalm 31:5	Luke 23:46		Acts 4:11
Psalm 32:1-2	Romans 4:7-8		1 Peter 2:7
Psalm 34:12-16	1 Peter 3:10-12	Ps. 118:22-23	Matthew 21:42
Psalm 35:19	John 15:2		Mark 12:10-11
Psalm 36:1	Romans 3:18	Ps. 118:25-26	Matthew 21:9
Psalm 40:6-8	Hebrews 10:5-7		Mark 11:9-10
Psalm 41:9	John 13:18		John 12:13
Psalm 44:22	Romans 8:36	Psalm 118:26	Matthew 23:39
Psalm 45:6-7	Hebrews 1:8-9		Luke 13:35
Psalm 51:4	Romans 3:4		Luke 19:38
Psalm 53:1-3	Rom. 3:10-12	Psalm 132:11	Acts 2:30
Psalm 68:18	Ephesians 4:8	Psalm 140:3	Romans 3:13
Psalm 69:4	John 15:25		
Psalm 69:9	John 2:17	Prov. 3:11-12	Hebrews 12:5-6
	Romans 15:3	Proverbs 3:34	James 4:6
Psalm 69:22-23	Rom. 11:9-10		1 Peter 5:5
Psalm 69:25	Acts 1:20	Proverbs 11:31	1 Peter 4:18
Psalm 78:2	Matthew 13:35	Prov. 25:21-22	Romans 12:20
Psalm 78:24	John 6:31	Proverbs 26:11	2 Peter 2:22
Psalm 82:6	John 10:34		
Psalm 89:20	Acts 13:22	Isaiah 1:9	Romans 9:29
Psalm 91:11-12	Matthew 4:6	Isaiah 6:9	Luke 8:10
	Luke 4:10-11	Isaiah 6:9-10	Matt. 13:14-15
Psalm 94:11	1 Cor. 3:20		Mark 4:12
Psalm 95:7-8	Hebrews 3:15	Isaiah 6:9-10	Acts 28:26-27
	Hebrews 4:7	Isaiah 6:10	John 12:40
Psalm 95:7-11	Hebrews 3:7-11	Isaiah 7:14	Matthew 1:23
Psalm 95:11	Hebrews 4:3,5	Isaiah 8:8,10	Matthew 1:23
Ps. 102:25-27	Heb. 1:10-12	Isaiah 8:14	Romans 9:33
Psalm 104:4	Hebrews 1:7		1 Peter 2:8
Psalm 109:8	Acts 1:20	Isaiah 8:17	Hebrews 2:13
Psalm 110:1	Matthew 22:44	Isaiah 8:18	Hebrews 2:13
	Matthew 26:64	Isaiah 9:1-2	Matt. 4:15-16
	Mark 12:36	Isaiah 10:22-23	Rom. 9:27-28
	Mark 14:62	Isaiah 11:10	Romans 15:12
	Luke 20:42-43	Isaiah 22:13	1 Cor. 15:32
	Luke 22:69	Isaiah 25:8	1 Cor. 15:54
	Acts 2:34-35	Isaiah 27:9	Romans 11:27b
	Hebrews 1:13	Isaiah 28:11-12	1 Cor. 14:21
Psalm 110:4	Hebrews 5:6	Isaiah 28:16	Romans 9:33
	Heb. 7:17,21		Romans 10:11
Psalm 112:9	2 Cor. 9:9		1 Peter 2:6
Psalm 116:10	2 Cor. 4:13	Isaiah 29:10	Romans 11:8
Psalm 117:1	Romans 15:11	Isaiah 29:13	Matthew 15:8-9
Psalm 118:6	Hebrews 13:6		Mark 7:6-7

OT Passage:	Quoted in:	OT Passage:	Quoted in:
Isaiah 29:14	1 Cor. 1:19	Jer. 31:33-34	Heb. 10:16-17
Isaiah 40:3-5	Luke 3:4-6	Ezek. 20:34,41	2 Cor. 6:17
Isaiah 40:3	Matthew 3:3	Ezekiel 37:27	2 Cor. 6:16
	Mark 1:3		
	John 1:23	Daniel 7:13	Matthew 24:30
Isaiah 40:6-8	1 Peter 1:24-25		Matthew 26:64
Isaiah 40:13	Romans 11:34		Mark 13:26
	1 Cor. 2:16		Mark 14:62
Isaiah 42:1-3	Matt. 12:18-20		Luke 21:27
Isaiah 42:4	Matthew 12:21		
Isaiah 43:20	1 Peter 2:9	Hosea 1:10	Romans 9:26
Isaiah 43:21	1 Peter 2:9	Hosea 2:23	Romans 9:25
Isaiah 45:21	Mark 12:32	Hosea 6:6	Matthew 9:13
Isaiah 45:23	Romans 14:11		Matthew 12:7
Isaiah 49:6	Acts 13:47	Hosea 10:8	Luke 23:30
Isaiah 49:8	2 Cor. 6:2	Hosea 11:1	Matthew 2:15
Isaiah 49:18	Romans 14:11	Hosea 13:14	1 Cor. 15:55
Isaiah 52:5	Romans 2:24		
Isaiah 52:7	Romans 10:15	Joel 2:28-32	Acts 2:17-21
Isaiah 52:11	2 Cor. 6:17	Joel 2:32	Romans 10:13
Isaiah 52:15	Romans 15:21		
Isaiah 53:1	John 12:38	Amos 5:25-27	Acts 7:42-43
	Romans 10:16	Amos 9:11-12	Acts 15:16-17
Isaiah 53:4	Matthew 8:17		
Isaiah 53:7-8	Acts 8:32-33	Jonah 1:17	Matthew 12:40
Isaiah 53:9	1 Peter 2:22		
Isaiah 53:12	Luke 22:37	Micah 5:2	Matthew 2:6
Isaiah 54:1	Galatians 4:27	Micah 7:6	Matt. 10:35-36
Isaiah 54:13	John 6:45		
Isaiah 55:3	Acts 13:34	Habakkuk 1:5	Acts 13:41
Isaiah 56:7	Matthew 21:13	Hab. 2:3-4	Heb. 10:37-38
	Mark 11:17	Habakkuk 2:4	Romans 1:17
	Luke 19:46		Galatians 3:11
Isaiah 59:7-8	Rom. 3:15-17		
Isaiah 59:20-21	Rom. 11:26-27	Haggai 2:6	Hebrews 12:26
Isaiah 61:1-2	Luke 4:18-19		
Isaiah 62:11	Matthew 21:5	Zechariah 8:16	Ephesians 4:25
Isaiah 64:4	1 Cor. 2:9	Zechariah 9:9	Matthew 21:5
Isaiah 65:1	Romans 10:20		John 12:15
Isaiah 65:2	Romans 10:21	Zechariah 11:12-13	Matt. 27:9-10
Isaiah 66:1-2	Acts 7:49-50	Zech. 12:10	John 19:37
			Matthew 26:31
Jeremiah 9:24	1 Cor. 1:31	Zechariah 13:7	Mark 14:27
	2 Cor. 10:17		
Jeremiah 31:15	Matthew 2:18	Malachi 1:2-3	Romans 9:13
Jer. 31:31-34	Hebrews 8:8-12	Malachi 3:1	Matthew 11:10

OT Passage:	Quoted in:	OT Passage:	Quoted in:
Malachi 3:1	*Mark 1:2* *Luke 7:27*		